D0475872

Opiate Receptors, Neurotransmitters, & Drug Dependence: Basic Science-Clinical Correlates

Opiate Receptors, Neurotransmitters, & Drug Dependence: Basic Science-Clinical Correlates is part of the *Advances in Alcohol & Substance Abuse* series of thematic journal issues.

Series Editor: Barry Stimmel, MD, Dean for Academic Affairs, Mount Sinai School of Medicine of the City University of New York

Other titles in this series:

Biologic Approach to Alcoholism: 1980 Update

The Effects of Parental Drug Dependency Upon Children

Alcohol & Drug Misuse, Abuse, & Dependence in the Elderly

Opiate Receptors, Neurotransmitters, & Drug Dependence: Basic Science-Clinical Correlates

Barry Stimmel, MD, Editor

Volume 1, Number 1, Fall 1981
Advances in Alcohol & Substance Abuse

The Haworth Press
New York

ADVANCES IN ALCOHOL & SUBSTANCE ABUSE is a quarterly journal dedicated to providing up-to-date articles on topics considered to be of concern to those working in the field of alcohol and substance abuse.

Each issue will be thematic and, where appropriate, will include basic research as well as clinical studies. One of the major goals of the journal is to provide health professionals in the field with a basic foundation of the biological principles pertaining to substance abuse as these principles relate to the clinical setting.

ADVANCES IN ALCOHOL & SUBSTANCE ABUSE is published quarterly in Fall, Winter, Spring, and Summer. Articles are abstracted or indexed in *BioSciences Information Services of Biological Abstracts. Advances in Alcohol & Substance Abuse* is the successor title to *Drug Abuse & Alcoholism Review,* Volumes 1-3, 1978-1980.

MANUSCRIPTS should be submitted in triplicate to Barry Stimmel, MD, Dean for Academic Affairs, Mount Sinai School of Medicine, Annenberg 5, 1 Gustave L. Levy Place, New York, NY 10029. Editorial inquiries should be directed to the Editor.

BUSINESS OFFICE. All subscription and advertising inquiries should be directed to The Haworth Press, 149 Fifth Avenue, New York, NY 10010. Telephone (212) 228-2800.

SUBSCRIPTIONS are on an academic year, per volume basis only. Payment must be made in U.S. or Canadian funds only. $45.00 individuals, $60.00 institutions, and $90.00 libraries. Postage and handling: U.S. orders, add $1.75; Canadian orders, add $6.00 U.S. currency or $6.50 Canadian currency. Foreign rates: add $40.00 (includes postage and handling).

CHANGE OF ADDRESS. Please notify the Subscription Department, The Haworth Press, 149 Fifth Avenue, New York, NY 10010 of address changes. Please allow six weeks for processing; include old and new addresses, including both zip codes.

ISSN: 0270-3106
ISBN: 0-86656-103-X

Second-Class postage paid at New York, NY and additional mailing offices.

POSTMASTER: Send address changes to The Haworth Press, 149 Fifth Avenue, New York, NY 10010.

Library of Congress Cataloging in Publication Data
Main entry under title:

Opiate receptors, neurotransmitters & drug dependence.

(Advances in alcohol & substance abuse, ISSN 0270-3106 ; v. 1, no. 1)
Includes bibliographic references.

1. Endorphins—Receptors. 2. Neurotransmitters. 3. Narcotic habit.
I. Stimmel, Barry, 1939- . II. Series. [DNLM: 1. Receptors, Endorphin—Metabolism.
2. Neuroregulators—Metabolism. 3. Substance dependence—Metabolism. 4. Narcotics
—Metabolism. 5. Endorphins—Metabolism. W1 AD432 v. 1 no. 1 / QV 89 061]

QP51.E5064   615'.78   81-7011
ISBN 0-86656-103-X   AACR2

Opiate Receptors, Neurotransmitters, & Drug Dependence: Basic Science-Clinical Correlates

Advances in Alcohol & Substance Abuse
Volume 1, Number 1, Fall 1981

EDITORIAL

THE IMPORTANCE OF SCIENCE
IN CLINICAL PRACTICE

Over the decades major advances in health care have for the most part been preceded by confirmation of basic research with subsequent application of these findings to the clinical setting. The advantages of a good relationship between "bench" and "field" have been well recognized in most areas of medicine. This interrelationship is facilitated by journals publishing papers addressing basic pathophysiology as well as clinical studies.

Unfortunately, in the field of alcoholism and substance abuse an understanding of the importance of basic science knowledge has been the exception rather than the rule. Although there is a high quality of basic research in these areas, all too frequently a link does not exist between those involved in the laboratories and those active in clinical management. This is most regrettable as there are few disorders that can be studied more accurately in the animal model than dependence, tolerance, and withdrawal. In addition, over the past several years exciting basic advances have been made in the study of dependence and related phenomena, culminating with the identification of opiate receptors and endogenous opiates as natural components of our internal milieu.

Advances in Alcohol & Substance Abuse is dedicated toward providing both the basic researcher and the practitioner in the health sciences with up-to-date information concerning alcohol and substance abuse. Rather than a presentation of unrelated papers, each issue of *Advances* will focus on a specific topic of concern, emphasizing the importance of and interrelationship between existing basic research and clinical findings. The papers will cover a broad range of topics as well as disciplines. It is considered no less important for the psychologist to understand the basic pathophysiology of the disorder being treated than for the physician to be aware of the multiple psychologic phenomena surrounding an illness.

It is indeed appropriate that the first issue of *Advances* addresses the role

Advances in Alcohol & Substance Abuse, Vol. 1(1), Fall 1981

1

of neuromodulators and opiate receptors in alcohol and drug dependence. In the introductory paper, Morgan reviews the current clinical concepts of dependence, tolerance, and withdrawal. Only by first understanding the basic terminology can one clearly focus on the possible causes of dependence and addiction as well as the rationale to be used in their therapy.

The paper by Simon provides an excellent, comprehensive review of our current knowledge of the endogenous opiates, their interactions with the opiate receptors, and the potential relationship that these substances might have in promoting the development of dependence, tolerance, and withdrawal. An understanding of the endorphins and their receptors can lay the foundation for potential explanations not only of dependence but also of analgesia as well as psychological disorders.

The translation of the basic physiologic findings occurring during withdrawal to treatment of withdrawal symptoms in the clinical setting is provided by Gold and Pottash in their paper detailing the use of clonidine in detoxification of narcotic addicts. As one might predict, if an increase in norepinephrine secretion is responsible for withdrawal symptoms, pharmacologic suppression of norepinephrine secretion will result in alleviation of symptoms, allowing a rapid detoxification from narcotic drugs. Clonidine, a drug widely used in the treatment of hypertension, has been demonstrated to effectively inhibit norepinephrine release. However, a knowledge of clonidine's action would predict that side effects such as fatigue, sedation, episodes of light-headedness, and dizziness would accompany its use. Development of similar agents not associated with these adverse effects may offer a valuable alternative to the current detoxification process using methadone.

An understanding of the basic biochemical mechanisms presented by Simon and Gold and Pottash also allows for an understanding of maintenance therapy or the use of narcotic antagonists in the treatment of heroin addiction. Saturation of the opiate receptors with a long-acting narcotic such as methadone suppresses self-administration of morphine or heroin. The slow elevation of the tolerance threshold, accompanied by increasing methadone dosage, also aids in extinguishing drug-seeking behavior by preventing euphoria following injection of street heroin.[1,2] The depressant effect of methadone on the locus coeruleus suppresses norepinephrine secretion and allows the individual to remain comfortable, thereby extinguishing the operant behavior associated with withdrawal.

The displacement of the opiates from the receptor by a narcotic antagonist prevents euphoria from being experienced with heroin injection, thus eliminating the reinforcement accompanying repeated heroin injections. Continued administration of an antagonist also interrupts the operant behavior associated with heroin use, resulting in a diminution of drug-seeking behavior and, hopefully, an extinction of previously conditioned responses.[1] One of the basic problems with narcotic antagonists has been the need to detoxify from narcotics prior to beginning their use. This period may be associated with a relapse to heroin. Gold and Pottash present a physiological explanation for the rationale of using clonidine and naltrexone in such a setting to accelerate the detoxification process without undue discomfort.

The use of antagonists in the treatment of opiate dependency, however, has not met with great success. Cyclazocine, the antagonist initially used, was associated with a number of untoward side effects due to partial agonist activity.[3,4] Most recently, naltrexone, a long-acting antagonist that need be taken only three times a week, has been studied for its efficacy in management of narcotic dependency. Unfortunately, the use of this drug is associated with an extremely high dropout rate.[5] In addition, the advantages of clonidine-naltrexone therapy have also been questioned. Nonetheless, a knowledge of the biochemical rationale underlying the use of these agents is quite helpful in better understanding addictive behavior.

The prominence of the hypothalamus and the pituitary gland in production of endogenous opiates, as well as in exerting a modulating influence over endocrine function, suggests an involvement of both of these systems in narcotic dependence. The paper by Cushman describes the neuroendocrine effects of narcotics. A knowledge of the relationship among endorphins, releasing factors, tropic and stimulating hormones, and exogenous narcotics can facilitate understanding of some of the clinical phenomena observed in narcotic-dependent persons.

It is obvious that the use of either maintenance therapy or narcotic antagonists in the treatment of heroin addiction influences only the operant behavior surrounding self-administration of narcotics. If anxiety still exists, other mood-altering drugs will be taken, most frequently those in the alcohol/barbiturate/tranquilizer group. Alcohol use has been commonly observed not only in patients in methadone programs but also among heroin addicts, especially those attempting to detoxify from narcotics. Although alcohol and opiates have long been thought to exert completely different effects upon the organism with little (if any) interactions, as clearly described in the paper by Ho and Allen, compelling evidence now exists that such interactions can be demonstrated in the laboratory as well as in the clinical setting.

Acute administration of alcohol to laboratory animals will result in an elevation of plasma endorphins similar in magnitude to that seen following acute morphine administration. This release can be reversed by the narcotic antagonist naloxone. Naloxone in turn has been shown to inhibit alcohol-induced dependence, exacerbate symptoms of alcohol withdrawal, and decrease the intoxicating effects of alcohol and other central nervous system depressants.

Naloxone-induced withdrawal in morphinized rats can be suppressed by the administration of alcohol, the degree of the suppression being dose-related. Similarly, acute administration of morphine can suppress alcohol-induced withdrawal convulsions as well as the consumption of alcohol during morphine withdrawal. All of these phenomena are helpful in explaining clinical observations of alcohol use in narcotic dependency.

In addition to an ability to produce euphoria, narcotics have been long known to exert a mild sedative or tranquilizing effect. Correspondingly, some persons stabilized on methadone maintenance have undergone extreme anxiety reactions or even psychotic breaks upon detoxification. Although this has been viewed as a "panic reaction" upon being suddenly forced to be drug free, it is possible that in such individuals methadone is primarily functioning as a tranquilizer or antipsychotic drug. In his paper, Verebey advances the intriguing hypothesis that endorphins are responsible for maintaining a healthy psychological milieu. An imbalance in endorphin homeostasis is responsible for psychological disorders and ultimately even psychosis. This possibility has excited many scientists active in the investigation of the biochemical basis of emotional disorders.

Finally, in recognition of the limited amount of time available for scholarly activity, each issue of *Advances* will end with a contribution focusing on the best way to research the topics. The use of major printed and computer-referenced indexing and abstracting services will be described, as well as available tertiary informational sources such as bibliographies and available current-awareness services. The field of library sciences is currently undergoing a technical revolution. It is appropriate that these advances be part of any educational or scientific endeavor.

In summary, the recent advances in the knowledge of endogenous opiates, other neurotransmitters, and opiate receptors allow for a much greater understanding of the clinical phenomena surrounding alcohol and narcotic use. It is hoped that the relevance of recently confirmed alcohol-opiate interactions will also serve as a stimulus to develop a better relationship between professionals in these fields, easing the all to frequently apparent divisiveness.

Barry Stimmel, MD

REFERENCES

1. Stimmel B, Glick SD: Animal-human correlates of narcotic dependence: A brief review. *Am J Psychiatry* 135:821-825, 1978.
2. Wikler A: Dynamics of drug dependence: Implications of a conditioning theory for research and treatment. *Arch Gen Psychiatry* 28:611-616, 1973.
3. Jaffe JH, Brill L: Cyclazocine, a long-acting narcotic antagonist: Its voluntary acceptance as a treatment modality by narcotic abusers. *Int J Addict* 1:99-123, 1966.
4. Freedman AM, Fink M, Sharoff R et al: Cyclazocine and methadone in narcotic addiction. *JAMA* 202:191-194, 1967.
5. Resnick RB, Washton AM: Clinical outcome with naltrexone: Predictor variables and follow-up status in detoxified heroin addicts. *Ann NY Acad Sci* 311:241-246, 1978.

CURRENT CLINICAL CONCEPTS
OF DEPENDENCE TOLERANCE
AND WITHDRAWAL

John P. Morgan, MD

ABSTRACT. There are "clinical" concepts of dependence tolerance and withdrawal in relationship to psychoactive drugs. These concepts are identified and outlined so as to be of use to physicians and other clinicians who care for patients whose involvement with psychoactive drugs has necessitated intervention. The clinical concepts do not stand apart from but are intertwined with and modified by other definitions of human interaction with drugs. Clinicians must understand and interpret scientific, social, behavioral and even anecdotal and prejudicial concepts of these terms in order to do right and not be led astray. The following discussion is essentially one of definitions and exclusions with an eye both to truth and practical meaning for clinicians and other intervenors.

Drug Use, Misuse, and Abuse of Psychoactive Agents

Using drugs to change consciousness, mood, or perception is America's and perhaps the world's pastime. Even in the Baptist church of my youth one of the deacons smoked cigarettes, more than a few members of the congregation used chewing tobacco, and the minister heavily consumed caffeine. Literally, I know no one who is completely abstinent from the use of psychoactive chemicals. Obviously, complex social rules govern the use of chemicals and in this society, like others, those who do not honor the rules of normative behavior are considered guilty of drug abuse. I hope my language has been clear. The term "drug abuse" has, in the main, social parameters and the term conveys social disapproval; "it is not necessarily descriptive of any particular pattern of drug use or its potential adverse consequences."[1] Clinically, it might be useful to extend the concept to encompass drug use, drug misuse, and drug abuse. An individual given a short term prescription for a phenethylamine as an anorexiant might use it appropriately* for a time and then use it because it relieves hypophoria (misuse) and finally escalate

---

Dr. Morgan is affiliated with the Sophie Davis School for Biomedical Education, The City College of New York, 138th Street and Convent Avenue, New York, NY 10031.

*Some would consider this use itself inappropriate.

Advances in Alcohol & Substance Abuse, Vol. 1(1), Fall 1981
5

the dose and purchase it on the street (abuse). Again, I cite the above possibilities because they might have clinical utility. The disapproval remains chiefly social because I have described only nonnormative behavior and (although the potential exists) not adverse physiological consequences.

Psychoactive Drugs

Psychoactivity is a critical issue for consideration. The culture and its medical and legal institutions are chiefly concerned with abuse of psychoactive drugs. An individual or a group may inappropriately utilize phenylephrine nasal spray or cephalothin, but the focus of concern is on agents that enter the human central nervous system and alter consciousness, mood, perception, and behavior. These terms are scarcely adequate to aid our understanding of desired effects. In fact, it often seems that drug users seek primarily a change in CNS function (or an alteration in consciousness) rather than a particular kind of change. The first individuals to inject psychostimulant amphetamine intravenously were intravenous heroin users.[2] Our current language, clinical or otherwise, is inadequate to explain the desired feelings users achieve or seek. Even if we assume that some chronic drug use is secondary to a need to combat withdrawal sequelae (see below), some chronic use and most early use reflects a pleasure that defies description. Our common terms (euphoria, tension relief) explain little and indeed have little empirical support.[3]

Another critical issue to our understanding is "psychotoxicity"—the consumed drug's ability to alter brain function sufficiently so that the user is intoxicated. An individual whose judgment and psychomotor function are so impaired frightens us, causes the passage of legislation to control him, and, of course, faces potential injury. Minor degrees of drug effect that do not cause intoxication are generally of little concern, hence the easy acceptance of the use of tobacco and caffeine, and in other cultures, betal, khat, and fly agaric. Again, this acceptance sheds no light on the potential harm of the agent to biological tissue.

Clinical Toxicity

Drugs and zenobiotica may damage tissue. Fortunately many drugs chosen for widespread recreational use, particularly at low dosage, have little toxicity. Tissue toxicity if present may have little or nothing to do with the pleasurable effects or the psychotoxicity. Alcohol is menacingly toxic at high dosage but minimally so at low dosage. Of course, the toxicity may relate chiefly to contaminants or the method of administration. A review of toxicity with commonly used drugs is beyond the scope of this article and the reader is referred elsewhere.[4]

Drug Sources

Not unlike other pleasures, people acquire their drugs where they find them. In agrarian societies bushes and trees may constitute the chief source, while in our society, a clandestine or legitimate laboratory may produce a purer and more dangerously potent drug. It is simplistic but perhaps necessary to point out that individuals in our culture may find it possible to obtain drugs from multiple sources: over-the-counter sellers, clandestine sellers, prescribing professionals, or family givers. Further, drugs may pass through more than one of these sources. The clinician cannot rely on the stated identity of a drug. The only truth that exists in the clandestine market is there by accident. I recently learned of a death by overdose of a young man who took more than 30 black capsules marked "Dex." The postmortem blood analysis revealed that he almost certainly died of a caffeine overdose.

Tolerance

The concept of tolerance is structurally simple. Many psychoactive drugs taken repeatedly lose effect. Conversely, an individual who wishes to achieve a remembered effect may need a much larger dose to reprovoke that effect. Traditionally, tolerance is viewed as having two mechanisms: drug dispositional or pharmacodynamic. In many animal experiments and a few human studies one can demonstrate that repeated exposure to a drug provokes improved disposition. Essentially this always relates to an improved metabolic capacity through hepatic enzyme induction.[5] Despite the demonstration of this potential and the widespread acceptance of the idea that drug dispositional tolerance occurs, I find little evidence that it is ever important in human tolerance to abused drugs. Most clinicians have had the experience of discharging an intoxicated individual from the emergency room and learning later that his blood alcohol level was greater than 400 mg per 100 cc of blood—a concentration that might be fatal to a nontolerant drinker. Human tolerance to abused drugs, particularly to important despressive psychoactive drugs (ethanol, sedative-hypnotics, and narcotic opiates), is mediated by a diminishing cellular response to the presence of the agent—so called "cellular" or "pharmacodynamic" tolerance. In other words, the diminished response is *not* concurrent with a diminished concentration of the drug at the site of action but is concurrent with the presence of the same or even greater concentration of the drug that earlier provoked effects.

CNS tolerance to both opioids and alcohol hypnotics can occur rapidly in experimental settings in animals and man. However, human *clinical* tolerance seems to occur only with prolonged exposure; its mechanisms may even vary from those that produce rapid CNS tolerance. Multiple theories exist as to the mechanisms of cellular tolerance. Several of these theories are discussed in Eric Simon's paper which follows in this journal.

Opiates

There are other important clinical aspects of tolerance. The character of tolerance to narcotic opiates varies from that to ethanol and sedative-hypnotics. Although tolerance to all effects of opiates does not occur, analgesic, euphoric, and sedative effects markedly decrease. This is logically accompanied by a marked increase in the lethal dose. Experimentally, the degree of tolerance to the lethal effects of opiates can be complete. Theoretically one can reach a state where no dose of narcotic would be fatal. Obviously, narcotic users with a developed state of tolerance do not die of overdose; most overdose deaths occur in new users and those recently out of incarceration or treatment. In recent years, the quality of street heroin has been low in most areas of the United States and many regular users have probably failed to achieve a large degree of tolerance.

Alcohol, Hypnotics, and Sedatives

Tolerance to alcohol, hypnotics, and sedatives may be profound, but it never reaches the degree of completeness described for opiates. This has two practical consequences. The user of these drugs can nearly always achieve a state of intoxication and is *not* protected from overdosage and death secondary to respiratory depression. Tolerant humans and animals apparently achieve only a modest increase in lethal blood concentration. Practically, this means that an individual who has achieved intoxication by overcoming a high degree of tolerance may need only a minimal dosage increase to die. I assume that this incompleteness of tolerance and lethal dosage convergence may occur in chronic alcoholics, but there are so many mechanisms for death in alcoholics that it is apparently seldom suspected or identified.

Tolerance to other abused drugs occurs. There is ample proof of tolerance to amphetamine and psychedelic drugs in humans, but the issue remains somewhat unsettled for cocaine.[6] An important clinical issue for the abuser of amphetamine and related sympathomimetics is the lack of tolerance to the psychotogenic effects. Users may develop profound tolerance to both the cardiovascular and euphoric effects but remain at high risk for the development of psychosis.[2]

Cross-Tolerance

Cross-tolerance exists between different narcotic opiates. An individual tolerant to heroin is tolerant to methadone or propoxyphene or fentanyl within the constraints previously described. There is no obvious cross-tolerance between narcotic opiates and other CNS depressants or analgesics. In a practical sense then, a patient on a methadone maintenance program who is injured will not be treatable with other narcotic analgesics, nor will he receive benefit from the methadone in his body.

Cross-tolerance in the broader class of alcohol-sedative-hypnotic drugs is pronounced. An individual tolerant to alcohol will be tolerant to barbiturates, meprobamate, benzodiazepines, and a lengthy list of nonbarbiturate depressants including methaqualone, ethchlorvynol, glutethimide, and the gaseous anesthetics, among others, although not to the phenothiazine antipsychotics. However, recent evidence presented in a subsequent paper suggests that previously held concepts concerning the exclusivity of alcohol-sedative-narcotic tolerance are now being questioned. Interactions between alcohol and opiates at the level of the opiate receptor may exist and may be shown to have clinical relevance.

Physical Dependence

Physical dependence simply refers to an altered physiological state produced by repetitive use of a drug which is manifest by the emergence of a withdrawal or abstinence syndrome upon cessation of drug use. The continued administration of the drug prevents emergence of the abstinence syndrome and may be a compelling reason why individuals continue chronic use of some agents. The most obvious and stereotyped withdrawal syndromes are associated with the depressant drugs: narcotic opiates, ethanol, and the sedative-hypnotics. As with tolerance, we can distinguish two types of physical dependence, both apparently related to the mechanisms by which tolerance develops. Both types of withdrawal syndromes are associated with central nervous system hyperactivity and in a simplistic manner seem to represent an expression of escape from the depressant actions of the drug.

Opiates

Withdrawal from opiates begins at various intervals after cessation of drug use, depending upon the particular opiate that has been utilized. The syndrome is often initiated by lacrimation, rhinorrhea, and sweating. With progression, pupillary dilitation, piloerection, restlessness, and tremor ensue and in the most severe syndromes may be accompanied by anxiety, irritability, nausea, vomiting, and muscle cramping. The severity of the syndrome and its duration both vary depending upon the individual opiate and the degree and duration of use. The syndrome may be easily precipitated by administration of an opiate antagonist, including these used inadvertently for analgesic effects. The opiate abstinence syndrome can range from mild to severe but it is important to realize that in the absence of other complicating illness it is not life-threatening. The syndrome does not constitute an emergency and many users have undergone it without therapy and without lasting sequelae. It is easily treated by administration of an opiate (methadone is most commonly used), but other treatments ranging from reassurance to benzodiazepines apparently have also been effective. The use of the non-opiate clonidine[7] has attracted much attention and is discussed elsewhere in this issue.

Alcohol, Hypnotics, and Sedatives

The withdrawal syndrome from alcohol or many of the hypnotic-sedatives can be severe and life-threatening and may demand emergency treatment. These syndromes have been thoroughly discussed[8] and will be reviewed only briefly. The emergence of the syndrome following cessation of drug use again varies relative to the drug and its duration and degree of use. It is important to note here that with drugs that persist for lengthy times in the body (some barbiturates and benzodiazepines), the onset of a abstinence syndrome may be delayed for many days. Gradually the user develops increasing agitation, tremor, restlessness, and insomnia. Orthostatic hypotension is common as is motor hyperactivity. The CNS excitation may lead ultimately to convulsions and in the most severe form to hyperpyrexia, toxic psychosis, and death.

In general, most clinicians have felt that early intervention with sedative drugs is appropriate although drug free withdrawal of some alcoholic patients is certainly possible.[9] Many agents may provoke this dependence and many may be used to treat it. Benzodiazepines are probably most commonly used today although a good case for phenobarbital has been made.[10] I think the use of phenothiazines is inappropriate and less effective.

Stimulants

Generally, physical dependence and withdrawal syndromes are not a part of chronic psychostimulant abuse. Adverse events may follow the cessation of chronic psychostimulant use but these have in general thought to be "due to stress of insomnia, fatigue, disturbances in metabolism and psychologic factors."[11] A group of studies apparently establish the presence of a physical dependence syndrome to coffee, particularly in high dose users.[12] It is safe to say however that physical dependence does not appear to be a strong motivation for chronic use of psychostimulant drugs.

Compulsive Relapsing Drug Use

The biological issues of tolerance, physical dependence, and abstinence outlined above are not sufficient to explain chronic drug use. This paper has almost been concluded without the use of the term "addiction." Like drug abuse, addiction has principally social parameters and is most often used to describe the complete expenditure of life resources in obtaining and using the beloved chemical. It often occurs with a background of physical dependence and when the drug is used in part to forestall the emergence of abstinence symptoms. Clearly, however, some users of psychostimulants (amphetamine and cocaine) act as addicts outside a setting of physical dependence. The presence of physical dependence does not in itself signal addiction. The use of narcotic opiates at full analgesic doses for 48 hours will be followed by a physical withdrawal syndrome, yet such patients do not act as or become addicts. Complex social, behavioral, political, and pharmacological forces come together in some individuals to lure them to psychoactive drug use as a cardinal rather than an incidental part of life. Clinicians need to accurately assess the biological events of drug use to discharge properly their medical responsibility to the intoxicated, overdosed, withdrawing, or organ-damaged drug user. The humanity and intellect of clinicians, like other human beings, should be brought to bear on some of the other issues when that initial responsibility is discharged.

REFERENCES

1. Jaffe, JH: Drug addiction and drug abuse, in Gillman AG, Goodman LS, Gillman A (eds.) *The Pharmacological Basis of Therapeutics*, ed 6. New York, Macmillan, 1980, 535.
2. Smith RC: Traffic in amphetamines: Patterns of illegal manufacture and distribution. *J. Psychedelic Drugs* 2: 20-24, 1969.
3. Cappell H: An evaluation of tension models of alcohol consumption, in Gibbons RJ, Israel Y, Kalant H, Popham RE, Schmidt W, Smart RG (eds.) *Research Advances in Alcohol and Drug Problems*. New York, Wiley, 1975, pp. 177-210.
4. Dupont, RI, Goldstein A, O'Donnell J (ed.): *Handbook on Drug Abuse*. NIDA US Government Printing Office, Washington, DC, 1979.
5. Misra PS, Lefevre A, Ishii H et al: Increases of ethanol, meprobamate, and pentobarbital metabolism after chronic ethanol administration in rats. *AM J MED* 51:346, 1976.
6. Castellani S, Ellinwood EH Jr, Kilbey MM: Behavioral analysis of chronic cocaine intoxication in the cat. *Biol Psy* 13:203-215, 1978.
7. Gold ME, Renard DC, Kleber HD: Clonidine blocks acute opiate-withdrawal symptoms. *Lancet* 2:599-607, 1978.
8. Mello NK, Mendelsohn JH: Clinical aspects of alcohol dependence, drug addiction I, in Martin WR (ed): *Handbook of Experimental Pharmacology*. Berlin, Springer Verlag, 1977, vol 45(1), p. 613-666.
9. Whitfield CL, Thompson G, Lamb A et al: Detoxification of 1024 alcoholic patients without psychoactive drugs. *JAMA* 239:1409-1410, 1978.
10. Smith DE, Wesson DR, Seymour RB: The abuse of barbiturates and other sedative-hypnotics, in Dupont RI Goldstein D, O'Donnell J (ed). *Handbook of Drug Abuse*. US GPO:NIDA, 1979, pp. 233-240.
11. Seevers MH: *Drug Dependence Vis-A-Vis Drug Abuse in Drug Abuse*. Philadelphia, Lea Febiger, 1972, p. 12.
12. Goldstein A, Kazen S: Psychotropic effects of caffeine in man, III. *Clin Parmocol & Therap* 10:477-488, 1969.

OPIATE RECEPTORS AND ENDORPHINS: POSSIBLE RELEVANCE TO NARCOTIC ADDICTION

Eric J. Simon, PhD

ABSTRACT. This review presents a chronological discussion of the discovery of opiate receptors and the endogenous opioid peptides. After a summary of the properties and distribution of the receptors and their endogenous ligands, the possible function of the endogenous opioid system is discussed. Evidence for a role of this system in endogenous pain modulation and in opiate addiction is presented. The nature of the evidence and the absence of definitive proof of a causal involvement of the opiate receptor-endorphin system are emphasized.

Introduction

Scientists have long been interested in elucidating the biochemical basis of the actions of drugs of abuse, particularly their tendency to produce addiction upon chronic use. For one group of addictive drugs, the opiates, there have recently been advances on the biochemical-pharmacological level that have created considerable excitement and have been widely hailed as breakthroughs that may lead to an understanding of opiate addiction as well as of analgesia and endogenous pain modulation.

In this paper I will review these developments briefly in a chronological manner and will then discuss critically the evidence that has given rise to the claims that have been made, particularly those pertaining to narcotic addiction. I will finish by summarizing my views as to where the field may be going and what we may hope to learn that may ultimately benefit clinical medicine and, in particular, the treatment and prevention of narcotic addiction.

The Discovery of Opiate Receptors

The hypothesis that narcotic analgesics must bind to highly specific sites or receptors in the central nervous system (CNS) in order to produce their

Dr. Simon is Professor, Departments of Psychiatry and Pharmacology, New York University Medical Center, 550 First Avenue, New York, NY 10016.

Advances in Alcohol & Substance Abuse, Vol. 1(1), Fall 1981

many well-known responses has been held by some investigators for several decades. The evidence for the existence of such receptor sites was compelling. It consisted primarily of the remarkable stereospecificity and, for certain parts of the molecules, structural specificity displayed by many of the pharmacological actions of narcotic analgesic drugs.

As thousands of analogues of morphine were synthesized in search of the still mythical nonaddictive analgesic it became clear that one enantiomer of a racemic mixture (usually the levo-rotatory one) was generally much more active than the other. Moreover, whereas some parts of the molecule could be drastically altered with relatively little change in potency, tampering with certain regions had dramatic effects. The most interesting and best studied such region is the substituent on the tertiary nitrogen, one of the functional groups essential for narcotic analgesic activity.

When the methyl group is substituted by a larger alkyl group, eg, an allyl or cyclopropylmethyl group, analgesic potency is reduced and the drug takes on the new pharmacological role of a potent, specific antagonist against many of the actions of morphine and related narcotics. Some drugs have both agonist and antagonist properties, while others, such as naloxone and naltrexone (the N-allyl and N-cyclopropylmethyl analogues, resp. of oxymorphone), are "pure" antagonists. The synthesis of mixed agonist-antagonist drugs as candidates for analgesics with low addiction liability has been a major enterprise in pharmaceutical company laboratories in recent years. Moreover, the pure antagonist naltrexone, which is longer acting than naloxone, has shown some promise for the treatment of heroin addicts.

The kinds of specificities described above are most easily explained by interaction with binding sites that exhibit complementary specificity. The search for such specific binding sites or opiate receptors began in the 1950s and bore fruit in the early 1970s. It was easy to show binding of opiates to cell constitutents[1] but to distinguish specific from nonspecific binding proved difficult.

It was the measurement of stereospecific binding that led to success. Ingoglia and Dole[2] were the first to apply stereospecificity to the search for receptors by injecting l- and d-methadone into the lateral ventricle of rats, but found no difference in the rate of diffusion of the enantiomers. Goldstein et al[3] devised a method for measuring stereospecific binding of ^{3}H-levorphanol in mouse brain homogenates. They reported that only 2% of the total binding was stereospecific and the properties and distribution of this binding turned out to be quite different from those of the subsequently discovered "receptors." Upon purification this binding material proved to be cerebroside sulfate.

In 1973 our laboratory[4] and the laboratories of Snyder[5] and Terenius,[6] using modifications of the Goldstein procedure, independently and simultaneously reported the observation in animal brain homogenates of stereospecific binding of opiates that represented the major portion of the total binding. The modifications involved the use of very low concentrations of labeled drugs, made possible by high specific activity, and washing homogenates pelleted or filtered, following incubation, in order to remove unbound and loosely bound contaminating radioactivity. Since that time stereospecific binding studies have been done in many laboratories and much evidence has been accumulated suggesting that these stereospecific sites are indeed receptors which are responsible for many of the pharmacological actions of the opiates. They have been found in man[7] and in all vertebrates studied so far. Very recently it has been reported that they also exist in some invertebrates.[8]

Properties and Distribution of Opiate Receptors

The properties of the opiate binding sites have been studied extensively and their distribution in the brain and spinal cord has been mapped in considerable detail by dissection and in vitro binding measurement[7,9] as well as by autoradiography.[10,11,12,13]

Stereospecific binding is saturable and total binding amount to 15-20 pmol of opiate per gram of rat brain. Affinities range from K_D of 0.025 nM for a potent fentanyl analogue[14] to little or no affinity for drugs devoid of opiate activity. The average dissociation constants for effective narcotic analgesics are in the 1-10 nM range. The pH optimum for binding is in the physiological range with a fairly broad optimum between 6.5 and 8.0. The addition of salts to the incubation mixture tends to reduce binding. Sodium represents an interesting exception which will be discussed later.

The inhibition of stereospecific binding by proteolytic enzymes [4,15] and a variety of protein reagents, including sulfhydryl reagents, suggests the involvement of protein moieties in opiate binding. The role of phospholipids is yet to be established. Binding is inhibited by some, although not all, phospholipase A preparations,[4,15] but not by phospholipases C or D. Moreover, we have shown[16] that inhibition by phospholipase A can be reversed by washing the membrane preparation with a solution of bovine serum albumin, suggesting that the nature of the phospholipid environment may be very important for the active conformation of the opiate receptor.

The extensive mapping studies can be summarized here only briefly. The highest levels of opiate receptors are found in areas of the limbic system and in the regions that have been implicated in the pathways involved in pain perception and modulation, such as the periventricular and periaqueductal gray areas, the medial thalamus, the nucleus raphe magnus and the substantia gelatinosa of the spinal cord. It has been suggested that the limbic system receptors may be involved in opiate-induced euphoria (or dysphoria) and in the affective aspects of pain perception.

Perhaps the most convincing evidence suggesting that stereospecific binding has pharmacological relevance comes from a number of studies that show excellent correlation between pharmacological potencies and in vitro binding affinities for a large number of drugs, varying in analgesic potencies over 5-6 orders of magnitude.[14,17]

Multiple Opiate Receptors

Various neurotransmitters such as acetylcholine, norepinephrine, and dopamine have been known for many years to have multiple types of receptors. The possibility of multiple opiate receptors has also been raised. Pharmacological differences between morphine, ketocyclazocine, and SKF 10,047 observed by Martin et al in chronic spinal dogs[18,19] suggested the presence of three types of opiate receptors: these were named μ, κ, σ after the respective drugs. After the isolation of the enkephalins, Kosterlitz's group found opposite potency differences between opiates and enkephalins in two bioassay systems.[20] While opiates were more potent than enkephalins in inhibiting electrically induced contractions in the guinea pig ileum, enkephalins were more potent in the mouse vas deferens. The authors concluded that the autonomic plexuses in the two tissues were relatively enriched in one of two different receptor types: a μ receptor in the guinea pig ileum favoring morphine-like compounds (possbily identical to the μ receptor of Martin), and a receptor having higher affinity for enkephalins, which they named the δ receptor, in the mouse vas deferens. The same group found significant differences in binding competitions in brain homogenates. When labeled opiates were used, unlabeled opiates competed more effectively for binding than enkephalins, while the unlabeled enkephalins were more effective competitors than opiates against labeled enkephalins.

This laboratory[21] and others[22] have confirmed these results. Like the bioassay findings, the binding competition experiments indicate that at least two different types of opiate receptors exist, with overlapping specificity but affinities that favor different ligands. However, the binding competition data do not rule out the possibility of opiates and enkephalins binding to a single class of receptor. The differences in competitive efficacy would then be due to differences in the way the ligands bind to the receptor, involving different types of chemical bonding and/or functional groups. Indeed, morphine (μ) and enkephalin (δ) receptors display similar chemical properties, such as having a single essential SH group and a similar 50% inactivation time by NEM. Their sensitivity to phospholipase A_2 and proteolytic enzymes is also similar. Yet two further lines of work support their distinctness.

One approach makes use of the ability of ligands to protect agains irreversible inactivation of receptor binding. Kosterlitz's group has used phenoxybenzamine as the irreversible inactivator,[28] while we have used NEM.[24] For both inactivators, opiate alkaloid ligands were more potent than enkephalins in protecting ³H-opiate binding, while enkephalins were more potent than opiates in protecting ³H-enkephalin binding. This is a very difficult phenomenon to explain in terms of different types of binding at a single receptor since for a single receptor, the relative protective efficacies of opiates and enkephalins should not vary with the labeled ligand used to measure residual binding. D-Ala² met-enkephalinamide, which has been shown to be equally effective against opiates and enkephalins in binding competition, suggesting similar affinity for the two receptor classes, is also equally effective in protecting opiate and enkephalin binding from inactivation.

The other confirmatory line of evidence is that binding competitions carried out in various brain regions indicate differing regional distributions for the two receptor classes.[21,25] In thalamus, opiates are strikingly more effective in competing against ³H-enkephalin binding than they are in the rest of the brain. This indicates that thalamus is markedly enriched in μ receptors and that in thalamus ³H-enkephalin binds largely to this class of receptors. Preliminary work using protection against NEM also supports this regional variation: in contrast to what is seen in whole brain, enkephalin is no more effective than opiate in protecting thalamic ³H-enkephalin binding from NEM inactivation (Smith, J. and Simon, E.J., unpublished results). Binding competition studies and other biochemical studies in rat brain have failed so far to distinguish the κ and σ receptors postulated by Martin.[26,27] Very recently, however, Kosterlitz (private communication) and collaborators have been able to demonstrate a significant number of κ receptors in guinea pig brain. After blocking μ receptors with a highly selective μ peptide and δ sites with Dala²-D-leu⁵-enkephalin, residual receptors were observed that bound ethylketocyclazocine and related benzomorphans preferentially.

In conclusion, the cautionary note should be made that though there is evidence for multiple opiate receptor types and multiple endorphins have been demonstrated, it is not known whether a given receptor type bears any special functional relationship to one endorphin as opposed to another. However, the elucidation of the number of classes of opiate receptors and their functions has very important theoretical and practical implications.

Conformational Changes in Opiate Receptors

I mentioned that sodium is an exception to the rule that increased salt concentrations present during incubation will inhibit binding. An apparent discrepancy between results in Snyder's laboratory[5] and in our laboratory[4] led to the realization that sodium can distinguish between agonists and antagonists.[28,29] Whereas agonist binding is inhibited by sodium salts, the binding of antagonists is either unaffected or, in many instances, augmented by the presence of sodium. This remarkable discrimination by a small ion between closely related molecules (eg, morphine and nalorphine, oxymorphone and naloxone) is highly specific. It is exhibited, though less effectively, by lithium, but by none of the other alkali metals. In fact, no other inorganic or organic cations have been found that exhibit this effect.[28,29] A study of the mechanism of this sodium effect has produced evidence that sodium is an allosteric effector, the binding of which produces a conformational change in the receptor. The sodium conformer has a higher affinity for antagonists and a markedly reduced affinity for agonists.

The best evidence for an alteration in receptor conformation by sodium ions came unexpectedly from a study of the kinetics of receptor inactivation by the sulfhydryl alkylating reagent, N-ethylmaleimide (NEM), in our laboratory.[30] When a membrane fraction from rat brain was incubated with NEM for various periods followed by inactivation or removal of unreacted NEM, there was a progressive decrease in the ability of the membranes to bind opiates stereospecifically. The rate of receptor inactivation followed pseudo-first order kinetics consistent with the existence of one SH-group essential for binding per receptor. Protection against inactivation was achieved by the addition of low concentrations of opiates or antagonists during the preincubation with NEM, suggesting that the SH-group is located near the opiate binding site of the receptor.

Considerable protection was observed (half time of inactivation was increased to 30 minutes from 8 minutes) when inactivation was carried out in the presence of 100 mM NaCl. Since sodium salts were without effect on the alkylation of model SH-compounds, such as cysteine or glutathione, this suggested that the SH-groups were made less accessible to NEM by a conformational change in the receptor protein. The fact that this protection exhibited the same ion specificity (Na^+ protects, Li^+ protects partially, K^+, Rb^+, or Cs^+ not at all) and that the dose-response to Na^+ is the same as the differential changes in ligand affinities, suggests that the conformational change that masks SH-groups is the same as that which results in increased affinity of antagonists and decreased affinity of agonists.

These studies illustrate that the opiate receptor can alter its shape. The physiological function of this plasticity is not yet clear. A role in the coupling of opiate binding to subsequent physical or chemical events has been suggested as has a role for Na^+ ions in the action of opiates.

Isolation of Opiate Receptors

Brief mention should be made of research that is of great importance but has proved very difficult, namely the isolation and purification of opiate receptors. The tight association of these receptors with cell membranes requires as a first step a method for solubilizing them without denaturing them. The extreme sensitivty of opiate binding to very low concentrations of detergents, even the nonionic variety adds a further complication.

Several years ago our laboratory succeeded in solubilizing a complex of etorphine bound stereospecifically to a macromolecule from rat brain membranes using the detergent Brij 36T.[31] This complex has a molecular weight of about 400,000 and had all of the earmarks of being an etorphine-receptor complex. However, this preparation was unable to exchange or rebind ^{3}H-etorphine in solution. Subsequently an enkephalin-macromolecular complex was solubilized by the same procedure and a portion of it was stabilized by Zukin and Kream[32] by a covalent cross-linking reagent as a possible preliminary to purification and characterization.

Using 1% digitonin, Ruegg, Hiller, and Simon[38] recently have solubilized an active opiate receptor from cell membrane fractions from the brain of the toad, *Bufo marinus*, though this technique and many others fail to solubilize an active receptor when mammalian brains are used. This work was stimulated by an analogous species difference that exists for the β adrenergic receptor, which was solubilized in active form with digitonin from frog[34] and turkey[35] erythrocyte membranes but could not so far be solubilized in active form from various mammalian tissues.[36]

For the toad brain, saturable stereospecific binding of ^{3}H-diprenorphine, representing 50%-60% of total binding, was obtained in the solubilized fraction. Up to 30%-40% of the original stereospecific opiate binding activity and 20%-30% of the membrane protein had been solubilized from the membranes. As is also true for the membrane-bound receptor, trypsin, NEM and heat readily inactivated binding activity of the solubilized receptor, indicating the importance of protein components in the receptor. By column chromatography the solubilized receptor has been purified 6-8-fold.

Recently two other laboratories published accounts of the solubilization of an active opiate receptor using different techniques. Simonds et al solubilized such a receptor from the membranes of neuroblastoma x glioma cells in culture using the new detergent CHAPS, a zwitterionic derivative of cholic acid.[37] They also reported some success with rat brain membranes. Bidlack and Abood[38] reported solubilization of a receptor from rat neural membranes using the detergent Triton X-100, which subsequently was removed with Bio-beads SM-2. A similar procedure carried out in other laboratories, including our own, had been unsuccessful.

The solubilization of an active opiate receptor took over five years to achieve, but the stage is now set for its purification to homogeneity. This will permit delineation of the chemical composition and subunit structure of the receptor molecule. Moreover, it will enable us to produce antibodies to the receptor. The injection of such antibodies into animal brain should help clarify the functional role of the opiate receptors and their ligands.

Discovery of Endogenous Opioid Peptides

The evidence that the brains of all vertebrates investigated, from the hag fish to man, contains opiate receptors led investigators to raise the question why such receptors for plant-derived substances exist in the CNS and have survived eons of evolution. A physiological role for opiate receptors that confers a selective advantage on the organisms seemed probable, suggesting the presence of an endogenous opiate-like ligand for the receptor. This notion was reinforced by the finding in the early 1970s that electrical stimulation of certain brain areas was able to mobilize an endogenous pain-relieving system, resulting in long-lasting analgesia.[39,40]

None of the many known neurotransmitters or neurohormones was found to exhibit high affinity for opiate receptors. A number of laboratories therefore initiated a search for new opiate-like substances in extracts of animal brain. This search was successful first in the laboratories of Hughes and Kosterlitz[41] and of Terenius and Wahlström.[42] At about the same time, Goldstein and his collaborators[43] reported opioid activity in extracts of pituitary glands. Hughes utilized the in vitro bioassays for opiates, namely naloxone-reversible inhibition of electrically evoked contraction of the mouse vas deferens or the guinea pig ileum, while Terenius assayed endogenous opioid activity by measuring the ability of brain extracts and fractions to compete with labeled opiates for receptor binding.

These studies culminated in the identification by Hughes et al[44] of the opioid substances in extracts of pig brain. They reported that the activity resided in two pentapeptides, Tyr-Gly-Gly-Phe-Met and Tyr-Gly-Gly-Phe-Leu, which they named methionine (met) and leucine (leu) enkephalin. Hughes et al also reported the interesting observation that the sequence of met-enkephalin was present as amino acid residues 61-65 in the pituitary hormone β-lipotropin (βLPH). This hormone had been isolated in 1965 from pituitary glands by C. H. Li.[45] It possessed weak lipolytic activity which was never seriously thought to be its real function. The report of Hughes et al, along with the Goldstein group's report of the existence of opioid activity in the pituitary gland, led Guillemin to examine the extracts of pig hypothalami and pituitary glands (remaining in his freezer from his Nobel prize-winning identification of hypothalamic releasing factors). Two polypeptides with opioid activity were found and sequenced.[45] They proved to have structures identical with amino acid sequences 61-76 and 61-77 of βLPH. Meanwhile, potent opioid activity was found in the C-terminal fragment of βLPH (LPH 61-91) in two laboratories[47,48] while the intact βLPH molecule was inactive. The proliferation of endogenous peptides with opioid activity caused the author of this paper to suggest the term "endorphin" (a contraction of "endogenous" and "morphine") which has been widely accepted. The C-terminal fragment was renamed β-endorphin by Li, while LPH 61-67 and 61-77 were named α and γ-endorphin, respectively, by Guillemin.

Recently, a number of additional peptides with opioid activity has been reported. One of the most important of these is a peptide from the pituitary characterized by A. Goldstein and collaborators.[49] The peptide was named dynorphin by the authors because of its potent opioid activity in bioassay systems. It has been found in certain areas of the CNS in addition to the pituitary.

All the opioid peptides exhibit opiate-like activity when injected intraventricularly. This activity includes analgesia, respiratory depression, and a variety of behavioral changes including the production of a rigid catatonia. The pharmacological effects of the enkephalins are very fleeting, presumably due to their rapid destruction by peptidases. The longer-chain endorphins are more stable and produce long-lived effects. Thus, analgesia from intraventricular administration of β-endorphin can last three to four hours. All of the responses to endorphins are reversible by opiate antagonists, such as naloxone. There have been reports that certain analogues of enkephalin can produce analgesia after systemic injection or even oral ingestion.[50]

Distribution of enkephalins has been studied by biochemical[51] as well as by bioassay[52] and immunohistochemical techniques.[53,54] The distribution of enkephalins in the CNS shows considerable though not complete correlation with the distribution of opiate receptors. Thus, the globus pallidus has a very high density of enkephalin (or at least enkephalin-like immunoreactive material) while it is low in opiate receptors. Certain cortical areas dense in opiate receptors have low levels of enkephalin.

In the earlier studies of Hökfelt and colleagues[53] the immunofluorescence was all found in nerve fibers and terminals but not in cell bodies. In a more recent paper this group[55] utilized colchicine which is known to arrest axonal transport. After such treatment it was possible to find immunofluorescence in cell bodies after treatment with antiserum to met-enkephalin. More than 20 cell groups containing enkephalin have so far been observed in the brain and spinal cord, a number somewhat larger than the 15 catecholamine cell groups known to exist in rat brain. The authors felt that their results indicate that these perikarya possess the machinery for enkephalin biosynthesis. This raises the interesting question whether enkephalin is always derived from large endorphin precursors, since levels of β-lipotropin and β-endorphin are very low in some of the areas that are found to have high enkephalin levels.

Studies on the distribution of β-endorphin in the laboratories of Guillemin[56] and Watson[57] have provided convincing evidence for a distribution that is very different from that of the enkephalins. This has led to the suggestion that the CNS has separate enkephalinergic and endorphinergic neuronal systems. β-Endorphin is present in the pituitary, where there is little or no enkephalin, as well as in certain regions of the brain. Brain β-endorphin seems to originate in a single set of neurons located in the periarcuate region of the hypothalamus, with axons projecting throughout the brain stem.

Pain and Its Modulation

Since it was work on the opiate analgesics that led to the discovery of the endorphins and their receptors it was natural to postulate that they may be involved in pain modulation. The fact mentioned earlier that all CNS regions implicated in the conduction of pain impulses have high levels of opiate receptors supports this hypothesis, as does the finding that opiates seem to inhibit selectively the firing of nociceptive neurons in the substantia gelatinosa of the dorsal spinal cord.[58] Moreover, as mentioned earlier, the intraventricular injection of all known opioid peptides produces analgesia. These findings did not prove that endogenous opioids are involved in the pain pathway, but were sufficiently suggestive to encourage further testing of this hypothesis.

Attempts were made to demonstrate by the use of the opiate antagonist naloxone the role of the natural opioid system in pain perception. It was postulated that if receptor occupancy by endorphins was involved in pain modulation, the administration of an opiate antagonist should lower the threshold or exacerbate perceived pain. Such an effect has been suprisingly difficult to demonstrate conclusively. Out of a great number of attempts on animals, only those of Jacob et al[59] were successful in demonstrating a lowering of pain threshold by naloxone (decreases in latency period before rats or mice jumped off a hotplate). The results have recently been replicated in other laboratories.[60] Attempts to show exacerbation of experimental pain or lowering of pain threshold in human volunteers have been unsuccessful.[61,62]

Better success was achieved by studying the effect of naloxone on several types of analgesia that do not involve the use of drugs. Analgesia produced by electrical stimulation of the periaqueductal gray area of both animals[63] and humans[64] has been shown to be at least partially reversed by the administration of naloxone.

A more dramatic reversal by naloxone has been observed with analgesia resulting from electroacupuncture in mice[65] and from acupuncture in human subjects.[66] The involvement of opiate receptors and endorphins in electroacupuncture has received additional support, not involving naloxone, from the findings that the CXBK strain of mice, which is deficient in opiate receptors, shows poor analgesia in response to electroacupuncture.[67]

Recently there has been a report[68] indicating that analgesia due to "placebo effect" is also reversed by naloxone in patients with postoperative pain after extraction of impacted third molars. In this regard it is of interest that analgesia produced by hypnosis was found not to be affected by naloxone.[69]

These results, though indirect, are supportive of the idea that the endorphin system may be involved in an endogenous pain modulation system. Such a system is likely to be of considerable survival value to the organism since it will permit it to experience pain as an important warning of tissue damage without the suffering, except in pathological states, of unbearable, disabling pain. The importance of pain to the individual is best demonstrated by a disease called congenital insensitivity to pain. Individuals with this condition are unable to feel pain from either visceral or superficial tissue damage. This is a serious pathology which results in a significantly shortened life expectancy. A number of laboratories including our own are currently studying such patients to determine whether an abnormality in the opiate receptor-endorphin system may play a role in this inborn error.

There have indeed been two brief reports suggesting that naloxone may have an effect on these patients. Dehen et al[70] report that the flexion-reflex threshold, which was 350% higher in the patient than in controls, fell dramatically by 67% within ten minutes of naloxone administration. Yanagida[71] reports that tooth pulp evoked potentials (TPEP) are absent in patients with congenital insensitivity to pain. However, ten minutes after administration of naloxone (10 mg, IV) some TPEP were observed, especially after stimuli of 15 mA (the highest used). The patient was able to recognize these stimuli as pressure sensations without apparent distress. These reports are still preliminary and the effects observed are minimal. Nevertheless, they suggest that the endorphin system could play a role in this disease. The administration of large amounts of a long-acting antagonist should be attempted as a possibly beneficial treatment of this serious pathology.

To prove conclusively the involvement of endorphins in endogenous pain regulation requires direct demonstration of changes in endorphin level or turnover during severe acute or chronic pain and during analgesia. Terenius and Wahlström[72] found decreases in opioid activity in the CSF of patients suffering chronic pain due to trigeminal neuralgia when compared to patients who were not in pain. More recently this group[73] also reported an increase in level of opioid activity after analgesia by electroacupuncture in patients with intractable pain. These reports have the drawback that the opioid activity in the CSF represents as yet poorly characterized chromatographic fractions that seem to differ from all of the known and well-characterized endorphins.

Reports on the release of well-characterized endorphins during analgesia have also appeared. Richardson et al[74] have reported good success in relieving intractable pain in patients by electrical stimulation with electrodes implanted in the periventricular gray region. The region found to be most effective and also the one at which the least side effects were seen was a site near the posterior commissure, adjacent to the ventricular wall at the level of the nucleus parafascicularis. This method is adaptable for pain relief by periodic self-stimulation by the patient over a period of months or even years. The analgesia so produced was found to be partially reversible by naloxone administration. More recently Akil et al[75] have shown that stimulation analgesia is followed after 15-20 minutes by a small ($<$ 2-fold) but significant increase in release of met-enkephalin into the ventricular CSF, measured by several techniques including bioassay, receptor binding, and radioimmunoassay. The same group[75] has reported a more dramatic release of β-endorphin-like immunoreactive material under identical conditions of analgesia. Baseline release was undetectable ($<$ 25 fmol per ml of CSF), while the level measured during stimulation-produced analgesia in five patients ranged from 319-481 fmol/ml, an increase of at least 13-20-fold.

Thus an impressive array of at least circumstantial evidence is accumulating suggesting the involvement of the enkephalins and probably also brain β-endorphin in an endogenous analgesic system.

At this point it may be appropriate to say a word about stress. Guillemin et al[77] have shown a parallel and equimolar secretion of ACTH and β-endorphin into the blood of rats that have been severely stressed. The involvement of pituitary β-endorphin in stress is further supported by the exciting discovery by Mains et al[78] that ACTH and β-endorphin are synthesized via a common large precursor peptide of molecular weight 31000. The question of the relationship between pituitary endorphin, evidently involved in reaction to stress, and the brain enkephalins and β-endorphin, which appear to play a role in pain modulation, is a very interesting and as yet unanswered one. The significance of the question is further enhanced by reports that certain types of stress can produce analgesia.

Narcotic Addiction

There were and continue to be great expectations that the discovery of opiate receptors and their endogenous ligands will result in major advances in our understanding of the mechanism of drug addiction. To date, progess in this area has been disappointing. In fact, evidence that the endogenous opioid system participates in aspects of the addictive process is, as can be seem from this brief discussion, still very indirect.

All opioid peptides will produce tolerance and physical dependence when injected repeatedly. Cross-tolerance with plant alkaloid opiates has also been shown.This does not prove that tolerance/dependence develop to endogenously produced and released endorphins nor that these peptides and their receptors are involved in the formation of tolerance and dependence to narcotics.

A theory that predated the biochemical demonstration of opiate receptors is one that suggests changes in either the number or binding characteristics of opiate receptors. A change in binding affinities similar to that seen when sodium concentration is increased during in vitro binding is especially attractive, since sensitivity to agonists decreases during tolerance formation while sensitivity to antagonists increases dramatically. Klee and Streaty[79] examined this question in whole rat brain and found no changes in the number or affinities of opiate binding sites. We felt that this might be explicable by a "drowning out" of changes occurring in only a few brain regions. However, an examination of receptor number and binding affinities in the medial thalamus, periventricular gray region, and caudate nucleus in collaboration with K. Bonnet[80] gave equally negative results. Whereas these three areas have high levels of receptors and/or have been implicated in various aspects of opiate action, the possibility still remains that these were not the appropriate areas to examine. However, it is at least equally possible that detectable changes in receptors do not occur during chronic morphinization.

The absence of changes in opiate binding during chronic morphinization of animals has given rise to the notion that the alterations occur in steps subsequent to the binding of opiates to their receptor. Support for this idea comes from studies on a cell culture system the relevance of which to the CNS of intact animals has yet to be established. Neuroblastoma x glioma hybrid cells in culture were shown to contain opiate receptors.[81] The receptor binding of opiates and endogenous opioids results in inhibition of basal as well as prostaglandin E_1-stimulated adenylate cyclase. When these cultures are grown in the presence of morphine, inhibition of adenylate cyclase requires increasing concentrations of opiates, a finding that has been suggested as the cellular equivalent of tolerance. It is due to an increase in enzyme activity that seems to be induced by the presence of opiate in the culture medium. Moreover, a putative cellular equivalent of withdrawal is also observed. When cells grown in morphine are placed in drug-free medium or treated with naloxone there is a dramatic overproduction of cyclic AMP (cAMP).

Observations of Collier and his collaborators provide further evidence that cAMP may play a role in chronic effects of opiates. Treatment of naive animals with inhibitors of phosphodiesterase, the enzyme that destroys cAMP, results in symptoms that closely resemble the withdrawal syndrome from opiates. This has been termed quasi morphine withdrawal syndrome (QMWS) by Collier who suggests that it results from increased brain levels of cAMP.

The possibility that a change in endorphin level might be observed during tolerance/dependence has also received attention. A report by Simantov and Snyder[83] that enkephalin levels are elevated in brains of tolerant rats has been refuted by experiments from the same laboratory.[84] The earlier work which had been done using a radioreceptor assay was not supported when the much more specific radioimmunoassay was used.

Herz's group[85] found little change in the level of β-endorphin immunoreactivity ten days after morphine pellet implantations in rats. However, when the period of exposure to morphine was extended to one month or longer, a 60% decrease of β-endorphin-like immunoreactivity from the intermediate/posterior lobe of the pituitary was observed. There was also a decrease in some brain areas such as septum and midbrain, but the level in the hypothalamus was unaltered. Some decrease in enkephalin levels in the striatum and the pituitary was also reported. The authors admit that interpretation of these data is difficult, especially since attempts to repeat these experiments with the potent narcotic analgesic etorphine were unsuccessful.

Recently there has been a report[86] that the intravenous administration of 4 mg of human β-endorphin to human addicts led to dramatic improvement in severe abstinence syndromes. There was no euphoria and little adverse effect. In a double-blind study it was found that subjects were able to distinguish morphine and β-endorphin. After endorphin treatment they felt thirsty, dizzy, sleepy, warm, and had "a strange feeling throughout the body." However, all these symptoms disappeared in 20 minutes while the beneficial effects of endorphin on the withdrawal syndrome lasted for several days. The long-lasting suppression of especially the most severe symptoms of abstinence (vomiting, diarrhea, tremor, and restlessness) by a single dose of β-endorphin suggested to the authors the possibility that this endogenous peptide may indeed have a role in the mechanism of tolerance/dependence development to opiates.

An exciting recent discovery that could have a bearing on our understanding of the role of the endogenous opioid system in addiction was made simultaneously in Paris and at Stanford University. Malfroy et al[87] and Sullivan et al[88] reported the existence of a membrane-bound peptidase that appears to be relatively specific for the breakdown of enkephalins. This "enkephalinase" is a carboxydipeptidase, ie, it splits enkephalin between the glycine in position 3 and the phenylalanine. The Schwartz group reported that the level of this enzyme increases significantly during chronic morphinization of rats. Other groups have found less dramatic changes, but this finding deserves watching. An enzyme, called by the authors enkephalinase A, has recently been purified by Gorenstein et al.[89]

For completeness I should like to mention two recent developments of considerable interest in which the relationship to the opiate receptor is still unknown.

Walter et al[90] reported that is was possible to suppress the abstinence syndrome when rats were withdrawn from chronic morphine by administration of the dipeptide Z-Pro-D-Leu. There was no effect on the analgesic response to morphine. The mechanism of this phenomenon is not understood.

Based on the abundant literature which seems to implicate catecholamines in the actions of opiates, Gold et al[91] treated human heroin addicts with clonidine. In a double-blind, placebo-controlled study, clonidine eliminated objective signs and subjective symptoms of opiate withdrawal for four to six hours in all addicts. In an open pilot study the same patients did well while taking clonidine for one week. All of the patients had been addicted to opiates for six to ten years and had been on methadone for six to sixty months at the time of the study. The authors suggest that their success with clonidine indicates that abstinence may be produced by an interaction between opioid receptors and alpha-2 adrenergic receptors in the mediation of effects by endogenous opiates in noradrenergic areas such as the locus coeruleus.

Comments and Conclusions

This review was written as a contribution to the first issue of *Advances in Alcohol and Substance Abuse*. The reader may well wonder whether the topic covered represents an advance in our understanding of substance abuse. A reasonably complete review of developments in the neuropharmacology of opiates has been presented. The reader who is not in this research domain should be able to appreciate the current state of the art and to form his own opinions regarding the possible relevance of opiate receptors and endogenous opioids to substance abuse and to other areas of human neurobiology and pathology. My own bias will be evident in the following remarks.

It is generally accepted that the disoveries of the opiate receptors and of the endogenous opioid peptides represent major advances in neuroscience. The influx of large numbers of distinguished investigators into this research area bears witness to the importance scientists attach to these discoveries and to the high expectations they entertain regarding the progress that will become possible in our understanding of brain function and behavior.

The way the opioid peptides in the nervous system function is not yet understood. There is evidence suggesting that they represent neurotransmitters or neuromodulators. The latter term implies that the release of enkephalins or endorphins regulates the release of other neurotransmitters.

At the present time the strongest and, at least to me, most convincing evidence for participation of the opiate receptor-opioid system exists for the pathways of pain perception and modulation. This evidence was summarized in some detail in an earlier section. Briefly, it consists of the ability of the opiate antagonist naloxone to reverse a variety of analgesic states produced without intervention by exogenous opiate analgesics. More recently evidence has also been reported for the release of enkephalins and β-endorphin into ventricular CSF during electrical stimulation analgesia in a patient with chronic pain. This is the most direct evidence for involvement of endogenous opioids and their receptors in the body's system of pain modulation. Definitive proof for or against such involvement should not be far away.

As can be seen from the discussion, the situation is far more embryonic when it comes to establishing a role for the endogenous opioid system in drug addiction. There is a conviction among investigators that if an endogenous opioid system exists it must have a role in mediating the effects of exogenous opioids, acute as well as chronic. There is just enought "teasing" evidence to keep this idea alive.

Attempts to explain chronic effects of opiates by changes in the number or properties of opiate receptors or of levels of endorphins have been disappointing, but such changes have not been completely ruled out. In the event that these changes do not occur a number of other possibilities exist and are being explored. One such possibility already mentioned is that the alterations occur in the "black box" of events between the binding of drugs to receptors and the observed pharmacological responses. Another is that changes in opiate receptor occupancy due to the presence of exogenous opiates are reflected primarily in other neurotransmitter systems with which the opioid system interacts. The symptoms observed during opiate withdrawal certainly seem to fall into this category. The changes we are seeking may also occur in the turnover, rather than tissue levels of opioid peptides. The increase in the enzyme enkephalinase observed by Schwartz belongs in this general category and is of great interest if confirmed. Methods for measuring enkephalin and endorphin turnover are currently being developed. Finally, we must not forget the new peptides with opioid activity that have recently been and are still being discovered. Changes in the level or turnover of these novel peptides, eg, dynorphin, have not yet been explored.

To complicate matters, it must be admitted that most biochemical studies, except for some work with human addicts, are not really concerned with addiction or substance abuse as they are usually defined. The phenomena studied are tolerance and physical dependence (withdrawal), aspects of addiction that are amenable to pharmacological measurement in animals as well as man. Psychic dependence, compulsive drug seeking, and abuse are much more difficult to study and there is no agreement as to what constitutes a suitable animal model for studies of these phenomena which are central to drug addiction.

I have presented the state of the art and would now like to end up on an optimistic note by speculating a bit about where I believe the field is going.

Within the next few years the neurotransmitter or neuromodulator function of the opioid peptides should be firmly established (or disproved). Methods for measuring their biosynthesis, release, and breakdown will become available and this may facilitate the elucidation of their role in opiate addiction and in other behavior.

There is much preliminary evidence suggesting that the endogenous opioid system has a role far beyond pain modulation and narcotic addiction. A function in normal and abnormal behavior, sexual performance, overeating, and certain mental diseases have all been suggested. The areas in which the endorphins and their receptors do indeed play a role should be delineated in the not too distant future.

Within the last year evidence has come to light that suggests the existence of several somewhat different types of opiate receptors. This finding is not only of considerable theoretical importance but could have great practical implications. Thus, preliminary evidence suggests that one of the receptors is primarily concerned with the analgesic function of opiates and opioid peptides, while another receptor may be responsible for their addiction liability. If this proves correct, molecules could be tailor-made to fit one but not the other receptor. Such an approach would provide a rational basis for the hitherto empirical search for analgesics of low addiction liability and for drugs useful in the treatment of addicts.

The day when drug addiction can be either prevented or treated in a rational manner may not yet be around the corner, but the enormous research activity that the recent discoveries have given rise to in the opiate field augurs well. If and when the molecular basis of the addictive process for opiates is understood, it may serve as a model for the elucidation of the mechanism of addiction to alcohol, nicotine, and other substances currently abused in this country and elsewhere.

REFERENCES

1. Van Praag D, Simon, EJ: Studies on the intracellular distribution and tissue binding of dihydromorphine-7,8-³H in the rat. *Proc Soc Exp Biol Med* 122:6-11, 1966.
2. Ingoglia NA, Dole VP: Localization of *d*- and *l*-methadone after intraventricular injection into rat brains. *J Pharmacol Exp Therap* 175:84-87, 1970.
3. Goldstein A, Lowney LI, Pal, BK: Stereospecific and nonspecific interactions of the morphine congener levorphanol in subcellular fractions of mouse brain. *Proc Natl Acad Sci USA* 68:1742-1747, 1971.
4. Simon EJ, Hiller JM, Edelman I: Stereospecific binding of the potent narcotic analgesic ³H-etorphine to rat brain homogenate. *Proc Natl Acad Sci USA* 70:1947-1949, 1973.
5. Pert CB, Snyder SH. Opiate receptor: Demonstration in nervous tissue. *Science* 179:1011-1014, 1973.
6. Terenius L: Stereospecific interaction between narcotic analgesics and a synaptic plasma membrane fraction of rat cerebral cortex. *Acta Pharmacol Toxicol* 32:317-320, 1973.
7. Hiller JM, Pearson J, Simon EJ: Distribution of stereospecific binding of the potent narcotic analgesic etorphine in the human brain: Predominance in the limbic system. *Res Commun Chem Pathol Pharmacol* 6:1052-1062, 1973.
8. Stefano GB, Kream RM, Zukin RS: Demonstration of stereospecific opiate binding in the nervous tissue of the marine mollusc *Mytilis edulis*. *Brain Res* 181:440-445, 1980.
9. Kuhar MJ, Pert CB, Snyder SH: Regional distribution of opiate receptor binding in monkey and human brain. *Nature* 245:447-450, 1973.
10. Pert CB, Kuhar MJ, Snyder SH: Autoradiographic localization of the opiate receptor in rat brain. *Life Sci* 16:1849-1854, 1975.
11. Atweh SF, Kuhar MF: Autoradiographic localization of opiate receptors in rat brain. I. Spinal cord and lower medulla. *Brain Res* 124:53-67, 1977.
12. Atweh SF, Kuhar MJ: Autoradiographic localization of opiate receptors in rat brain. II. The brainstem. *Brain Res* 129:1-12, 1977.
13. Atweh SF, Kuhar MJ: Autoradiographic localization of opiate receptors in rat brain. III. The telencephalon. *Brain Res* 134:393-406, 1977.
14. Stahl KD, van Bever W, Janssen P, Simon EJ: Receptor affinity and pharmacological potency of a series of narcotic analgesic, antidiarrheal and neuroleptic drugs. *Eur J Pharmacol* 46:199-205, 1977.
15. Pasternak GW, Snyder SH: Opiate receptor binding: Effects of enzymatic treatment. *Mol Pharmacol* 10:183-193, 1973.
16. Lin H-K, Simon EJ: Phospholipase A inhibition of opiate receptor binding can be reversed by albumin. *Nature* 271:383-384, 1978.
17. Wilson RS, Rogers ME, Pert CB, Snyder SH: Homologous N-alkylnorketobemidones. Correlation of receptor binding with analgesic potency. *J Med Chem* 18:240-242, 1975.
18. Gilbert PE, Martin WR: The effects of morphine and nalorphine-like drugs in the non-dependent and cyclazocine-dependent chronic spinal dog. *J Pharmacol Exp Therap* 198:66-82, 1976.
19. Martin WR, Eades CG, Thompson JA, Huppler RE, Gilbert PE: The effects of morphine- and nalorphine-like drugs in the nondependent and morphine-dependent chronic spinal dog. *J Pharmacol Exp Therap* 197:517-532, 1976.
20. Lord JAH, Waterfield AA, Hughes J, Kosterlitz HW: Endogenous opioid peptides: Multiple agonists and receptors. *Nature* 267:495-499, 1977.
21. Simon EJ, Bonnet KA, Crain SM, Groth J, Hiller JM, Smith JR: Recent studies on interaction between opioid peptides and their receptors, in Costa E. Trabucchi M (eds). *Advances in Biochemical Psychopharmacology*. New York, Raven Press, 1980 pp. 335-346.
22. Chang K-J, Cuatrecasas P: Multiple opiate receptors. Enkephalins and morphine bind to receptors of different specificity. *J Biol Chem* 254:2610-2618, 1979.
23. Robson LE, Kosterlitz HW: Specific protection of the binding sites of Dala²-D-leu⁵ enkephalin (δ receptors) and dihydromorphine (μ receptors). *Proc R Soc Lond* B205:425-432, 1979.

24. Smith J, Simon EJ: Selective protection by receptor ligands of stereospecific enkephalin and opiate binding from inactivation by N-ethylmaleimide: Evidence for two classes of opiate receptors. *Proc Natl Acad Sci USA* 77:281-284, 1980.

25. Chang K-J, Cooper BR, Hazum E, Cuatrecasas P: Multiple opiate receptors: Different regional distribution in the brain and differential binding of opiates and opioid peptides. *Mol Pharmacol* 16:91-104, 1979.

26. Hiller JM, Simon EJ: Specific, high affinity ^{3}H-ethylketocyclazocine binding in rat central nervous system: Lack of evidence for κ receptors. *J Pharmacol Exp Therap* 214:516-519, 1980.

27. Pasternak GW. Multiple opiate receptors: ^{3}H-ethylketocyclazocine receptor binding and ketocyclazocine analgesia. *Proc Natl Acad Sci USA* 77:3691-3694, 1980.

28. Pert CB, Snyder SH: Opiate receptor binding of agonists and antagonists affected differentially by sodium. *Mol Pharmacol* 10:868-879, 1974.

29. Simon EJ, Hiller JM, Groth J, Edelman I: Further properties of stereospecific opiate binding sites in rat brain: On the nature of the sodium effect. *J Pharmacol Exp Therap* 192:531-537, 1975.

30. Simon EJ, Groth J: Kinetics of opiate receptor inactivation by sulfhydryl reagents: Evidence for conformational change in presence of sodium ions. *Proc Natl Acad Sci USA* 72:2404-2407, 1975.

31. Simon EJ, Hiller JM, Edelman I: Solubilization of a stereospecific opiate-macromolecular complex from rat brain. *Science* 190:389-390, 1975.

32. Zukin RS, Kream RM: Chemical cross-linking of a solubilized enkephalin-macromolecular complex. *Proc Natl Acad Sci USA* 76:1593-1597, 1979.

33. Ruegg UT, Hiller JM, Simon EJ: Solubilization of an active opiate receptor from *Bufo marinus*. *Europ J Pharmacol* 64:367-368, 1980.

34. Caron MG, Lefkowitz RJ: Solubilization and characterization of the β-adrenergic receptor binding sites of frog erythrocytes. *J Biol Chem* 251:2374-2384, 1976.

35. Vauguelin G, Geynet P, Hanoune J, Strosberg AD: Isolation of adenylate cyclase-free, β-adrenergic receptor from turkey erythrocyte membranes by affinity chromatography. *Proc Natl Acad Sci USA* 74:3710-3714, 1977.

36. Strauss WL, Ghai G, Fraser CM, Venter JC: Detergent solubilization of mammalian cardiac and hepatic β-adrenergic receptors. *Arch Biochem Biophys* 196:566-573, 1979.

37. Simonds WF, Koski G, Streaty RA, Hjelmeland LM, Klee WA: Solubilization of active opiate receptors. *Pros Natl Acad Sci USA* 77:4623-4627, 1980.

38. Bidlack JM, Abood LG: Solubilization of the opiate receptor. *Life Sci* 27:331-340, 1980.

39. Reynolds DV: Surgery in the rat during electrical analgesia induced by focal brain stimulation. *Science* 164:444-445, 1969.

40. Mayer DJ, Wolfle, TL, Akil H, Carder B, Liebeskind, JC: Analgesia from electrical stimulation in the brain stem of the rat. *Science* 174:1351-1354, 1971.

41. Hughes J: Isolation of an endogenous compound from the brain with properties similar to morphine. *Brain Res.* 88:295-308, 1975.

42. Terenius L, Wahström, A: Inhibitor(s) of narcotic receptor binding in brain extracts and cerebrospinal fluid. *Acta Pharmacol Toxicol* 35(suppl 1): 55, 1974.

43. Teschemacher H, Opheim KE, Cox BM, Goldstein A: A peptide-like substance from pituitary that acts like morphine. I. Isolation. *Life Sci* 17:1771-1776, 1975.

44. Hughes J, Smith TW, Kosterlitz H, Fothergill LA, Morgan BA, Morris HR: Identification of two related pentapeptides from the brain with potent opiate agonist activity. *Nature* 258:577-579, 1975.

45. Li CH: Lipotropin: A new active peptide from pituitary glands. *Nature* 201:924, 1964.

46. Ling N, Burgus R, Guillemin R: Isolation, primary structure, and synthesis of α-endorphin and γ-endorphin, two peptides of hypothalamic-hypophysial origin with morphinomimetic activities. *Proc Natl Acad Sci USA* 73:3942-3946, 1976.

47. Bradbury AF, Smyth DG, Snell CR, Birdsall NJM, Hulme EC: C fragment of lipotropin has a high affinity for brain opiate receptors. *Nature* 260:793-795, 1976.

48. Cox BM, Goldstein A, Li CH: Opioid activity of a peptide, β-lipotropin(61-91), derived from β-lipotropin. *Proc Natl Acad Sci USA* 73:1821-1823, 1976.

49. Goldstein A, Tachibana S, Lowney LI, Hunkapiller M, Hood L: Dynorphin (1-13), an extraordinarily potent opioid peptide. *Proc Natl Acad Sci USA* 76:6666-6670, 1979.

50. Roemer D, Buescher HH, Hill RC, Pless J, Bauer W, Cardinaux F, Closse A, Hauser D, Huguenin R: A synthetic enkephalin analogue with prolonged parenteral and oral analgesic activity. *Nature* 268:547-549, 1977.

51. Simantov R, Kuhar MJ, Pasternak GW, Snyder SH: The regional distribution of a morphine-like factor enkephalin in monkey brain. *Brain Res* 106:189-197, 1976.

52. Hughes J, Kosterlitz HW, Smith TW: The distribution of methionine-enkephalin and leucine-enkephalin in the brain and peripheral tissues. *Brit J Pharmacol* 61:639-647, 1977.

53. Elde R, Hökfelt T, Johansson O, Terenius L: Immunohistochemical studies using antibodies to leucine-enkephalin: Initial observations on the nervous system of the rat. *Neuroscience* 1:349-351, 1976.

54. Simantov R, Kuhar MJ, Uhl GR, Snyder SH: Opioid peptide enkephalin: Immunohistochemical mapping in rat central nervous system. *Proc Natl Acad Sci USA* 74:2167-2171, 1977.

55. Hökfelt T, Elde R, Johansson O, Terenius L, Stein L: The distribution of enkephalin-immunoreactive cell bodies in the rat central nervous system. *Neurosci Lett* 1:25-31, 1977.

56. Rossier J, Vargo TM, Minick S, Ling N, Bloom FE, Guillemin, R: Regional dissociation of beta-endorphin and enkephalin contents in rat brain and pituitary. *Proc Natl Acad Sci USA* 74:5162-5165, 1977.

57. Watson SJ, Barchas JD, Li CH: β-lipotropin: Localization of cells and axons in rat brain by immunocytochemistry. *Proc Natl Acad Sci USA* 74:5155-5158, 1977.

58. Duggan AW, Hall JG, Headley PM: Suppression of transmission of nociceptive impulses by morphine: Selective effects of morphine administered in the region of the substantia gelatinosa. *Brit J Pharmacol* 61:65-76, 1977.

59. Jacob JJ, Tremblay EC, Colombel M-C: Facilitation de réactions nociceptives par la naloxone chez le souris et chez le rat. *Psychopharmacologia* 37:217-223, 1974.

60. Frederickson RCA, Burgis V, Edwards JD: Hyperalgesia induced by naloxone follows diurnal rhythm in responsivity to painful stimuli. *Science* 198:756-758, 1977.

61. El-Sobky A, Dostrovsky JD, Wall PD: Lack of effect of naloxone on pain perception in humans. *Nature* 263:783-785, 1976.

62. Grevert, P, Goldstein A: Endorphins: Naloxone fails to alter experimental pain or mood in humans. *Science* 199:1093-1095, 1978.

63. Akil H, Mayer DJ, Liebeskind JC: Antagonism of stimulation-produced analgesia by naloxone, a narcotic antagonist. *Science* 191:961-962, 1976.

64. Hosobuchi Y, Adams TF, Linchitz R: Pain relief by electrical stimulation of the central gray matter in humans and its reversal by naloxone. *Science* 197:183-186, 1977.

65. Pomeranz B, Chiu D: Naloxone blockade of acupuncture: Endorphin implicated. *Life Sci* 19:1757-1762, 1976.

66. Mayer DJ, Price DD, Rafii A: Antagonism of acupuncture analgesia in man by the narcotic antagonist naloxone. *Brain Res* 121:368-372, 1977.

67. Peets JM, Pomeranz B: CXBK mice deficient in opiate receptors show poor electroacupuncture analgesia. *Nature* 273:675-676, 1978.

68. Levine JD, Gordon NC, Fields HL: The mechanism of placebo analgesia. *The Lancet* pp. 654-657, September 23, 1978.

69. Goldstein A, Hilgard ER: Failure of the opiate antagonist naloxone to modify hypnotic analgesia. *Proc Natl Acad Sci USA* 72:2041-2043, 1975.

70. Dehen H, Willer JC, Prier S, Boureau F, Cambrier J: Congenital insensitivity to pain and the "morphine-like" analgesic system. *Pain* 5:351-358, 1978.

71. Yanagida H: Congenital insensitivity and naloxone. *Lancet* Sept 2 pp. 520-521, September 2, 1978.

72. Terenius L, Wahlström A: Morphine-like ligand for opiate receptors in human CSF. *Life Sci* 16:1759-1764, 1975.

73. Sjolund B, Terenius L, Erikson M: Increased cerebral spinal fluid levels of endorphins after electroacupuncture. *Acta Physiol Scand* 100:382-384, 1977.

74. Richardson DE, Akil H: Pain reduction by electrical brain stimulation in man. Part I: Acute administration in periaqueductal and periventricular sites. *J Neurosurg* 47:178-183, 1977.

75. Akil H, Richardson DE, Hughes J, Barchas JD: Enkephaline-like material elevated in ventricular cerebrospinal fluid of pain patients after analgetic focal stimulation. *Scienc* 201:463-465, 1978.

76. Akil H, Richardson DE, Barchas JD, Li CH: Appearance of β-endorphin-like immunoreactivity in human ventricular cerebrospinal fluid upon analgesic electrical stimulation. *Proc Natl Acad Sci USA* 75:5170-5172, 1978.

77. Guillemin R, Varga T, Rossier J, Minick S, Ling N, Rivier C, Vale W, Bloom F: β-Endorphin and adrenocorticotropin are secreted concomitantly by the pituitary gland. *Science* 197:1367-1369, 1977.

78. Mains R, Eipper E, Ling N: Common precursor to corticotropin and endorphins. *Proc Natl Acad Sci USA* 74:3014-3018, 1977.

79. Klee WA, Streaty RA: Narcotic receptor sites in morphine-dependent rats. *Nature* 248:61-63, 1974.

80. Bonnet KA, Hiller JM, Simon EJ: The effects of chronic opiate treatment and social isolation on opiate receptors in rodent brain, in *Opiates and Endogenous Opioid Peptides*, Proceedings of the International Narcotic Research Conference Meeting, Aberdeen, U.K. Amsterdam, North Holland, 1976 pp. 335-343.

81. Sharma SK, Nirenberg M, Klee WA: Morphine receptors as regulators of adenylate cyclase activity. *Proc Natl Acad Sci USA* 72:590-594, 1975.

82. Collier HOJ, Frances DL, Henderson G, Schneider C: Quasi morphine-abstinence syndrome. *Nature* 249:471-473, 1974.

83. Simantov R, Snyder SH: Elevated levels of enkephalin in morphine-dependent rats. *Nature* 262:505-507, 1976.

84. Childers SR, Simantov R, Snyder SH: Enkephalin: Radioimmunoassay and radioreceptor assay in morphine dependent rats. *Eur J Pharmacol* 46:289-293, 1977.

85. Herz A, Höllt V, Przewlocki R: Endogenous opioids and addiction, in Wuttke W, Weindl A, Voigt KH, Dries RR (eds). *Brain and Pituitary Peptides.* Basel, S Karger, 1979, pp. 183-189.

86. Su CY, Lin SH, Wang YT, Li CH, Hung LH, Lin CS, Lin BC: Effects of β-endorphin on narcotic abstinence syndrome in man. *J Formos Med Assoc* 77:133-141, 1978.

87. Malfroy B, Swerts JP, Guyon A, Roques BP, Schwartz JC: High-affinity enkephalin-degrading peptidase in brain is increased after morphine. *Nature* 26:523-526, 1978.

88. Sullivan S, Akil H, Barchas JD: In vitro degradation of enkephalin: Evidence for cleavage at the Gly-Phe bond. *Commun Psychopharmacol* 2:525-531, 1978.

89. Gorenstein C, Snyder SH: Characterization of enkephalinases, in Way EL, (ed). *Endogenous and Exogenous Opiate Agonists and Antagonists.* New York, Pergamon, 1980, pp. 345-348.

90. Walter R, Ritzmann RF, Bhargava HN, Rainbow TC, Flexner LB, Krivoy WA: Inhibition by Z-Pro-D-Leu of development of tolerance to and physical dependence on morphine in mice. *Proc Natl Acad Sci USA* 75:4573-4576, 1978.

91. Gold M, Redmond DE Jr, Kleber HD: Clonidine blocks acute opiate-withdrawal symptoms. *Lancet* pp. 599-601, September 16, 1978.

ENDORPHINS, LOCUS COERULEUS, CLONIDINE, AND LOFEXIDINE: A MECHANISM FOR OPIATE WITHDRAWAL AND NEW NONOPIATE TREATMENTS

Mark S. Gold, MD
A. L. C. Pottash, MD

ABSTRACT. We review the rodent, primate, and human data which have supported an endorphin-locus coeruleus (LC) disinhibition hypothesis and noradrenergic neuroanatomy for opiate withdrawal. This norepinephrine (NE) hyperactivity hypothesis can explain a large body of clinical and preclinical data and newer and more effective nonopiate treatments. Neuroanatomical, neurochemical, and neurobehavioral data which supported this norepinephrine (NE) hypothesis led to our demonstration of potent antiwithdrawal efficacy for clonidine and lofexidine in withdrawal and naturally occurring panic and anxiety states. We tested the efficacy of clonidine and lofexidine in opiate withdrawal not only to demonstrate that these medications might be new and important treatments for addicts but also to see which physiological and affective variables would be completely reversible and thereby attributable to specific agonistic effects on presynaptic alpha-2 receptors on the LC. Near complete opiate withdrawal reversal or opiate substitution by clonidine and lofexidine supports the NE hyperactivity hypothesis. Clonidine and lofexidine have a number of distinct advantages as antiwithdrawal agents. These clinical advantages of clonidine in drug abuse are summarized. We present additional data which supports the hypothesis that chronic exogenous opiate administration may have antiendorphin effects. These data suggesting endorphin dysfunction may explain the protracted abstinence syndrome and high relapse rate among recently detoxified methadone addicts.

We have suggested that the opiate withdrawal syndrome might be better understood from the point of view of the critical (symptom-generating) neurobiological events.[1-4] The critical neural events we were interested in were those which follow the discontinuation of chronic opiate administration and directly result in clinical signs and symptoms.[3,4] In this paper, we review the rodent, primate, and human data which have supported an endorphin-locus

Dr. Gold is Director of Research, Fair Oaks Hospital, Psychiatric Diagnostic Laboratories of America, Inc., Summit, NJ 07901 and Lecturer, Yale University School of Medicine, Department of Psychiatry, New Haven, CN 06521. Dr. Pottash is Lecturer, Yale University School of Medicine, Department of Psychiatry; Medical Director, Psychiatric Diagnostic Laboratories of America, Inc.; and Associate Director, Fair Oaks Hospital.

Advances in Alcohol & Substance Abuse, Vol. 1(1), Fall 1981
© 1981 by The Haworth Press, Inc. All rights reserved.

coeruleus (LC) disinhibition hypothesis and noradrenergic neuroanatomy for opiate withdrawal.[1,3,5] This norepinephrine (NE) hyperactivity hypothesis can explain a large body of clinical[5-10] and preclinical data and may be useful in predicting newer and more effective nonopiate treatments.[4] We will review the neuroanatomical, neurochemical, and neurobehavioral data which supported this norepinephrine (NE) hypothesis because they led to our demonstration of potent antiwithdrawal efficacy for clonidine and lofexidine and may lead to even better nonopiate treatments for drug withdrawal and naturally occurring panic and anxiety states. Therefore, we expect that clonidine and lofexidine will be but the first in a series of noradrenergic-inhibitor medications which will become available to increase drug abuse treatment options and allow for rapid and safe nonopiate detoxification. We will review the clinical use and implications of clonidine treatment itself and for naltrexone, drug-free, and other drug rehabilitation programs and physicians. Finally, we will present additional data which supports the hypothesis that chronic exogenous opiate administration may have antiendorphin effects. These data suggesting endorphin dysfunction may explain the protracted abstinence syndrome and high relapse rate among recently detoxified methadone addicts.

Endorphin—LC Connection

The effects of opiates on catecholamine neurons have been reported elsewhere[11-15] but have tended to show that opiates can decrease NE activity and turnover.[14,16,17] Studies of the brain's major noradrenergic nucleus, nucleus locus coeruleus (LC), have clearly demonstrated that the prototype opiate, morphine, causes a marked reduction in the normal LC neuronal firing rate.[17] These LC neurons are known to respond to a painful stimulus with an increased firing rate and this pain-induced effect can be blocked by morphine.[17] These data demonstrated an important opiate-NE interaction and suggested the possibility that some of the effects of opiates might be mediated by opiate-induced decreases in LC activity and NE release.[17,18] The discovery of specific opiate receptors in the brain,[19-24] the data by Pert et al[21] and Simon[22] demonstrating very dense opiate receptor accumulations in the LC and the use of naloxone reversal in electrophysiological studies as a means of identifying effects which could be attributable to opiate receptor stimulation[14,19,25] allowed LC-endorphin, LC-enkephalin, and LC-opiate interactions to be expanded and more clearly understood. Investigators using single neuronal recording techniques and microiontophoresis reported that endogenous opiates and exogenous opiates decreased LC firing rates and that this effect was specifically reversed by the opiate antagonist naloxone.[14,26] These data suggested that the specific opiate receptors on the LC which might normally utilize endorphins as a natural neurotransmitter inhibit LC firing rate and modulate ascending NE activity.[14,26] These data suggested that this LC-opiate interaction was not tonic; that is, endorphins do not tonically inhibit LC activity but rather endorphins are released in response to neural or environmental events. These data suggested to us that a critical endorphin-LC connection might exist and be related to some opiate effects and possibly play a critical role in opiate withdrawal.[1-5] Chronic exogenous opiate administration would tonically inhibit the LC and compromise endorphin biosynthesis or functional integrity.[1,4] Acute opiate abstinence might be due to a rebound NE hyperactivity and protracted abstinence due to slow endorphin recovery and incomplete functional inhibition of spontaneous or environmentally produced LC hyperactivity.[4]

While it is well established that NE cells of the LC are inhibited by systemic and iontophoretic administration of opiates[14,17] and enkephalins,[26,27] the endorphin-LC neural pathway has only been recently elucidated. Since the original discovery of opiate receptors[20-22] and the isolation of endogenous opiate compounds by Hughes,[20] two independent endogenous opioid systems have now been delineated. A β-endorphin system emanating from a group of cells within or slightly lateral to the arcuate nucleus of the hypothalamus which sends long axons to midbrain and limbic structures[28] and a short axon enkephalin system with multiple cell groups throughout the spinal cord, brain stem, and diencephalon[29,30] have been described. Opiate receptors within the locus coeruleus (LC)[21,27] appear to mediate the effects of endorphins concentrated in nerve terminals which surround the neurons.[27,28] The major source of these terminals is believed to be the β-endorphin-containing cell bodies of the hypothalamus.[31] These data support an important endorphin-LC connection in opiate action, tolerance, and opiate withdrawal.

The existence of LC cell body receptors for norepinephrine (NE) and epinephrine (E) were also suggested by single neuronal electrophysiological and microiontophoretic studies by Aghajanian and co-workers[32-35] and confirmed in binding-affinity studies.[36] LC neurons responded to the alpha-2 adrenergic agonist clonidine with a decrease in LC firing[33,34] resulting in a marked decrease in NE release[37,38] and turnover[39,40] in whole brain, cortex, and more recently arteriovenous-difference studies.[41] This depressant effect of clonidine on LC neurons could be reversed by the alpha-2 adrenergic antagonist piperoxane but not by other drugs (B-blockers, naloxone) without specificity for this alpha receptor.[33,34] These data suggested that LC activity may be tonically modulated, under normal physiological conditions, by presynaptic NE or E release. These studies clearly demonstrated that in very low doses clonidine decreases LC activity and piperoxane increases LC activity and that these drugs influence LC activity by their interaction with inhibitory alpha-2 adrenergic on the LC.[33,34] In higher doses this specificity is lost and clonidine has effects on postsynaptic NE and other receptors.[42,43]

These data suggest that the LC was under, at least, the dual inhibitory control of NE and endorphins and that inhibitory pharmacological manipulation of the LC could be effected through either system. This hypothesis was tested in nonhuman primates.

Locus Coeruleus Activation Studies

Piperoxane was given to nonhuman primates[44] and doses (1 mg/kg; 2.5 mg/kg) which were previously shown to increase noradrenergic activity in rats[20] and turnover in these nonhuman primates.[45] Piperoxane produced a behavioral syndrome which resembled spontaneous opiate withdrawal[44] suggesting a common NE hyperactivity in these states. A virtually identical primate "panic" syndrome was evoked by yohimbine, a drug similar in neurochemical action to piperoxane.[46] Piperoxane-administration studies suggested that noradrenergic augmentation might be a model system for studying the neuroanatomy, neurophysiology, and neurochemistry of opiate withdrawal which related to specific physiological and affective parameters. We also demonstrated the piperoxane-induced increase in these specific monkey behaviors and physiological signs could be reversed by morphine and the synthetic M-Enkephalin FK 33-824[8,47,48] through an opiate receptor-mediated mechanism, as assessed by naloxone reversal. Clonidine was also demonstrated to block or reverse the effects of piperoxane.[44] This effect was not antagonized by naloxone. These behavioral data suggested that the noradrenergic LC is under the dual control of inhibitory alpha-2 and opiate receptors. This conclusion was supported by our demonstration that yohimbine (2.5 mg/kg) produced a similar behavioral syndrome in the monkeys which could be blocked or reversed by morphine or clonidine.[48]

As an additional test of these hypotheses, we more specifically augmented noradrenergic activity by electrical stimulation (biphasic, bipolar 0.2—0.4 MA, 0.5 mSec, 5-50 HZ) of the locus coeruleus. Electrical stimulation produced a behavioral syndrome with physiological changes which were very similar to that produced by piperoxane.[48,49] Electrical stimulation-induced changes could be completely blocked or reversed by opiate receptor stimulation as assessed by naloxone reversal of the effects of morphine or FK 33-824.[44,50-52] These electrical stimulation changes could also be blocked or reversed by clonidine.[44,49]

The Opiate Withdrawal Hypothesis

We hypothesized that chronic exogenous opiate administration might cause a decrease in endogenous opiate release and synthesis or derangement of the endorphin system's functional activity.[1,4] Abrupt discontinuation of chronic opiate administration would, according to our model system, result in the absence of exogenous opiate-mediated inhibition of ascending NE activity. As a result of this release from chronic exogenous inhibition and absence of adequate inhibitory neurotransmitters at the level of the NE nucleus,[4] there would be a resultant large increase in NE activity, release, and turnover.[1,5] Attempts to use endorphin stores to autoreglate this profound LC firing increase would be too little too late, as the stores of available endogenous opiates would be of insufficient quantity, the receptor sensitivity would be too low to augment the available endorphin, and/or the endorphin-LC system would be virtually nonfunctional due to chronic exogenous opiate administration (eg, methadone maintenance). In addition, it is likely that other available inhibitory presynaptic neurotransmitters such as E and NE would be of insufficient quantity to interact with receptors which are themselves abnormal to reverse the NE "rebound" release from opiate-mediated inhibition.[4]

We tested the efficacy of clonidine in opiate withdrawal not only to demonstrate that clonidine might be a new and important treatment for addicts but also to see which physiological and affective variables would be clonidine-reversible and thereby attributable to clonidine's agonistic effects on presynaptic alpha-2 receptors on the LC. The more complete the opiate withdrawal reversal or opiate substitution by clonidine, the more support for the NE hyperactivity hypothesis. We had speculated that clonidine would reverse in man the behaviors and affective state produced by electrical or pharmacological activation of the LC as we had demonstrated in primates. Our LC or NE hyperactivity hypothesis was supported by knowledge of LC neuroanatomy.[53-57] The known anatomical connections of the LC suggested an important role for this structure as a "panic button" in the coordination of the wide variety of behaviors and physiological changes which accompany drug-withdrawal and spontaneous panic states. The LC also receives afferents from serotonergic, adrenergic, peptidergic, and noradrenergic neurons, the hypothalamus, and may have transducer cells to receive and relay hormonal messages.[56,57] This LC neuroanatomy supports an important coordinating role for the LC and does not necessitate the direct involvement of numerous brain systems in the feeling state, cardiovascular, sympathetic, parasympathetic, and many other manifestations of opiate withdrawal states.[1,4]

After we administered orally in matching vehicles to five male opiate (methadone) addicts 5 ug/kg of the imidazoline derivative clonidine and placebo double-blind, we recognized that clonidine was effective for the full spectrum of acute withdrawal signs, symptoms, and affects. In a study of 11 methadone addicts[2] and a study of five male heroin and five male methadone addicts[5] we demonstrated that clonidine reversed the signs, symptoms, and effects of acute opiate withdrawal. Clonidine effectively reversed withdrawal in patients addicted for many years to high doses of methadone.[2] Finally, in two well-controlled studies, one small[6] followed by another large[9] inpatient study, we delineated a safe and near-100% effective protocol for rapid non-opiate detoxification which demonstrated that clonidine blocked and reversed acute withdrawal demonstrated that clonidine blocked and reversed acute withdrawal and continued (nearly completely) to suppress the reemergence of withdrawal symptoms after abrupt discontinuation of chronic opiate addiction. This series of studies demonstrated that clonidine could be substituted for opiates and discontinued without withdrawal signs of its own. We will return to these clinical studies shortly. However, for the purposes of the NE or LC hyperactivity hypothesis, the efficacy of clonidine offered strong support for the hypothesis on the basis of the known inhibitory effects of low dose clonidine on the LC and NE release and turnover.

Additional Support for the Hypothesis

All of this clinical data[1,2,5-10] served to support an important endorphin-LC interaction and NE hyperactivity as the most critical event in the generation of withdrawal symptoms on the basis of clonidine's known effects on the LC and NE activity when given in low doses. This NE hypothesis could only be directly investigated in animal studies. In rodent and primate studies it was demonstrated that clonidine decreased NE activity, release, and turnover as assessed by changes in the brain's major NE metabolite MHPG.[41] Morphine and endogenous opiates were found to have a similar effect through interaction with LC opiate receptors as assessed by naloxone reversal. Finally, Aghajanian[58] demonstrated that chronic exogenous opiate administration produced tolerance of LC neurons to suppression. He also demonstrated that tolerance develops in the LC inhibition response to chronic opiates (in opiate addiction) and that naloxone-precipitated withdrawal was accompanied by the predicted[1,2] nora-adrenergic hyperactivity.[58] He demonstrated in a single neuronal electro-physiological and microionto-phoresis study that this NE hyperactivity could be reversed by clonidine.[58] This study confirmed the hypothesized LC hyperactivity in withdrawal and supported our notion[3,4,59] that NE was an important neurotransmitter in the generation of withdrawal symptoms. Our studies and the studies in the literature[1,2,4,60,61] did not exclude an important or at least significant role for other brain monoamine nuclei[59] and neurotransmitters in opiate withdrawal. However, we did hypothesize that the NE hyperactivity could be directly related to the generation and amelioration of withdrawal signs, symptoms, and effects[1,2] in studies of man.

Recent data reported in the literature also support a NE hypothesis. Our pilot data on the major metabolite of NE, MHPG,[8] offer tentative support for the hypothesized NE hyperactivity and relationship of NE activity to symptom generation and relief. These data are supported by recent data in rodents and primates which demonstrate increase in MHPG in withdrawal and clonidine reversal of the MHPG increases.[62-64] Clonidine withdrawal itself has significant phenomenological similarities to opiate withdrawal[65,66] and would be expected to result, in part, from chronic exogenous inhibition of the LC through alpha-2 receptor stimulation. Clonidine withdrawal results in increases in MHPG and may be treatable with clonidine or opiates.[67] Clonidine, while not an opiate drug and having no affinity for opiate receptors,[68] has a number of opiate-like properties including analgesia, miosis, hypotension, sedation, antianxiety, and decreased respiration.[69-74] These data suggest that the effects of exogenous alpha-2 or opiate agonists which tonically inhibit brain areas like the LC may be responsible for tolerance and the development of withdrawal symptoms after abrupt discontinuation of chronic administration.

Additional support for this NE hyperactivity hypothesis comes from neuroendocrine studies of withdrawal. Significant decreases in serum PRL are normally attributable to direct stimulation of DA receptors or increased DA release or neurotransmission.[75-77] The decreased serum PRL for patients in withdrawal supports underlying DA hyperactivity in withdrawal.[59,78] These data were consistent with animal studies showing decreases in PRL in opiate withdrawal.[79] However, in our studies the serum PRL levels did not return to baseline after clonidine-induced amelioration of symptoms.[59,78] This suggested that DA hyperactivity continues even though clonidine markedly relieves symptoms. Therefore, we have suggested that DA hyperactivity is present but is not related to symptoms or symptom relief.

Further Implications and Tests of the Hypothesis

Known drugs which we believe inhibit NE activity at the level of the LC and which may have antiwithdrawal efficacy are shown in Fig 1. Therefore, nonalpha adrenergic drugs and neural peptides may be found to be safe for use in humans, and to decrease LC activity. These medications may be safely developed for use in withdrawal. Nonaddicting opiate receptor agonists, vasopressin, or GABA agonists like baclofen may be found to have potent antiwithdrawal efficacy, but without hypotensive effects and with significantly less sedation than clonidine. These drugs would be without alpha-2 activity but might be expected to have antiwithdrawal activity by decreasing LC activity. These new possibilities would thus provide additional tests for the NE hyperactivity hypothesis for opiate withdrawal as well as possibly adding new, safe, and effective nonopiate treatments to the treatment armamentarium.

What would be an important test of the NE neurotransmitter hypothesis from the clinical point of view would be the ability to develop an alpha-2 agonist, like clonidine, which decreases LC activity and NE release and has

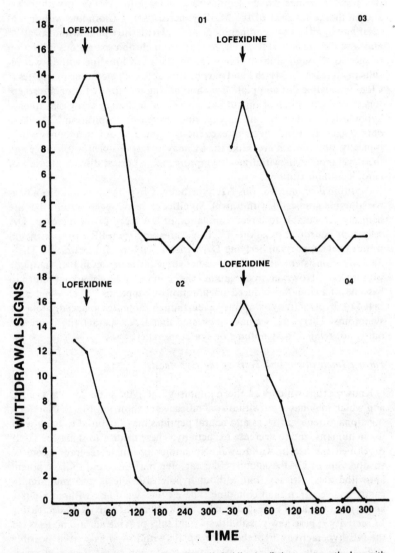

FIGURE 1. Four patient examples. The effect of lofexidine (ug/kg) on acute methadone withdrawal signs and symptoms.

potent antiwithdrawal efficacy but does not produce other clonidine effects such as extreme sedation and hypotension. It may be that potent alpha-2 nonopiate drugs which reverse withdrawal from high doses of chronic opiate administration must produce sedation and decrease blood pressure because of other alpha-2 effects or that the LC is the common final neurotransmitter pathway in these pheonomenon. However, we have recent data from five male methadone addicts addicted to > 30 mg of methadone for > six months which clearly demonstrates potent antiwithdrawal activity for Lofexidine (see Fig 1). Lofexidine, an imidazoline derivative which is a structurally related analogue of clonidine with substantial affinity for alpha-2 (clonidine) binding sites in brain, produced a marked and significant decrease in acute methadone-withdrawal signs, symptoms, and affects without marked hypotension and sedation. These data offer additional support for the NE and LC hyperactivy hypothesis and again suggest that new nonopiate treatments can be predicted on the basis of inhibitory effects at the level of the LC (see Fig 2). Other neural peptides and medications listed in this Figure may be found to have a potent antiwithdrawal action on the basis of potent LC-inhibitory activity. Again, the NE hyperactivity or LC hypothesis would predict that other drugs, which are potent at specifically inhibiting the LC by an action at specific presynaptic LC receptors, will be found to have marked antiwithdrawal efficacy in man.

Finally, it should be mentioned that the discovery of opiate receptors, their density in the LC, and the parallel function of alpha-2 and opiate receptor stimulation at the level of the LC have suggested the efficacy of clonidine in withdrawal and the possibility that NE hyperactivity may be responsible for the effects—anxiety and panic—as well as the physiological

"ANTIWITHDRAWAL" MODEL NEURON

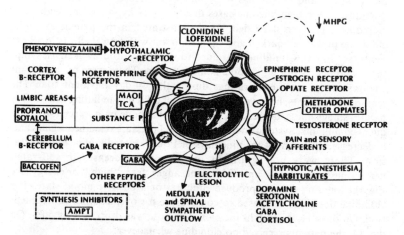

FIGURE 2. Antiwithdrawal model neuron. Medications and neural peptides which may be expected to have antiwithdrawal efficacy.

changes associated with withdrawal.[4,5,52,80] This raises the question of naturally-occurring panic and anxiety states and whether these states share LC hyperactivity as a final common neurobiological pathway.[3] NE hyperactivity might then also provide a model for studying naturally and drug-related panic states and lead to a neural construct for these states which could yield new treatment possibilities including opiates, endorphins, and clonidine.[3,5,61]

Clinical Use and Limitations of Nonopiate Treatments

We have recently reported clinical utility data from an inpatient clonidine detoxification study of 100 chronic methadone addicts. After abrupt opiate discontinuation, the patients took 6 ug/kg of clonidine or placebo orally in matching vehicles to demonstrate the effect of clonidine on opiate withdrawal signs and symptoms to assess the changes in blood pressure produced by this dose of clonidine. After the initial clonidine and placebo administration, patients without precipitous blood pressure declines were given clonidine 17 ug/kg/day for at least nine days. Clonidine dose was gradually decreased to zero by day 14. Naloxone (1.2 mg) was given intravenously to assess for naltrexone readiness. All patients were excluded who had a previous history of cardiac arrhythmias, hypotension, vasomotor instability, psychiatric illness, or hospitalization.[81]

On the first day of clonidine administration, the patients were given 6 ug/kg as a test dose and then 6 ug/kg at bedtime. Thereafter, 17 ug/kg/day of clonidine was given in divided doses of 7 ug/kg at 8:00 AM and 3 ug/kg at 4:00 PM and 7 ug/kg at 11:00 PM. Each day vital signs and nurses' abstinence ratings and self-ratings were done as described previously.[1-3] Clonidine doses were held in some cases due to severe hypotension. Additional clonidine was given if needed. As demonstrated in the patient example, clonidine produced marked and significant antiwithdrawal effects in all patients (see Fig 3). Clonidine continued to suppress withdrawal signs, symptoms, and effects during chronic administration. There were no significant changes in the abstinence ratings during this 14-day inpatient trial. The majority of patients, however, complained of difficulty in falling asleep. Dry mouth, sluggishness, depression, and occasional bone pain were more infrequent complaints. Systolic and diastolic blood pressure remained significantly decreased throughout the nine days of 17 ug/kg of clonidine administration. There were no significant increases or decreases in self-rated nervousness, irritability, uninvolvement, anger, fear, "high," or energy (see Fig 4).Clonidine did not produce euphoria or a positive mood state. The clonidine dose was decreased to compensate for oversedation or hypotension. On days 11, 12 and 13 the clonidine dose was decreased by 50%. On day 14, the patients received no clonidine whatsoever.

None of the patients showed any increase in opiate withdrawal signs or symptoms or had the emergence of clonidine withdrawal symptoms using

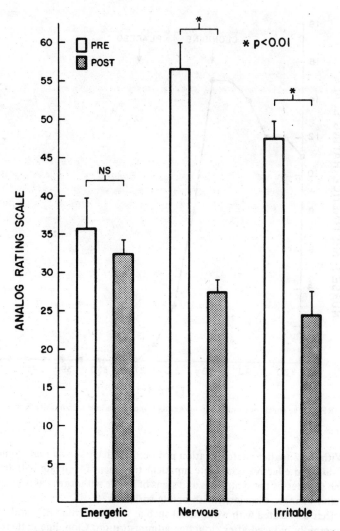

FIGURE 3. The effects of clonidine (6 ug/kg) on acute methadone withdrawal.

this protocol. One patient eloped from the hospital on day five of the study. On day 14 all patients were given naloxone (1.2 mg) intravenously to assess for residual opiates of dependence. All naloxone test responses were negative. Ninety-nine of the 100 patients completed the 14-day inpatient study and were naltrexone ready.

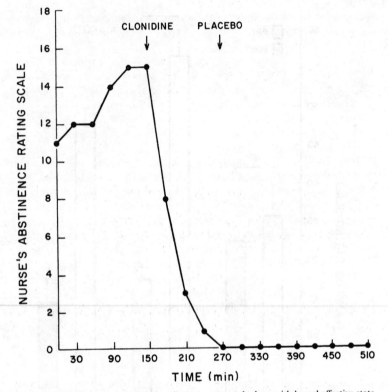

FIGURE 4. The effects of clonidine (6 ug/kg) on acute methadone withdrawal affective state.

With this inpatient detoxification protocol, we have shown that clonidine is a safe and effective nonopiate inpatient treatment for opiate withdrawal which suppresses the symptoms and signs of opiate withdrawal as well as the affective changes associated with opiate withdrawal.

Affects associated with withdrawal such as anxiety, irritability, and anger were rapidly reduced after clonidine administration. Clonidine is therefore extremely useful as a noreuphorogenic treatment for detoxification. This 14-day inpatient clonidine detoxification protocol could be useful in the treatment of selected opiate addicts. For example, clonidine detoxification could be linked to maintenance on long-acting opiate antagonists such as naltrexone. Clonidine, being a nonopiate, allows the patient to abrubtly discontinue opiate administration and be opiate-free long enough to initiate maintenance treatment with naltrexone. Clonidine detoxification may allow the detoxification of patients maintained on methadone who have had previous unsuccessful attempts to detoxify due to the morbidity of current slow detoxification practices. Clonidine is also potentially useful in the treatment of iatrogenic addictions and the protracted abstinence syndrome where the risk of exposure to opiates might be reduced. Clonidine appears most useful in the treatment of working patients, iatrogenic addictions, nondrug-using methadone maintenance patients, and patients with family and work support systems who are also good candidates for naltrexone.

Clonidine has a number of distinct advantages as an antiwithdrawal agent. These clinical advantages of clonidine in drug abuse treatment are summarized in Table 1.

These clinical implications and the clinical utility of clonidine will become more evident and well suited as investigators with divergent patient groups begin to use clonidine as a nonopiate treatment. Results from others[84-87] and the results of our outcome studies suggest clonidine is an efficacious antiwithdrawal treatment. Clonidine-aided withdrawal appears well suited for highly motivated, working, middle-class and upper-class addicts. Clonidine is also ideal for coupling with intensive drug-free or naltrexone treatment.

Clonidine is by no means the most ideal drug for the rapid nonopiate treatment of withdrawal. Its sedative and hypotensive effects limit its usefulness in outpatient programs and make outpatient detoxification more difficult and more dangerous than methadone detoxification. In addition, clonidine's antiwithdrawal effects may be time-limited, making its use in slow detoxification difficult, if not impossible, for this reason and also because of "rebound" effects reported after longer-term clonidine administration.[65,66]

TABLE 1. Advantages Of Detoxification From Opiates With Clonidine

1. Abrupt discontinuation of opiates and treatment through nonopiate receptor system may allow normalization (more rapid) of opiate and alpha-2 receptors.[82]
2. Detoxification from 15-50-75 or even 100 mg of chronic methadone can be readily accomplished with relatively equal ease in 14 days.[83]
3. Noneuphorogenic clonidine detoxification can be readily linked to naltrexone induction and maintenance.[82]
4. Enhancement of role of physician and physician-patient relationship which relates to compliance and using naltrexone in a model similar to prophylactic administration of lithium carbonate to manic-depressive patients.
5. Increase in treatment options available to patients, especially the methadone-addicted patients who may believe it difficult, if not impossible, to detoxify from methadone.
6. Availability to methadone-maintained patients of a viable alternative to prolonged methadone detoxification, with a chance to be drug-free or maintained on naltrexone in less than 14 days.
7. Possible treatment of choice for iatrogenic addictions and addictions in working individuals with significant job jeopardy.
8. Possible use in "opiate holidays" and reversal of tolerance in cancer/pain patients.
9. Treatment of other drug withdrawal and naturally-occurring panic/anxiety states.
10. Use in treatment of conditional withdrawal episodes or acute manifestations of the protracted abstinence syndrome.

While these disadvantages are real and limit its general utility, clonidine is an extremely useful new treatment, especially in facilitating the transition from opiate addiction to naltrexone maintenance.[10] This use of clonidine in the transition from opiate addiction to naltrexone may add viability to naltrexone, a troubled but potentially valuable treatment. Some real and potential advantages of naltrexone are summarized in Table 2.

Demonstration of Endorphin Deficiency or Impairment in Man

We have postulated that chronic exogenous opiate administration might be associated with a prolonged decrease in the availability of endorphins (or functional integrity of the endorphin system) which may be responsible for both the acute and protracted[1-8] opiate withdrawal syndrome in man. This derangement of the endorphin system's functional integrity might result from negative feedback effects exerted by potent, exogenous opiate self-administration (eg, methadone). The hypothesis that chronic opiate administration may decrease endorphins in the brain, has been difficult to test due to methadological difficulties in direct measurement of endorphins.[88] In addition, chronic methadone treatment might produce a localized endorphin derangement or deficit at the noradrenergic locus coeruleus which is rich in endorphins and opiate receptors and has been suggested as the possible neural substrate for the signs and symptoms of opiate withdrawal.[1-8]

An endogenous opioid neurotransmitter system whose activation mimics exogenous opiate action had been postulated for many years but only recently described. There is now compelling evidence that corticotropin (ACTH) and β-lipotropin/β-endorphin are formed from a larger precursor protein which has been called pro-ACTH/endorphin.[89-92] Studies reported in the literature have shown that ACTH and β-LPH/β-endorphin are located and

TABLE 2. Potential Advantages Of Naltrexone

1. Antagonizes or blocks euphoric effects of opiates.
2. Antagonizes or blocks development of physical dependence to opiates.
3. nonaddicting with insignificant opiate-like effects or abuse potential.
4. Tolerance to antagonist effects does not develop.
5. Absence of toxicity or serious side effects with chronic use.
6. Can be taken orally at reasonable cost.
7. Extinguishes opiate-seeking behavior.
8. Reduces opiate craving.
9. Promotes deconditioning to external environmental cues which provoke conditioned abstinence syndrome.
10. May replenish or help normalize opiate-induced depletion or derangement of endorphin system.
11. Provides needed opiate-free time to allow for alteration in life course and psychological change in a structured psychotherapeutic milieu.
12. Allows for early reentry of recovering addict into the work place.

stored in the same cells and secretory granules within the pituitary. More recently, it has been demonstrated that under stimulatory and inhibitory conditions all fragments are secreted together during secretion by granule extrusion.[90-92] Studies in animals have shown that the major source of plasma β-LPH/β-endorphin is the pituitary gland so that a reduced concentration in the pituitary causes reductions in circulating blood levels of β-LPH, β-endorphin, ACTH, and cortisol.[92]

The effects of opiates (eg, morphine, methadone) on neuroendocrine function has been utilized to provide evidence for the action of exogenous opiates and the role of endorphins in the brain. A number of neuroendocrine functions are influenced by the administration of exogenous opiates, endogenous opioids, and opiate antagonists (eg, Naloxone).[93-97] The infusion of the exogenous opiate, methadone, has been demonstrated to produce a decrease in plasma cortisol levels in man.[98] These, and other data[97,99] suggest that opiate receptor stimulation by exogenous opiates may, through a feedback mechanism, cause a decrease in the release and possible the synthesis and available stores of pro-/ACTH/endorphin and therefore decreases ACTH and cortisol. We have preliminary provocative test data from methadone addicts which suggest that endorphin and ACTH reserve may be compromised by chronic methadone treatment.

The subjects were five male methadone addicts who had been addicted to ≥ 30 mg of methadone for one to eight years, and five normal, age-matched male opiate-naive volunteers. All subjects gave written informed consent to the study. The methadone addicts had their chronic methadone abruptly discontinued and clonidine suppression of withdrawal signs and symptoms as reported previously.[1-5] Clonidine was given according to a fixed dose regimen for ten days and discontinued within 14 days. All subjects were opiate and clonidine-free at least 16 days after their last methadone dose for the endorphin-ACTH reserve test. All subjects were NPO past midnight and were at rest in bed for the placement of an indwelling venous catheter at 800 h. Small samples of venous blood was taken for the measurement of plasma cortisol in duplicate by radioimmunoassay[94] through the catheter at -30, 0, 15, 30, 45, 60, 75, 105, and 135 minutes after 20 mg of naloxone was administered intravenously at 930 h. Two subjects reported mild withdrawal complaints consisting of nervousness, perspiration, and yawning immediately after naloxone administration.

In our group of five methadone addicts (see Fig 5) naloxone caused a small and insignificant (paired t test, t = 1.64, NS) increase in plasma cortisol levels from a baseline of 19.3 ± 2.5 ug/dl to peak of 23.1 ± 1.9 ug/dl at 45 minutes after naltrexone administration. Mean Δ cortisol for the normal controls was 9.7 ± 2.1 ug/dl. The two groups had a significantly (t test p = 3.9 < 0.01) different cortisol responses to naloxone.

We have suggested here and elsewhere[1-8] that opiate withdrawal may

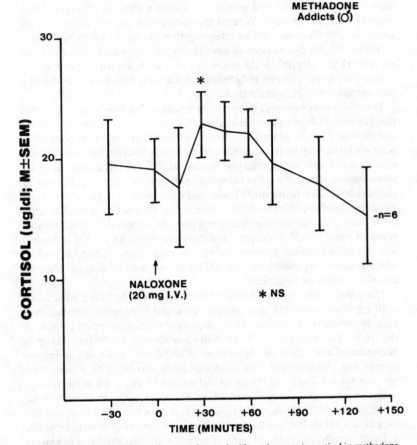

FIGURE 5. Naloxone (20 mg) fails to produce a significant increase in cortisol in methadone addicts.

result from a sudden lack of exogenous opiates and an inadequate endorphin reserve releasing the noradrenergic LC from chronic inhibition. Thus far tests of this hypothesis have involved nonadrenergic augmentation in primates and the administration of clonidine and lofexidine to man. However, the specific opiate antagonists naltrexone and naloxone have been reported to cause a marked increase in plasma ACTH and cortisol levels in normal man.[94,97] Naloxone blocks opiate/endorphin receptor sites and through a feedback mechanism causes the release of available pro-ACTH/endorphin precursor stores to overcome the blockade. This results in large increases in plasma ACTH and cortisol levels.[94,97] This suggests that naloxone or naltrexone test response may be a measure of endorphin system function. The impaired response data reported here for recently detoxified addicts suggest that the endorphin precursor-endorphin-ACTH-cortisol is not functioning normally. The fact that this response was decreased even in addicts who had mild withdrawal symptoms and a stress response to the large dose of naloxone (which would be expected to increase ACTH and cortisol), suggests that chronic methadone administration decreases the synthesis, storage, and quantity of available pro-ACTH/endorphin and endorphin/endogenous opiate reserve. The preliminary data reported here support the endorphin-noradrenergic locus coeruleus hypothesis[1-8] which suggests that opiate withdrawal results from a loss of exogenous opiate-induced inhibition of the LC and an inability of the endogenous opioid systems to compensate for this loss. These data also suggest that prolonged abstinence, postdetoxification depression, and other affective symptoms which contribute to relapse may result from a prolonged endorphin deficiency. Chronic administration of an endorphin agonist like methadone might cause the brain to assume that there are more than adequate endorphin stores and that endorphin fuction is preserved and the brain may stimulate feedback mechanism to slow synthesis and inhibit function. Methadone being a potent and long-acting opiate agonist may have more potent antiendorphin effects than other opiates.

While these data rely on the measurement of cortisol, they are not likely to relate to adrenal factors since they are in agreement with previous studies in the literature which have demonstrated decreased ACTH in opiate addicts[99] and suggested that chronic exogenous opiate administration might cause an endorphin system imbalance.[1-6,94] These data are also consistent with animal data which have shown reduced brain β-endorphin immunoactivity in rats addicted to morphine for three months or longer[100] and decreased β-endorphin immunoactivity and Naltrexone test response in chronic male opiate addicts.[94] Additional larger studies of methadone addicts are necessary to confirm these data and to expand the biological measurements (before and after naloxone) to ACTH, endorphin, and β-lipotrophin. If these data are confirmed, studies are also necessary to determine whether there is a minimal dose of methadone necessary to cause an endorphin system dysfunction and whether methadone has more serious antiendorphin effects than other opiates.

REFERENCES

1. Gold MS, Redmond DE Jr, Kleber HD: Clonidine in opiate withdrawal. *Lancet* 1:929-930, 1978.
2. Gold MS, Redmond DE Jr, Kleber HD: Clonidine blocks acute opiate withdrawal symptoms. *Lancet* 2:599-602, 1978.
3. Gold MS, Kleber HD: A rationale for opiate withdrawal symptomatology. *Drug and Alcohol Dependence* 4:419-424, 1979.
4. Gold MS, Byck R, Sweeney DR, Kleber HD: Endorphin-locus coeruleus connection mediates opiate action and withdrawal. *Biomedicine* 30:1-4, 1979.

5. Gold MS, Redmond DE Jr, Kleber HD: Noradrenergic hyperactivity in opiate withdrawal supported by clonidine reversal of opiate withdrawal. Am J Psychiatry 136:100-102, 1979.
6. Gold MS, Pottash, ALC, Sweeney DR, Kleber HD: Opiate withdrawal using clonidine: A safe, effective and rapid nonopiate treatment for opiate withdrawal. JAMA 243:343-346, 1980.
7. Gold MS, Pottash ALC, Sweeney DR, Kleber HD: Clonidine detoxification: A fourteen day protocol for rapid opiate withdrawal, in Petersen R (ed): Problems of Drug Dependence. Rockville, NIDA Research Monograph 27:226-232, 1979.
8. Gold MS, Pottash ALC, Carter: The neurobiological implications of clonidine HCL. Ann NY Acad Sci, in press, 1980.
9. Gold MS, Pottash ALC, Extein I, Kleber HD: Clonidine in acute opiate withdrawal. New Engl J Med 302:1421-1422, 1980.
10. Gold MS, Pottash ALC, Extein I, Kleber HD: Clonidine and opiate withdrawal. Lancet II:1078-1079, 1980.
11. Eidelberg E: Possible action of opiates upon synapses. Prog Neurbiol 6:81-102, 1976.
12. Lal H: Narcotic dependence, narcotic action and dopamine receptors. Life Sci 17:483-496, 1975.
13. Roberts DCS, Mason S, Fibiger HC: 6-OHDA lesions to the dorsal noradrenergic bundle alters morphine-induced locomotor activity and catalepsy. Eur J Pharmacol 52:209-214, 1978.
14. Bird SJ, Atweh SF, Kuhar MJ: Microiontophoretic study of the effects of opiates on autoradiographically localized opiate receptors, in Kosterlitz H. (ed): Opiates and Endogenous Opioid Peptides. Amsterdam, Elsevier Press, 1976, pp. 199-204.
15. Fry JP, Herz A, Zieglgansberger W: A demonstration of naxolone-precipitated opiate withdrawal on single neurons in the morhpine-tolerant dependent rat brain. Br J Pharmacol 68:585-592, 1980.
16. Herz A, Blasig J, Papeschi R: Role of catecholaminergic mechanisms in the expresssion of the morphine abstinence syndrome in rats. Psychopharmacologia 39:121-143, 1974.
17. Korf J, Bunney BS, Aghajanian GK: Noradrenergic neurons: Morphine inhibition of spontaneous activity. Eur J Pharmacol 25:165-169, 1974.
18. Basbaum AI, Fields HL: Endogenous pain control mechanisms: Review and hypothesis. Ann Neurol 4:451-462, 1978.
19. Gold MS, Byck R: Endorphins, lithium, and naloxone: Their relationship to pathological and drug-induced manic-euphoric states, in Petersen R. (ed): The International Challenge of Drug Abuse. Rockville, NIDA Research Monograph 19:192-209, 1978.
20. Hughes J: Isolation of an endogenous compound in brain with pharmacological properties similar to morphine. Brain Res 88:295-308, 1975.
21. Pert CB, Kuhar MJ, Snyder SH: Autoradiographic localization of the opiate receptor in rat brain. Life Sci 16:1849-1954, 1975.
22. Simon EJ: Opiate receptor binding with 3H-etorphine. Neurosci Res Program Bull 13:43-50, 1975.
23. Hughes J, Smith TW, Kosterlitz HW, Fothergill LA, Morgan BA, Morris HR: Identification of two related pentapeptides from the brain with potent opiate agonist activity. Nature 258:577-579, 1975.
24. Pert CB, Snyder SH: Opiate receptors: Demonstration in nervous tissue. Science 179:1011-1014, 1973.
25. Kleber HD, Gold MS: Use of psychotropic drugs in treatment of methadone maintained narcotic addicts. Ann NY Acad Sci 311:81-98, 1978.
26. Kuhar, MJ: Opiate receptors: Some anatomical and physiological aspects. Ann NY Acad Sci 311:35-48, 1978.
27. Atweh SF, Kuhar MJ: Autoradiographic localization of opiate receptors in rat brain. II. The brain stem. Brain Research 129:1-12, 1977.
28. Bloom FE, Rossier J, Battenberg EL, Bayon A, French E, Hendricksen SJ, Siggins GR, Segal D, Browne R, Ling N, Guillemin R: Beta-endorphin: Cellular localization electrophysiological and behavioral effects. Advance Biochem Psychopharmacol 18:89-109, 1978.
29. Simantov R, Kuhar MJ, Uhl GR, Snyder SH: Opioid peptide enkephalin: Immunohistochemical mapping in rat central nervous system. Proc Nat Acad Sci 74:2167-2171, 1977.
30. Watson SJ, Akil H, Sullivan S, Barchas JD: Immunocytochemical localization of methionine enkephalin: Preliminary observations. Life Sci 21:733-738, 1977.
31. Ward DG, Grizzle WE, Gann DS: Inhibitory and facilitatory areas of the rostral pons mediating ACTH release in cat. Endocrinology 99:1220-1228, 1976.
32. Svensson TH, Bunney BS, Aghajanian GK: Inhibition of both noradrenergic and serotonergic neurons in brain by the alpha-adrenergic antagonist clonidine. Brain Res 92:291-306, 1975.
33. Cedarbaum JM, Aghajanian GK: Noradrenergic neurons of the locus coeruleus: Inhibition by epinephrine and activation by the alpha-antagonist piperoxane. Brain Res 112:413-419, 1976.
34. Cedarbaum JM, Aghajanian GK: Catecholamine receptors on locus coeruleus neurons: Pharmacological characteristics. Eur J Pharmacol 44:3765-385, 1977.
35. Cedarbaum JM, Aghajanian GK: Characterization of catecholamine receptors on noradrenergic neurons of the locus coeruleus. Neurosci Abstr 2:683, 1976.
36. Greenberg DA, U'Prichard DC, Snyder SH: Alpha-noradrenergic receptor binding in mammalian brain. Life Sci 19:69-76, 1976.
37. Schmitt H, Schmitt MME H, Fenard S: Evidence for an alpha-sympathomimetic component in the effects of Catapresan vasomotor centres: Antagonism by piperoxane. Eur J Pharmacol 14:98-100, 1971.
38. Starke K: Regulation of noradrenaline release by presynaptic receptor systems. Rev Physiol Biochem Pharmacol 77:1-124, 1977.
39. Bertilsson L, Haglund K, Ostman J, Rawlins MD, Ringberger VA, Sjoqvist F: Monoamine metabolites in cerebrospinal fluid during treatment with clonidine or alprenolol. Eur J Clin Pharmacol 11:125-128, 1977.
40. Strombom U: On the functional role of pre- and postsynaptic catecholamine receptors in brain. Acta Physiol Scand 431 (suppl.): 1-43, 1975.
41. Maas JW, Greene NM, Hattox SE, Landis DH: Neurotransmitter metabolite production by human brain, in Usdin E, Kopin IJ, Barchas J, (eds): Catecholamines: Basic and Clinical Frontiers. New York, Pergamon Press, 1979, pp 1878-1880.
42. Anden NE, Corrodi H, Fuxe K, Hokfelt B, Hokfelt T, Rydin C, Svensson T: Evidence for a central noradrenaline receptor stimulation by clonidine. Life Sci 9:513-523, 1970.
43. Sastuy B, Phillis J: Evidence that clonidine can activiate histamine H_2-receptors in rat cerebralcortex. Neuropharmacology 223-225, 1977.
44. Gold MS, Redmond DE Jr: Pharmacological activation and inhibition of noradrenergic activity alter specific behaviors in nonhuman primates. Nuerosci Abstr 3:250, 1977.
45. Maas JW, Hattox SE, Landis DH, Roth RH: The determination of a brain arteriovenous difference for 3-methoxy-4-hydroxyphenethylene glycol (MHPG). Brain Res 118:167-173, 1976.
46. Gold MS, Donabedian RK, Redmond DE Jr: Further evidence for alpha-2 adrenergic receptor mediated inhibition of prolactic secretion: The effect of yohimbine. Psychoneuroendocrinology 3:253-260, 1979.
47. Extein I, Goodwin FK, Lewy AJ, Schoenfeld RI, Fakhuri L, Gold MS, Redmond DE Jr: Behavioral and biochemical effects of FK 33-824, a parenterally and orally active enkephaline analogue, in Usdin E, (ed): Endorphins in Mental Health Research London, McMillan, 1979, pp 279-292.
48. Redmond DE Jr, Huang YH, Gold MS: Evidence for the involvement of a brain norepinephrine (NE) system in anxiety. Proc 4th Int Catecholamine Symposium, Pacific Grove, CA, 1978.
49. Redmond DE Jr, Huang YH, Gold MS: Anxiety: The locue coeruleus connection. Neurosci Abstr 3:258, 1977.
50. Remdond DE Jr, Huang YH, Baulu J, Gold MS: Evidence for the involvement of a brain norepinephrine system in anxiety, in Usdin E, Kopin I, Barchas J (eds): Catecholamines: Basic and Clinical Frontiers New York, Pergamon Press, 1979, vol 2, pp 1693-1695.

51. Redmond DE J, Gold MS, Huang YH: Enkephalin acts to inhibit locus coeruleus mediated behaviors. *Soc Neurosci Abstr* 4:413, 1978.
52. Sweeney DR, Gold MS, Pottash ALC, Davies RK: Neuro-biological theories, in Kutash IL, Schlesinger LB (eds): *The Handbook of Stress and Anxiety: Current Knowledge, Theory and Treatment*. San Francisco, Jossey Bass, 1980, pp 112-122.
53. Dahlstrom A, Fuxe AK: Evidence for the existence of monoamine containing neurons in the central nervous system. I. Demonstration of monoamines in the cell bodies of brain stem neurons. *Acta Physiol Scant* 62(suppl):1-55.
54. Loisou LA: Projections of the nucleus locus coeruleus in the albino rat. *Brain Res* 15:563-574, 1969.
55. Morrison JH, Molliver ME, Grazanna R: Noradrenergic innervation of cerebral cortex: Widespread effects of local cortical lesions. *Science* 205:313-316, 1979.
56. Halaris AE, McIlhany M, Moore RY: Ascending projections of the locus coeruleus in the rat: I & II. *Brain Res* 127:1-21, 23-53, 1977.
57. Sakai K, Touret M, Salvert D, Leger L, Jouvet M: Afferent projections to the cat locus coeruleus as visualized by the horseradish peroxidase. *Brain Res* 119:21-41, 1977.
58. Aghajanian GK: Tolerance of locus coeruleus neurones to morphine and suppression of withdrawal response by clonidine. *Nature* 276:186-188, 1978.
59. Gold MS, Sweeney DR, Pottash ALC, Kleber HD: Decreased serum prolactin in opiate withdrawal and dopaminergic hyperactivity. *Am J Psychiatry* 136:849-850, 1979.
60. Ary M, Cox B, Lomax P: Dopaminergic mechanisms in precipitated withdrawal in morphine-dependent rats. *J Pharmacol Exp Ther* 200:271-276, 1977.
61. Lal H, Hynes MD: Effectiveness of butyrophenones and related drugs in narcotic withdrawal, in Deniker P, Thomas A, Villeneuve D, Baronet-La Croix Aarcin F, (eds): *Neuropsychopharmacology*. Elmsford, Pergamon Press, 1978, pp 289-295.
62. Crawley JN, Laverty R, Roth RH: Clonidine reversal of increased norepinephrine metabolite levels during morphine withdrawal. *Eur J Pharmacol* 57:2-3, 1979.
63. Redmond DE Jr, Roth RH, Hattox, SE, Stogin JM, Baula J: 3-Methoxy-4-hydroxyphenethylene glycol (MHPG) in monkey brain, CSF, and plasma during naloxone precipitated morphine abstinence. *Neurosci Abstr* 5:1160, 1979.
64. Laverty R, Roth RH: Clonidine reverses the increased norepinephrine turnover during morphine withdrawal in rats. *Brain Res* 182:482-485, 1980.
65. Hansson L, Hunyor SN, Julius S, Hoobler SW: Blood pressure crisis following withdrawal of clonidine with special reference to arterial and urinary catecholamine levels, and suggestions for acute management. *Am Heart J* 85:605-610, 1973.
66. Hunyor SN, Hansson L, Harrison TS, Hoobler SW: Effects of clonidine withdrawal: Possible mechanisms and suggestions for management. *Br Med J* 2:209-211, 1973.
67. Tang SW, Helmeste DM, Staucer HC: The effect of clonidine withdrawal on total 3-methoxy-4-hydroxyphenethylene glycol in the rat brain. *Psychopharmacology* 61:11-12, 1979.
68. Simon E: Personal communication, 1979, Brescia, Italy
69. Koss MC: Topical clonidine produces mydriasis by a central nervous system action. *Eur J Pharmacol* 55:305-310, 1979.
70. Kobinger W, Pichler L: The central modulatory effect of clonidine on the cardiodepressor reflex after suppression of synthesis and storage of noradrenaline. *Eur J Pharmacol* 30:56-62, 1975.
71. Paalzow L: Analgesia produced by clonidine in mice and rats. *J Pharm Pharmacol* 26:361-363, 1974.
72. Farsang C, Kunos G: Naloxone reverses the antihypertensive effect of clonidine. *Br J Pharmacol* 161-164, 1979.
73. Fielding S, Wilker J, Jynes M, Szewczak M, Novick WJ, Lal H: A comparison of clonidine with morphine for antinociceptive and antiwithdrawal actions. *J Pharmacol Exp Ther* 207:899-905, 1978.
74. Paalzow G, Paalzow L: Involvement of both pre and postsynaptic catecholaminergic receptors in the mediation of analgesic activity—Possible implications for morphine. *Opiates and Endogenous Opioid Peptides*, 1976, pp 427-430.
75. Clemens JA, Smalstig EB, Sawyer BD: Antipsychotic drugs stimulate prolactin release. *Psychopharmacologia* 40:123-127, 1974.
76. Gold MS, Redmond DE Jr, Donabedian RK: The effects of opiate agonist and antagonist on serum prolactin in primates: Possible role for endorphins in prolactin regulation. *Endocrinology* 105:284-289, 1979.
77. Gold MS, Redmond DE Jr, Donabedian RK, Goodwin FK, Extein I: Increase in serum prolactin by exogenous and endogenous opiates: Evidence for antidopamine and antipsychotic effects. *Am J Psychiatry* 135:1415-1416, 1978.
78. Gold MS, Pottash ALC, Finn LB, Kleber HD, Extein I: Serum prolactin and opiate withdrawal. *Psychiatry Research* 2:205-210, 1980.
79. Lal H, Brown W, Drawbaugh R, Hynes M, Brown G: Enhanced prolactin inhibition following chronic treatment with haloperidol and morphine. *Life Sci* 20:101-106, 1977.
80. Gold MS, Pottash ALC, Sweeney DR, Davies RK, Kleber HD: Clonidine decreases opiate withdrawal-related anxiety: Possible opiate noradrenergic interaction in anxiety and panic. *Substance and Alcohol Misuse* 1:239-246, 1980.
81. Gold MS, Pottash ALC, Sweeney DR, Kleber HD, Redmond DE Jr: Rapid opiate detoxification: Clinical evidence of antidepressant and antipanic effects of opiates. *Am J Psychiatry* 136:982-983, 1979.
82. Gold MS, Pottash ALC, Extein I, Stoll A: Clinical utility of clonidine in opiate withdrawal. NIDA Research Monograph 34:95-100, 1981.
83. Gold MS, Pottash ALC, Sweeney DR, Kleber HD: The effect of methadone dosage on clonidine detoxification efficacy. *Am J Psychiatry* 137:375-376, 1980.
84. Korczyn AD: Clonidine for opiate withdrawal. *Lancet* 2:649, 1980.
85. Washton AM, Resnick RB, Rawson RA: Clonidine for outpatient opiate detoxification. *Lancet* 1:1078-1079, 1980.
86. Riordan CE, Kleber HD: Rapid opiate detoxification with clonidine and naloxone. *Lancet* 1:1079-1080, 1980.
87. Washton AM, Resnick RB: Clonidine for opiate detoxification: Outpatient clinical trials. *Am J Psychiatry* 137:1121-1123, 1980.
88. Suda T, Liotta AS, Krieger DT: Beta-endorphin is not detectable in plasma from normal human subjects. *Science* 202:221-223, 1978.
89. Pasternack GW: Endogenous opioid systems in brain. *Am J Med* 68:157-159, 1980.
90. Weber E, Martin R, Voigt KH: Corticotropin/β-endorphin precursor: Concomitant storage of its fragments in the secretory granules of anterior pituitary corticotropin/endorphin cells. *Life Sci* 25:1111-1118, 1979.
91. Adler MW: Opioid peptides. *Life Sci* 26:497-510, 1980.
92. Guillemin R, Vargo T, Rossier J, Minick S, Ling N, Rivier C, Vale W, Bloom F: Beta-endorphin and adrenocorticotropin are secreted concomitantly by the pituitary gland. *Science* 197:1367-1369, 1977.
93. Mendelson JH, Ellingboe J, Kenhnle JC, Mello NK: Effects of naltrexone on mood and neuroendocrine function in normal adult males. *Psychoneuroendocrinology* 3:231-236, 1979.
94. Gold MS, Pottash ALC, Extein I, Kleber HD: Anti-endorphin effects of methadone. *Lancet* II:973-974, 1980.
95. Gold MS, Redmond DE Jr, Donabedian RK: Prolactin secretion, a measurable central effect of opiate-receptor antagonists. *Lancet* I:323-324, 1978.
96. Volavka J, Mallya A, Bauman J, Pevnick J, Cho D, Reker D.James B, Dornbush R: Hormonal and other effects of naltrexone in normal men, in Ehrlich YH, Volavka J, Davis LG, Brunngraber EG (eds): *Modulators, Mediators, and Specifiers in Brain Function*. New York, Plenum, 1979, pp 291-305.
97. Volavka J, Cho D, Mallya A, Baumann J: Naloxone increases ACTH and cortisol levels in man. *N Engl J Med* 300:1056-1057, 1979.
98. Gold PW, Extein I, Pickar D, Rebar R, Ross R, Goodwin FK: Suppression of plasma cortisol in depressed patients by acute intravenous methadone infusion. *Am J Psychiatry* 137:862-863, 1980.

99. Ho WWK, Wen HL, Fung KP: Comparison of plasma hormonal levels between heroin addicts and normal subjects. *Clin Chim Acta* 75:415-419, 1975.
100. Ho WWK, Wen HL, Ling N: Beta-endorphin-like immunoactivity in the plasma of heroin addicts and normal subjects. *Neuropharmacology* 19:117-120, 1980.

ALCOHOL AND THE OPIATE RECEPTOR: INTERACTIONS WITH THE ENDOGENOUS OPIATES

Andrew K.S. Ho, PhD
John P. Allen, MD

ABSTRACT. Recent findings in the area of interactions among alcohol, opiates, and opiate receptors are reviewed. In the laboratory animal, alcohol dependency is associated with an increased intake of morphine as well as an increased sensitivity to morphine toxicity. Acute administration of alcohol is associated with elevations of plasma β-endorphin similar in magnitude to that seen with acute morphine administration. Opiate antagonists can precipitate alcohol withdrawal in the alcohol-dependent animal as well as decrease toxic reactions to alcohol and other central nervous system depressants. These data support the clinical observations of alcohol-opiate interactions in narcotic addicts as well as explain the increased morbidity seen with concurrent alcohol use in persons on methadone maintenance.

Introduction

The phenomenon of alcohol abuse among opiate addicts is a century-old problem.[1] Numerous clinical and epidemiologic studies have been reported in the literature dealing with the seriousness of sequential, concurrent, or alternating drug and alcohol abuse patterns.[2] However, until recently, the hazards of concurrent alcohol and drug abuse, especially with heroin addicts, have not been fully recognized. The synergistic action between these two CNS depressants may lead to acute intoxications, drug overdoses, and ultimately an increase in mortality.[3-7] Thus, the question of the potential hazards and the mechanisms of interactions between alcohol and the opiates is one of great importance.

Interaction between alcohol and other drugs including the opiates has been a subject of several reviews.[8-11] However, available data in the literature

Dr. Ho is in the Division of Pharmacology, Department of Basic Sciences and Dr. Allen is in the Department of Neurosciences, Peoria School of Medicine, University of Illinois, Peoria, IL 61605. The work was supported in part by a contract from NIDA ADM-45-74-220 and a Career Teacher's Development Award in Substance Abuse Grant T01-DA00218 to Dr. Ho. The authors wish to thank Dr. Monique Braude, Project Officer, for her support and guidance. Also gratefully acknowledged are the many colleagues and students who have contributed at various stages of the research and Ms. Evelyn Hodgkins for typing the manuscript.

on the mechanisms of alcohol-opiate interactions remain scanty. Pharmacologically, it is well documented that both alcohol and morphine are potent drugs with a wide spectrum of actions at multiple sites. The mechanism of action for either alcohol or morphine is not fully understood,[12] yet these chemically dissimilar agents produce similar addictive liabilities upon repeated use, with tolerance, physical dependence, and withdrawal all part of the pattern of their abuse. They are both membrane-active agents slowing nerve conduction. They alter permeability to electrolytes, such as sodium, potassium, and calcium. Their actions often involve the same neurotransmitters, and they have similar effects on endocrine systems.[13]

The major difference between the two agents is that, as of this time, no specific alcohol receptor has been identified. Consequently, many of the actions of alcohol have been attributed to its nonspecific effects on membranes.[14] On the other hand, opiate agonists are known to be stereospecific in their actions. Since 1973, two major advances have been made in opiate research, namely, the recognition of the presence of the opiate receptor(s)[15-18] and the identification and characterization of the endogenous opiate-like peptides, the enkephalins and endorphins,[19-20] in the central nervous system. These discoveries have generated a great deal of interest on the possible role of these opiate receptors and endorphins in alcoholism.

During the past several years, a number of laboratories have studied the interactions between alcohol and the opiates. This article reviews some of the recent findings as well as presents some new data on the possible involvement of the endogenous opioids and the opiate receptor(s) in the action of alcohol.

Endorphins and Opiate Receptors

The complexity and the lack of well-developed methodology to study the phenomenon of drug interactions have been major handicaps in the understanding of the mechanisms involved. Braude and Vessel[21] summarized the many variables which may influence the outcome of interacting drugs. These include the pharmacologic variables, affecting both pharmacodynamic and pharmacokinetic parameters, and various other internal and external environmental factors. In order to focus our attention on alcohol and the opiates, considerations are given mainly to the pharmacologic aspects of drug interactions. Since several of the interaction phenomena discussed involved behavioral end-points resulting from opiate agonist-antagonist interactions, our approach is to first review the literature on opiate receptor interactions in the central nervous system (CNS) and the gastrointestinal tract (GI).

The CNS is believed to be the major site of action of both alcohol and the opiates. Although alcohol is distributed throughout the CNS, the polysynaptic structures of the reticular activating system and areas of the cerebral cortex are particularly susceptible to the effects of alcohol.[22] In contrast, the pattern of distribution of the opiate receptor in human and monkey brains shows striking heterogeneity with the highest density in the amygdala, periaqueductal area of the brain, followed by the hypothalamus, medial thalamus, caudate nucleus, and the hippocampus. The cerebral cortex shows moderate density but with marked variations in different parts, and the lowest density is in the cerebellum.[23] The regions of high opiate receptor density, such as the limbic system, are also believed to be involved with pain perception[24] and the regulation of hormone release possibly through the endogenous opiates.[25]

In morphine-dependent rats, naloxone applied to specific areas of the brain through microcannules would precipitate an abstinence syndrome only when injected in certain brain regions including the medial thalamus and the diencephalic-mesencephalic junctures[26] but not in other areas of the limbic system including the hypothalamus where opiate receptor densities are high. The abstinence signs commonly used to describe opiate withdrawal in rodents include spontaneous jumping, "wet-shakes," body weight loss, diarrhea, teeth chattering, ptosis, hypothermia, and hyperirritability. The area responsible for wet-shake behavior was demonstrated to be located in medial subcortical structures such as the periaqueductal gray matter, the medial preoptic area, and the locus ceruleus.[27]

β-Endorphin and other enkephalins have also been reported to produce physical dependence in rats, with naloxone precipitating a typical morphine-like withdrawal syndrome.[28] In microiontophoretic studies in rats, it can be demonstrated that individual neurons in various brain parts develop a state of dependence following chronic administration of either opiate or β-endorphin. Naloxone, applied microiontophoretically, induced excitatory responses which have been suggested to be representative of the withdrawal state. The areas where single neuronal responses have been recorded include the medial thalamus,[29] frontal cerebral cortex,[30] locus ceruleus,[31] and the frontal cortex and the striatum.[32] The excitatory effects of naloxone appear to be mediated by actions at stereospecific opiate receptors since only the (−)-isomer of naloxone, but not the (+)-isomer, an enentiomer lacking specific pharmacologic activity, has been shown to elicit such responses.[33] These findings suggest that opiate receptor-agonist-antagonist interaction in individual neurons of the CNS are essential for the development of abstinence syndrome in opiate-dependent animals.

In man, the characteristic abstinence signs described include acute anxiety; abdominal pain; anorexia; goose flesh; hyperexcitability; emesis; lacrimation; nasal discharge; diarrhea; increase in respiration, blood pressure, heart rate, and muscle spasm. The cycle of morphine dependence is essentially similar to animals. Furthermore, opiate receptors have been described in the human brain and naloxone precipitates the typical abstinence syndrome.[34,35] It would, therefore, seem reasonable that opiate receptor-agonist-antagonist interactions exist in humans as well as in animals.

Alcohol withdrawal is characterized by anxiety, muscle pain, disorientation, or hallucinations. According to Seevers,[36] there is no evidence of specific cross-dependence or cross-tolerance between morphine and alcohol on the basis that morphine antagonists fail to antagonize alcohol intoxication or intoxicaton with drugs known to show cross-dependence with alcohol such as barbiturates and sedative hypnotics. The basic mechanisms of opiate dependence have been reviewed by Way[37] and of alcohol by Mendelson and Mello,[38] respectively. Although dependence on alcohol and on morphine are still considered independent phenomena, more recent evidence, however, suggests the existence of alcohol-opiate interactions.

Modification of Opiate Withdrawal by Alcohol

Our interest in the studies of alcohol modification on opiate withdrawal has derived from the epidemiologic surveys showing extensive use of alcohol by heroin addicts on methadone treatment.[39] Studies on the social and behavioral profiles of methadone clients have shown that alcoholism is a major complicating factor to the success of the methadone program.[40,41] The ready availability of alcohol is often cited as the reason for the increase in its use. Questions arise as to whether there is any pharmacologic basis for the narcotic addict to use alcohol. What is the potential hazard for a narcotic addict to become an alcoholic? Does cross-tolerance and dependence exist between the two compounds? What are the potential toxicity and lethality with such drug combinations?

In order to provide some insight into these questions, animal studies using rats have been carried out to evaluate the role of alcohol in opiate withdrawal. Rats were made physically dependent on morphine, either by pellet implantation (75 mg/rat) or by single subcutaneous injection of a bolus of morphine (150 mg mg/kg in oil). Control rats were treated either with a placebo pellet or vehicle solution. Physical dependence on the opiates was established by the characteristic abstinence syndrome following naloxone administration. Several of the behavioral end-points were assessed quantitatively, including withdrawal, jumping, and wet-shakes,[27] to estimate physical dependence.

In addition, a procedure was developed to assess quantitatively diarrhea during morphine withdrawal in rats.[42] Naloxone (0.005 to 1.0 mg/kg, s.c.) produces a dose-response relationship on morphine withdrawal diarrhea, with an optimal naloxone dose of 0.4 mg/kg. The severity of diarrhea is dependent on the interval after morphine withdrawal prior to naloxone administration. Using these procedures, we studied the effects of alcohol on morphine withdrawal. Alcohol given to rats 30 minutes before naloxone treatment at doses ranging from 0.5 to 2.0 g/kg, i.p., suppresses wet-shakes, jumping, teeth chattering, and irritability but enhances hypothermia, with the effects being dose dependent on alcohol (Table 1). These symptoms are attributable to the action of alcohol on the CNS. Since none of these abstinence signs studied was seen in rats given ethanol-naloxone, the effects may be attributable to alcohol-morphine interacting possibly involving the opiate receptor in the brain.

In addition to the centrally mediated effects, the action of alcohol on morphine withdrawal-induced diarrhea may be a more peripheral phenomenon. Our results show that alcohol (0.5 to 2.0 g/kg) suppresses diarrhea and GI motility in a dose-dependent manner. This suppression by alcohol (2 g/kg) is prolonged, lasting up to 20 hours, long after the disappearance of alcohol from the GI tract. There is also significant distribution of the opiate receptor in different parts of the gastrointestinal tract.

Naloxone by itself has no effect on those of alcohol on these parameters; it antagonizes the acute effects of morphine but not those of alcohol on the suppression of GI motility. The dose-response relationship exists with an optimal effect at 0.4 mg/kg, implying that the opiate receptors in the gut are readily saturable. Alcohol produces dose-dependent effects on the suppression of the naloxone precipitated morphine diarrhea. However, the effect of alcohol may be an indirect one on the opiate receptor since alcohol has also been shown to block the diarrhea induced by castor oil.[42]

Kosterlitz and co-workers[43] used the intramural, electrically stimulated, isolated guinea pig ileum to study the effects of opiate agonist and antagonist interactions and reported good correlation between the inhibitory effects of the opiate in the contraction of the ileum and their ability to produce analgesia in man. Furthermore, the relative potencies of opiate antagonists such as naloxone, as measured by their dissociation equilibrium constants, correlate well ($r = 0.986$) with their potencies to reduce stereospecific binding in rat brain homogenates as reported by Pert and Snyder.[44] These findings imply that opiate receptor antagonist (naloxone) interactions are present in the mediation of the opiate-induced effects.

Recently, Clement[45] studied the response of alcohol and morphine in the isolated longitudinal muscle strip of guinea pig ileum. This investigator suggested that the inhibition by alcohol on twitching response is at the postsynaptic site subsequent to receptor activation whereas the inhibition induced by morphine is thought to be both generated from presynaptic sites as well as interacting with the postsynaptic sites possibly at the calcium channel.[46] The effects of alcohol on the opiate withdrawal symptoms may involve the indirect actions on various neurotransmitters and local hormones release as well as on the opiate receptors.

Table I. EFFECTS OF INTRAPERITONEAL INJECTION OF ETHANOL ON
SOME MORPHINE ABSTINENCE SIGNS IN LONG EVANS HOODED RATS
(N=8) WITHIN 30 MINUTES AFTER NALOXONE (0.4 mg/kg)

Treatment*	Mean no. of Jumps in 30 minutes	Mean no. of Wet-shakes in 30 minutes	Mean no. of Chattering in 30 minutes
Placebo pellet removal	0	0	0
Ethanol (1 g/kg) plus placebo pellet removal	0	0	0
Morphine pellet removal	12.4 ± 2.9	12.1 ± 2.4	7.0 ± 1.6
Ethanol (1 g/kg) plus morphine pellet removal	10.7 ± 4.4++	1.5 ± 0.6**	7.4 ± 2.6
Ethanol (2 g/kg) plus morphine pellet removal	1.3** (0-11)+	2.2 ± 0.8** (0.6)	3.5 ± 0.8

*Pellet removed 2 hrs before naloxone treatment
+Only one out of eight rats showed sign
++Five out of eight rats showed jumping (mean no. of jumps in 30 min. for group of eight rats)
**Data expressed as mean ± S.E., statistically significant $p < 0.002-0.001$

Reproduced from Morphine withdrawal in the rat: assessment by quantitation of diarrhea and modification by ethanol. Pharmacology, 18:9-17 (1979).

Modification of Alcohol Withdrawal by Opiates

Several groups of investigators have reported interaction of opiate ago-nists and antagonists on alcohol dependence and withdrawal. For example, Blum et al[47] found that acute morphine administration significantly sup-presses the alcohol-induced withdrawal convulsions in mice utilizing the Goldstein-Pal inhalation technique which involved the use of treatment with pyrazole, an alcohol dehydrogenase inhibitor. The duration of suppresssion lasts for a period longer than the ordinary time-course of the analgesic effect of morphine. This same group of investigators also reported that naloxone significantly inhibits the alcohol-induced dependence in mice.[11]

Hemmingsen and Sorensen,[48] however, using intragastric feeding of 20% alcohol to Wistar rats to produce intoxication, reported that naloxone (2 mg/kg, i.p. every six hours) failed to affect signs of severe alcohol intoxi-cation or modify the withdrawal syndrome following chronic alcohol intoxi-cation. According to these investigators, one of the difficulties has been the exceedingly high mortality rate as a result of intragastric "drowning." These findings are in contrast to those reported in Blum et al[49] in mice using a different technique to produce physical dependence on alcohol.

Variations in the degree of tolerance and dependence may account for the differences in the effects of naloxone. In our laboratory the combined effects of chronic opiates and alcohol have been studied in neonatal Sprague-Daw-ley rats pretreated with either morphine or methadone daily using an incre-mental dose regimen for six weeks and followed by a forced-drinking sched-ule of alcohol.[50,51] Characteristic abstinence signs due to either morphine or alcohol were observed. The controls were pretreated either with opiate or saline. The rats treated with both opiate and alcohol showed significantly more severe withdrawal symptomatology compared with those given alcohol alone as evidenced by the various scores of withdrawal signs of alcohol in-cluding body weight loss, tremor, convulsions, jumping, clonic tonic convul-sions, coma, and death. The naloxone-precipitated opiate withdrawal signs were significantly reduced in rats given a combination of opiate and alcohol compared with opiate alone. Our observations also showed that opiate pre-treated rats consumed significantly less alcohol during the first two months of forced drinking. It is unlikely that the increase in withdrawal symptoms was due primarily to dependence on alcohol alone. Some degree of cross-tolerance and dependence between alcohol and morphine is apparent.

In support of this hypothesis are the recent studies by Khanna et al[52] who reported cross-tolerance between alcohol and morphine in the rat with re-spect to hypothermia during withdrawal. Mayer et al[53] studied the combined effects of morphine pellet implantation on the isolated longitudinal muscle/ myenteric-plexus preparation of the guinea pig ileum and demonstrated cross-tolerance to the in vitro inhibitory effects of morphine and alcohol on the electrically stimulated contractions. In another group of neonatal rats, naltrexone was given in combination with morphine for six weeks using a graded increase dose schedule and then exposed to alcohol on a forced drinking schedule. Naltrexone treatment significantly blocked not only the morphine withdrawal, but also the combined effects of morphine and alcohol on withdrawal.[54] Thus, opiate agonists and antagonists appear to influence the withdrawal of alcohol.

Interactions of Opiates, Opiate Antagonists and Alcohol: Effects on Alcohol Preference

While it is generally acknowledged that alcohol abuse prior to narcotic addiction or the continual abuse of alcohol is common among heroin addicts or methadone clients,[2] Few experimental data are available in the literature on alcohol-opiate interactions with reference to alcohol preference. Animals with a higher rate of alcohol consumption have also been shown to have an unusually high intake of morphine.[55] Shuster and Thompson[56] reviewed some of the intravenous self-administered drugs including morphine and alcohol for their positive reinforcing properties and suggested that dependence on these agents is responsible for their behavioral reinforcement. Killam et al,[57] in self-infusion studies in morphine-dependent monkeys, reported that treatment with alcohol (5 ml/kg of 70%) and l-alpha-acetyl methadol (LAAM) significantly increased morphine intake. Naloxone, naltrexone, and cyclazocine precipitated abstinence syndrome which the animals generally controlled by increased morphine intake.

Altshuler and co-workers[58] studied the effect of naltrexone, a longer acting opiate antagonist than naloxone, on the intravenous self-infusion of alcohol in eight drug-naive male rhesus monkeys. They reported that at doses ranging from 3 to 5 mg/kg, naltrexone induces a significant increase of alcohol self-infusion during the first five days followed by significant decreases during the next ten days. These investigators suggested that blockade of opiate receptors by naltrexone may decrease the reinforcement effects of alcohol. In rats, acute morphine has been shown to suppress consumption of alcohol.[59]

In our laboratory, the acute effects of morphine suppression on alcohol intake in rats and mice have been confirmed. In addition, we extended our observations to a number of other opiate agonists and antagonists.[50,51] Our results showed that morphine, methadone, LAAM, or levorphanol suppressed the volitional consumption of alcohol. This effect was not seen with dextrorphan. The antagonists, naloxone and naltrexone, produced a small but not significant increase in alcohol consumption following a single, acute injection.

The suppression of alcohol intake by the opiate agonists appear to be dose dependent. There is no significant alterations in food and water intake and in body weight. Furthermore, under the influence of the opiates, the animals are able to discriminate against alcohol and solutions of different tastes. Morphine-dependent rats show significant increases in alcohol preference during withdrawal in the volume, the amount of alcohol ingested, and the preference-aversion cut-off concentration reached. In a group of neonatal rats treated with both morphine and naltrexone daily on an incremental regimen, no significant increase in alcohol preference was observed during morphine-naltrexone withdrawal. These findings suggest that the increase in volitional alcohol consumption is dependent on the development of. tolerance and physical dependence on the opiate.[54]

To explore whether the endogenous opiate-like peptides are involved in alcohol preference, we studied the effects of enkephalin on the volitional consumption of alcohol.[60] Adult male Long-Evans hooded rats were screened for their alcohol selection (5%). A permanent indwelling canula was implanted into the lateral ventricle, and the rats were allowed to recover for two weeks. Daily consumption of alcohol (5%), water, and food were measured from 1 to 3 PM. Different doses of met-enkephalin (40 μg, 80 μg, and 200 μg in 20 μl) were infused into the brain under conscious conditions. Fig 1 shows a significant reduction in alcohol consumption ($p < 0.025$) lasting for

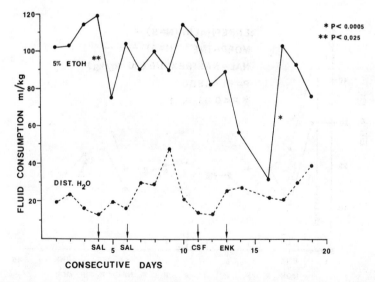

FIGURE 1.—Effects of met-enkephalin (ENK) on alcohol selections in the Long-Evans hooded rats. ENK (200 μg/rat) was infused into the lateral ventricle through an indwelling canula, 30 minutes before a two-hour daily session of alcohol (5%), water, and food. Data are expressed as mean daily consumption, eight rats used for each group. Injection days indicated as (↑), SAL = saline, CSF = artificial cerebral spinal fluid.

days. No such reduction in alcohol consumption was observed in the "sham"-operated controls given equivalent volume of artificial CSF. To study whether this effect can be blocked by naloxone, we repeated these observations in another group of rats injected daily with the placebo (CSF solution, 20 μl) for seven days, and on day 8, naloxone was given 30 minutes prior to met-enkephalin, the acute suppression of alcohol consumption was blocked by naloxone (Fig 2).

These preliminary findings on the suppression of alcohol consumption by acute met-enkephalin are consistent with our earlier observations that certain degree of specificity exists on the interactions between opiate and alcohol with respect to alcohol preference including stereospecificity of the opiates and antagonism by opiate antagonist. Since β-endorphin and met-enkephalin also interact with alcohol and morphine and their effects are antagonized by naloxone, one apparent interpretation of these findings is that alcohol-opiate receptor interactions may involve the endogenous opioids possibly as modulators on the various behavior parameters such as volitional consumption and withdrawal.

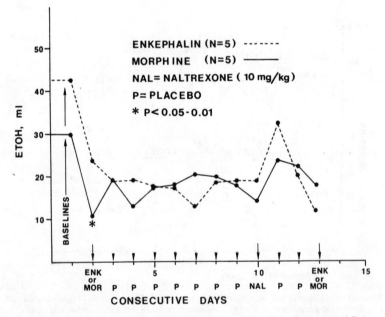

FIGURE 2.—Effects of enkephalin (200 μg/rat) and morphine (60mg/kg, s.c.) on daily consumption of alcohol. Treatment protocol as described in Fig 1. NAL: naltrexone (10 mg/kg, s.c.) given with morphine or enkephalin as indicated (↑).

Toxic Effects of Interactions Between Alcohol and Opiate Agonists and Antagonists

The toxicities and the potential hazards of alcohol-opiate interactions have been studied in animals. Venho and co-workers[61] reported that mice treated chronically with alcohol, develop supersensitivity and increase in lethality to morphine. Alcohol is known to produce hepatic dysfunction. Consequently, the ability to metabolize opiates may be greatly compromised. We have reported marked potentiation of alcohol toxicity in mice with acute opiate-alcohol combinations especially with the longer acting opiates such as LAAM and methadone. Treatment with various opiate agonists (morphine, LAAM, methadone, and levorphanol) reduces the rate of disappearance of alcohol in the blood and brain. This effect is not seen with dextrorphan or naloxone.

On the other hand, with acute or chronic treatment with alcohol at doses not greater than 4 g/kg, the morphine contents in the blood and brain are not significantly altered. It is interesting to note that chronic administration of methadone, morphine, and LAAM produced only a small but insignificant decline in the rate of disappearance of alcohol.[62,63]Development of tolerance to the effects of the opiates may have contributed to the lack of effects on the rate of alcohol disappearance. Naloxone has also been reported to antagonize the intoxication induced by alcohol.[64]

The effects of naloxone on narcosis and/or lethality induced by diazepam, methaqualone, lithium, phenobarbital either alone or in combination with alcohol have also been studied in mice. Interaction toxicities between alcohol and various psychotropic drugs including the opiates are dose dependent as is the degree of naloxone antagonism as evidenced by the reduction in narcosis and lethality.[65] The presence of naloxone antagonism to a variety of CNS depressants, as well as to the opiates, raises the question of naloxone acting on sites other than the opiate receptors. This possibility is furthered by the observation that the dose of naloxone required to elicit significant reversal of narcosis and lethality of these CNS depressants far exceeds those for specific opiate receptor interactions. At this level (5 to 10 mg/kg) naloxone is known to be a GABA antagonist.[66]

Another interesting observation was made by Freund[67] who reported that chronic alcohol consumption in mice induced the loss of anxiolytic receptors as measured by receptor binding assays using tritiated flunitrazepam. Freund suggested that the loss of such benzodiazepine receptors may enhance anxiety and the compensatory increase in consumption of alcohol. Naloxone has also been reported to antagonize general anesthetics.[68] Clinically, naloxone reversal of apnea in patients ingesting large doses of alcohol, barbiturates, and diazepam has been reported.[69,70]

Ethanol-Opiate Interaction on the Neuroendocrine System

In recent years, the effect of alcohol on endocrine function and the role of the opiates and their receptors have received increasing attention. However, the combined effects of opiates and ethanol on various indices of endocrine and neuroendocrine function are poorly understood. Despite the general argument by Nichols[71] in a treatise on the general theory of addiction that a common biologic mechanism was operant for either alcohol or opiate addiction, sufficient experimental data to support this hypothesis were lacking until recently.

Two major problems exist when considering ethanol-opiate interaction on endrocrine function. The first is separation of the acute effects of alcohol from those resulting from chronic alcoholic exposure. The second problem is the capacity to distinguish between the endocrinologic and metabolic effects of alcohol from those which are secondary to ethanol-induced tissue damage. The effect of ethanol on the endocrine system has been known for centuries. A summary of these interactions is given below.

Hypothalamic-Pituitary-Adrenal Axis

Following administration of ethanol, corticosterone levels rise in rats.[72,73] Direct evidence that this adrenal response was mediated through increased ACTH secretion was reported by Noble and colleagues[74] who showed that pituitary ACTH concentrations fell after acute administration of alcohol in mice. Tolerance to alcohol as assessed by endocrine parameters has been well studied. Ellis,[72] in his initial studies, demonstrated that the increase in plasma corticosterone was slightly reduced after injection of ethanol in rats. Crossland and Ratcliffe[75] reported that plasma corticosterone response following ethanol was significantly lower in those animals chronically addicted to alcohol, accompanied by a reduced corticosterone response to stress.

Noble, Kakihana, and Butte[74] confirmed those studies by showing that corticosterone was reduced after ethanol was injected in alcohol-dependent mice. With prolonged administration of alcohol, diurnal variation in plasma corticosterone is abolished.[76] Finally, glucocorticoids may play a role in the development of dependence upon and tolerance to alcohol. If alcohol-dependent mice are adrenalectomized, the number of withdrawal seizures is significantly reduced.[77] Rats treated with dexamethasone and alcohol showed antagonism to ethanol and greater tolerance to alcohol's depressive effects when compared with those treated with ethanol alone.[78]

In man, the effects of alcohol on the hypothalamic-pituitary-adrenal axis is extremely important. Recently several groups of investigators have reported a total of 17 patients with chronic alcoholism and clinical and biochemical features of Cushings' syndrome whose features disappeared after alcohol was withdrawn.[79-82] In some patients plasma ACTH levels were elevated whereas in others plasma ACTH levels were undetectable. Smols and Kloppenburg[83] found little correlation between plasma cortisol levels and liver damage.

The mechanism responsible for biochemical alterations accounting for the ethanol-induced pseudo-Cushings is unknown. Adrenalectomy is known to abolish the increase in liver alcohol dehydrogenase activity in mice dependent on alcohol although there is no induction of liver microsomal ethanol oxydizing system activity.[84] It is extremely unlikely that ethanol directly acts on the adrenal to alter steroid synthesis.[85] The acute administration of alcohol in man is known to result in increased cortisol production.[86-88] Pretreatment with morphine does not affect the subsequent increase in plasma cortisol levels following alcohol administration.

In alcoholic humans, resting plasma cortisol levels are higher than abstinent alcoholics.[89-91] Curiously, concurrent treatment with a barbiturate in a dose which alleviates withdrawal symptoms is associated with a fall in plasma cortisol in alcoholic patients. However, treatment with a benzodiazepine, which will also alleviate withdrawal symptoms, was not associated with any change in plasma cortisol.[92] These findings suggest that increased cortisol secretion is not the result of an acute stress, but rather is caused by alterations of, most likely, the hypothalamus and the limbic systems, which are involved in the regulation of corticotropin releasing factor and subsequently ACTH release. The additional effects of opiates on the physiologic effects of alcohol on the endocrine system are unknown.

Inasmuch as there have been few reports on the combined effect of ethanol and opiates on endocrine function, we decided to assess the effect of these two substances on β-endorphin and ACTH secretion in the male rat.[93,94] Adult male Sprague-Dawley rats, kept individually, were acutely treated with one of the following regimes: (1) morphine (10 mg/kg, s.c.); (2) alcohol (2 g/kg, i.p.); (3) naloxone (0.4 mg/kg, s.c.); (4) morphine (10 mg/kg, s.c.) and naloxone (0.4 mg/kg, s.c.); (5) alcohol (2 g/kg, i.p.) and naloxone (0.4 mg/kg, s.c.); and (6) controls (normal saline, 1 cc, i.p.). Naloxone was administered at 8:30 AM in groups 4 and 5. Fifteen minutes later either morphine or alcohol was injected. All rats were decapitated 30 minutes later. Trunk blood was collected and plasma β-endorphin determined by radioimmunoassay using kits supplied by New England Nuclear Corporation Mass.

The results obtained on the mean plasma levels in the various treatment groups are illustrated in Fig 3. Significant increases in the plasma level of β-endorphin was obtained for morphine ($p < 0.001$) or alcohol ($p < 0.01$) as compared with controls. This increase induced by either alcohol or morphine was significantly antagonized by naloxone pretreatment ($p < 0.01$). There was no significant difference in the mean plasma β-endorphin concentration between the naloxone and the saline treated control.

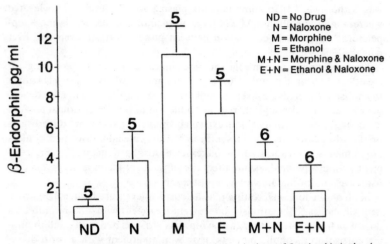

FIGURE 3.—Antagonism of alcohol or morphine induced release of β-endorphin in the plasma of male Sprague-Dawley rats. Naloxone (0.4 mg/kg, s.c.) was given 15 minutes before either morphine (10 mg/kg, s.c.) or ethanol (2 g/kg, i.p.) and the rats killed 30 minutes later. Data are expressed as mean value ± S.D. in pg/ml × 100. Significant increase in mean plasma β-endorphin was obtained with either morphine (p < 0.025) or ethanol (p < 0.02).

In chronic experiments, rats were made physically dependent on morphine by pellet implantations, and naloxone was used to precipitate morphine withdrawal. The mean plasma level of β-endorphin was suppressed significantly (p < 0.01) in the morphine-tolerant rats, and this suppression was reversed completely by naloxone (Fig 4). Naloxone by itself produced no significant alteration of β-endorphin level. In addition, ether given acutely completely restored suppression induced by morphine as well as significantly increased the mean plasma level of β-endorphin in the naloxone-precipitated, morphine-withdrawn rats.

Experiments are in progress on the acute effects of alcohol on β-endorphin. We have also presented preliminary data on other hormones in the plasma such as ACTH, corticosterone, prolactin, LH and testosterone levels in morphine-tolerant rats before and during naloxone-precipitated withdrawal.[94,95] The mean plasma levels of ACTH were significantly stimulated by naloxone alone and in morphine-tolerant rats, but the naloxone-precipitated withdrawal produced no significant change (Fig 5-6). The mean plasma level of corticosterone was lowered in morphine-tolerant rats, but naloxone produced no significant change in morphine-tolerant animals.

Acute adminstration of morphine and alcohol stimulates β-endorphin release as evidenced by an increase in the mean plasma levels. During morphine dependence, however, β-endorphin release is suppressed. Naloxone reversal of both alcohol and morphine stimulation of β-endorphin release suggests that the opiate receptor may be involved in this sequence of events. β-endorphin may therefore play an important role in alcohol-opiate interactions on the hypothalamic-pituitary-adrenal axis.

Hypothalamic-Pituitary-Gonadal Axis

The effects of prolonged administration of alcohol on the hypothalamic-pituitary-gonadal axis have been known for centuries and have been the subject of several reviews in recent years.[96-98] The biochemical bases for hypogonadism in subjects with liver damage include decreased concentration of total and free testosterone, decreased clearance of testosterone, decreased production rates of testosterone, decreased plasma concentration of dihydrotestosterone, increased androgen binding due to increase in sex hormone binding globulin, impaired testosterone response in human chorionic gonadotropin secretion, and clomiphene stimulation.

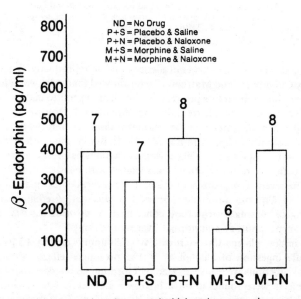

FIGURE 4.—Effects of morphine-tolerance and withdrawal on mean plasma concentration -endorphin in Sprague-Dawley rats implanted with morphine pellet (75 mg/rat) 72 hours prior to withdrawal with naloxone (0.4 mg/kg, s.c.) 30 minutes later. β-endorphin level was lowered significantly ($p < 0.01$) compared with the controls. Naloxone precipitated withdrawal completely reversed this decrease.

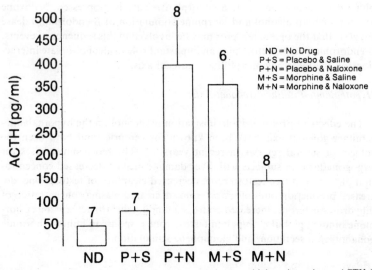

FIGURE 5.—Effects of morphine-tolerance and naloxone withdrawal on plasma ACTH in Sprague-Dawley rats. Treatment protocol as in Fig 4. Naloxone or morphine produced a significant increase in plasma ACTH ($p < 0.01$).

Initial studies on the effects of alcohol on the reproductive system were done by Chaudhury and Matthews[99] who showed that there was a fall in the number of litters in rabbits pretreated with alcohol prior to mating. They felt that the effect was not due to inhibition of ovulation. However, Kieffer and Ketchell[100] demonstrated that ovulation was inhibited in rats which could be reversed by prior administration of LH. It is well recognized that acute administration of ethanol to mice results in a biphasic effect on serum testosterone with low doses of ethanol associated with elevation of plasma testosterone levels. Large doses of ethanol, however, depress plasma testosterone.[101,102] Chronic administration of low dosages of ethanol results in lowering of plasma testosterone concentration associated with abnormal testicular morphology and normal liver morphology.[102-104]

In humans, plasma testosterone levels fall approximately 12 hours after the acute ingestion of alcohol.[105-106] The prolonged effects of alcohol on gonadal functions were investigated by Gordon and co-workers.[107] Some of the subjects were found to have increased LH levels whereas others had normal levels. In the former cases, a direct effect of alcohol on testicular function was suggested. Other findings included: an increase in hepatic testosterone A-ring reductase activity, an increase in metabolic clearance of testosterone with a concurrent fall in testosterone production rates, and fall in plasma testosterone binding. There was also a reduction in loss of the episodic pulsatile secretion of testosterone.

Further evidence which supports the hypothesis of a primary ethanol effect on the gonad was presented by Wright et al[108] who assessed the effect of leutinizing hormone releasing factor (LHRF) on pituitary gonadotropin secretion. In 6 of 13 noncirrhotic alcoholics, basal plasma LH levels were elevated, and an exaggerated response in LH secretion was noted following LHRF administration. The effects of alcohol on testicular function are therefore well documented in the absence of liver disease. The presence of hepatic dysfunction probably accentuates these abnormalities.

Prolactin

There is a paucity of data on the effects of alcohol on prolactin secretion. Ylikahri, Huttensen, and Harkonen[109] reported that acute ethanol administration stimulated prolactin secretion in man. The prolactin response to thyrotropin releasing hormone (TRH) administration was also enhanced after ethanol consumption. However, in alcoholics the effect of alcohol on prolactin secretion is quite different. Loosen and Prang[110] report basal pro-

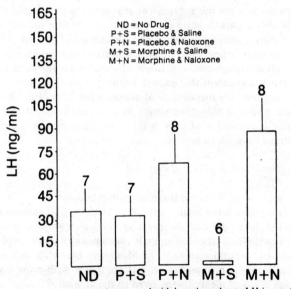

FIGURE 6.—Effects of morphine-tolerance and withdrawal on plasma LH in rats (treatment protocol as in Fig 4). Morphine-tolerant rats showed a significantly lowered plasma LH (p < 0.001) which was completely reversed by naloxone.

lactin levels to be slightly reduced with impairment in TRH-induced release of prolactin during times of withdrawal from ethanol compared with normal controls.

Growth Hormone

Alcohol affects growth hormone in a number of ways. Bellet et al, (1971) reported that growth hormone concentrations rose after an acute dose of alcohol in fasting subjects. In contrast, Toro et al[111] found no change in plasma levels of growth hormone, cortisol, prolactin, testosterone, or LH following the acute administration of alcohol. Similarly, Andreani, Tamburrano, and Javicoli[112] also failed to confirm Bellet's initial reports on fasting levels but did demonstrate an impaired growth hormone release to arginine infusion, a known stimulant of growth hormone release.

Alcohol administration to normal human subjects during prolonged fasting results in hypoglycemia and an increase in free fatty acids. During this time, growth hormone levels may fall,[113] remain unchanged, or undergo a modest rise.[112,114] It is suggested that the impaired growth hormone response to alcohol is due to the rise in free fatty acids which blocks the hypoglycemic-induced growth hormone response.[115,116] Subsequently, Priem, Shanley, and Malan[117] reported that the growth hormone response to insulin-induced hypoglycemia was diminished in those that consumed ethanol.

Alterations in growth hormone secretion in response to insulin-induced hypoglycemia in actively drinking, chronic alcoholics has not been reported.[118] However, Chalmers et al[119] have reported impaired growth hormone response after hypoglycemia in those who had been abstinent for several days. Thus it is apparent that growth hormone secretion can be altered by alcohol; however, the mechanism of action is far from clear. Whether the effects are mediated through changes in free fatty acids or alterations in hypothalamic regulation of growth hormone releasing factor and somatostatin release have yet to be clearly ascertained.

Hypothalamic-Pituitary-Thyroid Function

Initial studies investigating the relationship between alcohol and thyroid function were conducted in the early 1950s. Hypothyroid animals voluntarily increased their intake of alcohol compared with animals given propylthiouracil of thyroidectomized animals concomitantly treated with dessicated thyroid or triiodothyronine.[120-122] Moreover, blood alcohol levels were significantly lower in hypothyroid rats compared with hyperthyroid rats after equal doses of alcohol were given to the animal.[120]

In man, Goldberg[123,124] reported a high incidence of hypothyroidism in chronic alcoholics. Since those initial reports, other investigators have either failed to confirm those initial findings or found no consistent alteration in thyroid function. Whether the changes in thyroid function are due to poor nutrition giving rise to a "euthyroid sick syndrome" or the result of alcohol modification of controlling factors in thyroid physiology have yet to be clearly elucidated.

Role of Opiates on Neuroendocrine Function

Several recent reviews have summarized the effects of opiates on the neuroendocrine system in humans and animals.[125-127] This subject is discussed more fully in a following paper in this issue. Generally, morphine and the endogenous opiates stimulate growth hormone, prolactin and ACTH release whereas they inhibit LH, FSH, and TSH release. These effects can be reversed by naloxone administration. Moreover, stress-induced release of prolactin can be inhibited in the rat by prior administration of naloxone.[126] In a recent paper by Morley and co-workers,[128] morphine addiction and withdrawal in rats resulted in alterations in the concentration of a variety of peptides in the neurophil. Somatostatin, choleycystokinin, neurotensin, and substance P concentrations increased during morphine addiction. Following naloxone-induced withdrawal, decreased brain concentrations of TRF, somatostatin, neurotensin, and substance P occurred. Naloxone, alone, decreases thalamic substance P and neurotensin concentrations. There was no change in vasoactive intestinal peptide concentrations in any group. The fall in tissue concentrations of somatostatin during withdrawal correlated highly with a fall in circulating growth hormone.

These investigations have suggested that these various peptides in the central nervous system are important neuromodulators in morphine addiction and withdrawal. The combined effect of alcohol on this system or the effect of alcohol alone on these peptides has yet to be determined. Future research in this area should be directed toward a clear understanding of the regulating mechanisms through which addiction and withdrawal syndromes are mediated as well as the common mechanism through which alcohol and opiate addiction are operant.

Clinical Implications of Alcohol-Opiate Interactions

The prevalence of alcohol abuse by addicts maintained on methadone programs has been a major complicating factor greatly undermining the success of methadone and other regulated drug treatment programs.[129] The clinical implications of a combined alcohol/opiate interaction may be profound, as up to 50% of narcotic addicts may consume large amounts of alcohol, with 25% of these individuals having a history of alcohol dependence.[130-133] Stimmel et al[132,133] studying medical complications in methadone patients, suggested that alcohol abuse, rather than intravenous narcotic use, may be the major factor responsible for liver damage.

Kreek,[134] reviewing the medical complications in methadone patients, concluded that in over 10-14 years of follow-up studies in adult patients and 5-7 years of follow-up in adolescent patients, no toxic or serious adverse effects due to methadone itself could be demonstrated. The most common cause of serious medical complications in these patients during maintenance and following detoxication from methadone was alcohol abuse. The prevalence of alcoholism in narcotic addicts is therefore considerable, often greatly compromising ongoing therapy. A strong case can therefore be made for the development of combined therapy for alcoholism and narcotic abuse.[41]

Animal studies have confirmed the potential hazards of alcohol-opiate interactions. Toxicity data suggest that opiate pretreatment may alter various pharmacokinetic parameters of alcohol leading to retention in tissues such as the brain. On the other hand, liver dysfunction, induced by chronic alcohol, may compromise the ability of the animal or human to detoxify opiates, with a consequent increase in toxicity in individuals using such drug combinations. Evidence from animal studies suggest a reason why addicted individuals use alcohol excessively is that alcohol readily suppresses the discomforts of various opiate withdrawal signs. In addition, alcohol in combination with methadone or other opiates may facilitate th penetration of opiates and enhance the behavioral "high,"[9] thus reinforcing combined use of these drugs.

The fact that opiate antagonists, naloxone or naltrexone, antagonize not only acute opiate intoxication and precipitate opiate withdrawal but also effect intoxications from alcohol and other CNS depressants suggests the possible involvement of the opiate-receptors in the actions of alcohol and other CNS depressants.

On the basis of experimental findings, the possible use of opiate antagonists in the treatment of alcohol and other CNS depressants intoxications should be further explored. Preliminary findings, revealing the ability of exogenous opioids to modify voluntary alcohol consumption in rats, further suggest the possible role of such physiologically occurring substrates to modulate alcohol preference.

One may be tempted to speculate that individuals prone to become alcoholics or problem drinkers have biochemical aberrations with some "alcohol drinking factors," possibly related to the opioid-like peptides or other substances as yet to be discovered. Thus, the ability of physicians to predict alcohol problem drinkers may be a future possibility. Our limited knowledge at this time on the mechanisms of opiate receptor interactions with opiates and alcohol should be viewed as new opportunities for researchers to engage in this fertile field of research.

REFERENCES

1. Mattison JB: A case of double narcotic addiction, opium and alcohol. Imbecility recovery. *Canada Lancet* 17:101-104, 1884.

2. Carroll JFX, Malloy TE, Kendrick FM: Multiple substance abuse: A review of the literature, in Gardner SE (ed): *National Drug/Alcohol Collaborative Project: Issues in Multiple Substance Abuse.* NIDA Services Research Monograph Series, 1980, pp 9-24.

3. Halpern M, Rho Y: Deaths from narcotism in New York City. Incidence circumstances and post mortem findings. *New York State Journal of Medicine* 66(18):2391-2408, 1966.

4. Jackson GW, Richman A: Risk factors in mortality of narcotics addicts. Paper presented at the Annual Meeting of the American Public Health Association, Minneapolis, 1971.

5. Jackson GW, Richman A: Alcohol use among narcotic addicts. *Alcohol Health and Research World* 1:25-28, 1973.

6. Baden MM: Methadone related deaths in New York City, in Einstein S (ed): *Methadone Maintenance.* New York, Marcel Dekker Inc, 1971.

7. Baden MM: Narcotic Abuse: A medical examiner's view. *New York State Journal of Medicine* 72(7):834-840, 1972.

8. Forney, RB, Hughes FW: Interaction between alcohol and psychopharmacological drugs, in Tremolieres J (ed): *Int. Encyclopedia of Pharmac. and Ther.* vol 2, New York, Pergamon Press, 1970.

9. Kissin B: Interactions of ethyl alcohol and other drugs, in Kissin B, Begleiter H (eds): *The Biology of Alcoholism.* New York, Plenum Press, 1974, pp 109-161.

10. Smith CM: Interactions of drug of abuse with alcohol. *Ann N Y Acad Sci* 281:384-392, 1976.

11. Blum, K, Hamilton MG, Wallace JE: Alcohol and opiates: A review of common neurochemical and behavioral mechanisms, in Blum K (ed): *Alcohol and Opiate - Neurochemical and behavioral mechanisms.* New York, Academic Press, 1977, pp 203-236.

12. Kalent H: Comparative aspects of tolerance to, and dependence on, alcohol, barbiturates and opiates, in Gross MM (ed): *Alcohol Intoxication and Withdrawal;* vol 3b. New York, Plenum Press, 1977, p 169.

13. Goodman LS, Gilman AG: The pharmacological basis of therapeutics, 6th ed. Gilman AG, Goodman LS, and Gilman A (eds), 1980, pp 376-390 and pp 494-534.

14. Chin JH, Goldstein DB: Effects of low concentrations of ethanol on the fluidity of spin-labeled erythrocyte and brain membranes. *Mol Pharmacol* 13:435-441, 1977.

15. Goldstein A: The search for the opiate receptor, in Cochin J (ed): *Pharmacology and the Future of Man. Vol. I. Drug Abuse and Contraception.* (Proceedings of the 5th Int. Congr. on Pharmacol. San Francisco, July 1971). Basel, S Karger, 1973, pp 140-150.

16. Simon EJ: In search of the opiate receptor. *Am J Med Sci* 266:160-168, 1973.

17. Pert CB, Snyder SH: Opiate receptor: Demonstration in nervous tissue. *Science* 179:1011-1014, 1973.

18. Terenius L: Characteristics of the "receptor" for narcotic analgesics in synaptic plasma membrane fraction from rat brain. *Acta Pharmacol Toxicol* 33:377-384, 1973.

19. Goldstein A: Opioid peptides (endorphins) in pituitary and brain. *Science* 193:1081-1086, 1976.

20. Hughes J, Smith TW, Kosterlitz HW, Fothergill LA, Morgan BA, Morris HR: Identification of two related pentapeptides from the brain with potent opiate agonist activity. *Nature* 258:577-579, 1975.

21. Braude MC, Vesell EC: Interactions of drugs of abuse. *Ann NY Acad Sci* 281:vii-x, 1976.

22. Himwich AE, Callison DA: The effects of alcohol on evoked potentials of various parts of the central nervous system of the cat, in Kissin B, Begleiter H (eds): *The Biology of Alcoholism. Vol. 2, Physiology and Behavior.* New York, Plenum Press, 1972, pp 67-84.

23. Kuhar MJ, Pert CB, Snyder SH: Regional distribution of opiate receptor binding in monkey and human brain. *Nature* 245:447-450, 1973.

24. Snyder SH, Pert CB: Regional distribution of the opiate receptor, in Snyder SH, Matthysse S (eds): *Opiate Receptor Mechanisms.* Cambridge, Mass, The MIT Press, 1975, pp 35-38.

25. Holaday, Loh HH: Endorphin-opiate interactions with neurendocrine systems, in Loh HH, Ross DH (eds): *Neurochemical Mechanisms of Opiates and Endorphins* (Adv. Biochem. Psychopharmacol. Vol. 20). New York, Raven Press, 1979, pp. 227-258.

26. Wei E, Loh HH, Way EL: Neurochemical correlates of morphine dependence. *Science* 177:616-617, 1972.

27. Wei E, Sigel S, Way EL: Regional sensitivity of the rat brain to the inhibitory effects of morphine on wet shake behavior. *J Pharmac and Exptl Therap* 193:56-63, 1975.

28. Wei E, Loh HH: Physical dependence on opiate-like peptides. *Science* 193:1262-1263, 1976.

29. Frederickson RCA, Norris FH, Hewes CR: Effects on naloxone and acetylcholine on medial thalamic and cortical units in naive and morphine dependent rats. *Life Sci Oxford* 17:81-82, 1975.

30. Satoh M, Zieglgansberger W, Herz A: Actions of opiates upon single unit activity in the cortex of naive and tolerant rats. *Brain Res* 115:99-110, 1976.

31. Aghajanian GK: Tolerance of locus coeruleus neurons to morphine and suppression of withdrawal response by clonidine. *Nature, London* 276:186-188, 1978.

32. Nicole RA, Siggins GR, Ling N, Bloom FE, Guillemin R: Neuronal actions of endorphins and enkephalins among brain regions: A comparative microiontophoretic study. *Proc Natl Acad Sci USA* 74:2584-2588, 1977.

33. Fry JP, Herz A, Zieglgansberger W: *A Demonstration of Naloxone-Precipitated Opiate Withdrawal on Single Neurones in the Morphine-Tolerant/Dependent Rat Brain.* Baltimore, University Park Press, 1980, pp 45-61.

34. Martin WR: Assessment of the dependence producing potentiality of narcotic analgesics, in Lasagna L (ed): *Int. Encyclopedia of Pharmacol and Ther Sec 6, Vol. 1. Clinical Pharmacol.* Glasgow, Scotland, Pergamon Press, 1966 pp 155-180.

35. Martin WR, Gorodetsky CW, Thompson WD: Receptor dualism; Some kinetic implications, in Kosterlitz HW, Collier HOJ, Villarreal JE (eds): *Agonist and Antagonist Actions of Narcotic Analgesic Drugs.* Baltimore, University Park Press, 1973, pp 30-44.

36. Seevers MH: Morphine and ethanol physical dependence: A critique of a hypothesis. *Science* 170:1113-1114, 1970.

37. Way EL: Basic mechanisms in narcotic tolerance and physical dependence, in Kissin B, Lowinson JG, Millman RB (eds): Recent Developments in Chemotherapy on Narcotic Addiction. *NY Acad Sci* 311:61-68, 1978.

38. Mendelson JH, Mello NK: Basic mechanisms underlying physical dependence upon alcohol, in Kissin B, Lowinson JH, Millman RB (eds): Recent Developments in Chemotherapy on Narcotic Addiction. *Ann NY Acad Sci* 281:311-320, 1976.

39. DuPont RL: Polydrug abuse and the maturing national drug abuse data base. *Ann NY Acad Sci* 273:624-628, 1976.

40. Freedman L: Methadone and alcohol, in Seixas FA, Eggleston S (eds): Work in Progress on Alcoholism. *Ann NY Acad Sci* 273:624-628, 1976.

41. Stimmel B: Drug and alcohol treatment, in DuPont R, Goldstein A, O'Donnell J. (eds): *Handbook on drug abuse.* NIDA Publication, 1979, pp 175-180.

42. Ho AKS, Chen RCA, Kreek MJ: Morphine withdrawal in rat: Assessment by quantitation of diarrhea and modification by ethanol. *J Pharmacol* 18:9-17, 1979a.

43. Kosterlitz HW, Lord JAH, Watt AJ: Morphine receptor in the myenteric plexus of the guinea-pig ileum, in Kosterlitz HW, Collier HOJ, Villarreal JE (eds): *Agonist and Antagonist Actions of Narcotic Analgesic Drugs*, 1973. pp 45-61.

44. Pert CB, Snyder SH: Properties of opiate-receptor binding in rat brain. *Proc Nat Acad Sci* 70:2243-2247, 1973.

45. Clement JG: Investigations into the mechanism of morphine and ethanol inhibition in the guinea pig ileum longitudinal muscle strip. *Can J Physiol and Pharmacol* 58:265-270, 1980.

46. Paton WDM: Transmural and field stimulation of nerve smooth muscle preparations, in Daniel EE, Paton DM (eds): *Methods in Pharmacology, Vol. 3. Smooth muscle*. New York, Plenum Press, 1975, pp 313-320.

47. Blum K, Eubanks JD, Wallace JE, Schwerter HA: Morphine suppression of ethanol withdrawal in mice. *Experientia* 32:79-82, 1976.

48. Hemmingsen R, Sorensen SC: Absence of an effect of naloxone on ethanol intoxication and withdrawal reactions. *Acta Pharmacol Toxicol* 46:62-65, 1980.

49. Blum K, Wallace JE, Futterman SL: Naloxone induced inhibition of ethanol dependence in mice. *Nature* 49:265-267, 1976.

50. HO AKS, Chen RCA, Morrison MJ: Interactions of narcotics, narcotic antagonists, and ethanol during acute, chronic states, in Vescell ES, Braude MC (eds): Interactions of Drugs of Abuse. *NY Acad Sci* 281:297-310, 1976.

51. Ho AKS, Chen RCA, Morrison MJ: Opiate-ethanol interaction studies, in Blum K (ed): *Alcohol and Opiates: Neurochemical and Behavioral Mechanisms*. New York, Academic Press, 1977, pp. 189-202.

52. Khanna JM, Lê AD, Kalant H, LeBlanc AE: Cross-tolerance between ethanol and morphine with respect to their hypothermic effects. *Europ J Pharmac* 59:149-49, 1979.

53. Mayer JM, Khanna JM, Kalant H, Spero L: Cross-tolerance between ethanol and morphine in the guinea-pig ileum longitudinal-muscle/myenteric-plexus preparation. *Europ J Pharmac* 63:223-227, 1980.

54. Ho AKS: Interaction of alcohol and narcotics, in Messiha F, Tyner G (eds): *Alcoholism: A perspective*. New York, JDP Publications, 1980a, pp 309-327.

55. Nichols JR, Hsiao S: Addiction liability of albino rats: Breeding for quantitative differences in morphine drinking. *Science* 157:561-563, 1967.

56. Shuster CR, Thompson T: Self-administration of and behavioral dependence on drugs. *Ann Rev Pharmac* 9:483-502, 1969.

57. Killam KF Jr, Brocco MJ, Robinson CA: Evaluation of narcotic and narcotic antagonist interactions in primates. *Ann NY Acad Sci* 281:331-335, 1976.

58. Altshuler HL, Phillips PE, Feinhandler DA: Alteration of ethanol self-administration by naltrexone. *Life Sciences* 26:679-688, 1980.

59. Sinclair JD, Adkins J, Walker S: Morphine-induced suppresssion of voluntary alcohol drinking in rats. *Nature* 246:425-427, 1973.

60. Ho AKS, Rossi N: Suppression of alcohol consumption by met-enkephalin in rats. *J Pharmac and Pharmacol*, to be published.

61. Venho IL, Ernola R, Venho EV, Vartiarnen O: Sensitization to morphine by experimentally induced alcoholism in white mice. *Ann Med Exp Biol Finn* 33:249-252, 1955.

62. Ho AKS, Chen RCA, Ho CC: Interaction toxicity between ethanol and narcotics in mice with reference to alpha-l-acetylmethadol (LAAM). *Pharmac Biochem and Behav* 9:195-200, 1978a.

63. Howd RA, Pryor GT: Effect of chronic morphine on the response to and disposition of other drugs. *Pharmac Biochem and Behav* 12:577-586, 1980.

64. Sorenson SC, Mattison K: Naloxone as an antagonist in severe alcohol intoxication. *Lancet* 112:688-689, 1978.

65. Ho AKS, Ho CC: Toxic interactions of ethanol with other central depressants: Antagonism by naloxone to narcosis and lethality. *Pharmac Biochem and Behav* 11:111-114, 1979.

66. Dingledine R, Iversen LC, Breuker E: Naloxone as GABA antagonist: Evidence from iontophoretic, receptor binding and convulsant studies. *Europ J Pharmac* 47:19-27, 1978.

67. Freund G: Benzodiazepine receptor loss in brains of mice after chronic alcohol consumption. *Life Sciences* 27:987-992, 1980.

68. Finck AD, Ngai SH, Berkowitz BA: Antagonism of general anesthesia by naloxone in the rat. *Anesthesia* 46:241-245, 1977.

69. Moss LM: Naloxone reversal of non-narcotic induced apnea. *J Am Col Emer Phys* 1:46-48, 1973.

70. Bell EF: The use of naloxone in the treatment of diazepam poisioning. *J Pediat* 87:803-804, 1975.

71. Nichols JR: Alcoholism and opiate addiction: Theory and evidence for a genetic link between the two, in Forsander O, Eriksson K (eds): Biological Aspects of Alcohol Consumption. *Finn Found of Alc Stud Helsinki* 1972, pp 131-134.

72. Ellis FW: Effects of ethanol on plasma corticosterone levels. *Journal of Pharmacology and Experimental Therapeutics* 153:121-127, 1966.

73. Jenkins JS, Connolly J: Adenocortical response to ethanol in man. *J Br Med J* 2:804-805, 1968.

74. Noble, EP, Kakihana R, Butte JC: Corticosterone metabolism in alcohol-adapted mice, in Roach MK, McIsaac WM, Creaven PJ, (eds): *Biological Aspects of Alcohol*. Dallas, University of Texas Press, 1971, pp 389-417.

75. Crossland J, Ratcliffe F: Some effects of chronic alcohol and administration in the rat. *British Journal of Pharmacology and Chemotherapy* 32:413-414, 1968.

76. Kakihana R, Moore JA: Circadian rhythm of corticosterone in mice the effect of chronic consumption of alcohol. *Psychopharmacology* 46:301-305, 1975.

77. Sze PY, Yanai J, Ginsburg BE: Adrenal glucocorticoids as a required factor in the development of ethanol induced withdrawal seizures in mice. *Brain Research* 80:155-159, 1974.

78. Wood WG: Facilitation by dexamethasone of tolerance to ethanol in the rat. *Psychopharmacology* 52:67-72, 1977.

79. Feajria A: Alcohol induced pseudo-Cushings' Syndrome. *Lancet* 1:1050-1051, 1977.

80. Paton A: Alcohol-induced Cushings' Syndrome. *B Med J* ii:1504, 1976.

81. Rees LN, Besser GM, Jeffcoate WJ, Goldie DJ, Marks V: Alcohol induced pseudo-Cushings' Syndrome. *Lancet* 1:726-728, 1977.

82. Smols A, Kloppenburg P, Njo KT, Knohen JM, Ruland CM: Alcohol induced Cushings' Syndrome. *British Med Journal* ii:1298, 1976.

83. Smols AG, Kloppenburg P: Alcohol induced pseudo Cushings' Syndrome. *Lancet* 1:1369, 1977.

84. Sze PY: The permissive effect of glucocorticoids in the induction of liver alcohol dehydrogenase by ethanol. *Biochemical Medicine* 14:156-161, 1975.

85. Ayromlodi J, Essman WB: Fetal adreno stereodogenisis: Drug effects in sheep. *J Reprod Med* 24:23-25, 1980.

86. Merry J, Marks V: Plasma hydrocortisone response to ethanol in chronic alcoholics. *Lancet*1:921-923, 1969.

87. Bellet A, Roman L, DeCastro O, Henerva M: Effect of acute ethanol intake on plasma 11-hydroxycorticosteroids. *Metabolism* 19:664-667, 1970.

88. Bellet S, Yoshimine N, DeCastro O, Roman L, Parmar SS, Sandberg H: Effects of alcohol ingestion on growth hormone levels: Their relation to 11-hydroxycorticoid levels and serum FFA. *Metabolism* 20:762-769, 1971.

89. Margraf HW, Moyer CA, Ashford LE, Lavelle LW: Adrenocortical function in alcoholics. *Journal of Surgical Research* 7:55-62, 1967.

90. Mendelson JH, Stein S: Serum cortisol levels in alcoholic and nonalcoholic subjects during experimentally-induced ethanol intoxicaton. *Psychosomatic Medicine* 28:616-626, 1966.

91. Mendelson JH, Ogata M, Mello NK: Adrenal function and alcoholism. 1. Serum cortisol. *Psychosomatic Medicine* 33:145-157, 1971.
92. Merry J, Marks V: The effect of alcohol barbiturates and diazepam on hypothalamic-pituitary-adrenal function in chronic alcoholics. *Lancet* ii:990-992, 1972.
93. Ho AKS, Allen JP: Alcohol-opiate interactions on β-endorphin release in rats. *Experientia*, to be published.
94. Allen J, Kepic T, Ho AK, Ho CC, Vaughn M, Falvo R: Opiate regulation of gonadotrophin & prolactin. *Endo Sci* 6/80.
95. Ho, AK, Allen JP, Kepic TK, Ho CC: Opiate Regulation of β-endorphin and ACTH secretion. *Fed Proceed* 39:300, 1980.
96. Adlercreutz H: Hepatic metabolism of estrogens in health and disease. *New England Journal of Medicine* 290:1081-1083, 1974.
97. van Thiel DH, Lester R: Alcoholism: Its effect on hypothalamic pituitary gonadal function. *Gastroenterology* 71:318-327, 1976.
98. Green, JRB: Mechanism of hypogonadism in cirrhotic males. *Gut* 18:843-853, 1977.
99. Chaudhury R, Matthews M: Effects of alcohol on the fertility of female rabbits. *Journal of Endocrinology* 34:275-276, 1966.
100. Kieffer JD, Ketchell MM: Blockade of ovulation in the rat by ethanol. *Acta Endocrinologica* 65:117-124, 1970.
101. Cicero TJ, Badger TM: Effects of alcohol on the hypothalamic pituitary-gonadal axis in the male rat. *J Pharmac Exp Ther* 201:427-433, 1977.
102. Anderson R, Willis BR, Oswald C, Reddy JM, Beyler SA, Zaneveld LJD: Hormonal imbalance and alterations in testicular morphology induced by chronic ingestion of ethanol. *Biochem Pharm* 29:1409-1419, 1980.
103. Van Thiel DH, Gavalier JS, Lester R, Goodman D: Alcohol induced testicular atrophy. An experiment model for hypogonadism occurring in chronic alcoholic men. *Gastroenterology* 69:326-332, 1975.
104. Klassen RW, Pirsand TVN: Influence of alcohol on the reproductive system of the male rat. *Int J Fert* 23:176, 1978.
105. Mendelson JH, Mello NK, Ellingboe: Affects of acute alcohol intake on pituitary-gonadal hormones in normal human males. *J Pharm Exp Ther* 202:676-682, 1977.
106. Ylikahri R, Huttenen M, Harkonen M, Adlercreutz H: Hangover and testosterone. *British Medical Journal* ii:445, 1974.
107. Gorahan GG, Altman K, Southren AL, Rubin E, Lieber CS: Effect of alcohol administration on sex hormone metabolism in normal men. *N Engl J of Med* 295:793-797, 1976.
108. Wright JW, Jerry J, Fry D, Marks V: Pituitary function in chronic alcoholism, in Gross MM (ed): *Alcohol Intoxication and Withdrawal. Advances in Experimental Medicine and Biology.* New York, Plenum Press, 1976, pp 253-255.
109. Ylikahri RH, Huttenen MO, Harkonen M: Effect of alcohol on anterior pituitary secretion of trophic hormones. *Lancet* i:1353, 1976.
110. Loosen PT, Prange AJ: Alcohol and anterior pituitary secretion. *Lancet* 2:985, 1977.
111. Toro G, Koloday RC, Jacobs LS, Masters WH, Daughaday WH: *Clinical Research* 21:505, 1973.
112. Andreani D, Tamburrano G, Javicoli M: Alcohol hypoglycaemia: Hormonal changes, in Adreani D, Lefebvre P, Marks V (eds): *Hypoglycaemai: Proceedings of the European Symposium, Rome 1974. Hormone and Metabolic Research Supplement Series.* Stuttgart, Gerog Thieme, 1976, pp 99-105.
113. Arky R, Freinkel N: The response of plasma growth hormone in insulin and ethanol induced hypoglycaemia in two patients with isolated adrenocorticotrophic defect. *Metabolism* 13:547-550, 1964.
114. Bagdade JD, Gale CC, Porte D: *Hormone-fuel interrelationships during alcohol hypoglycaemia in man.* Proceedings of the Society for Experimental Biology and Medicine 141:540-542, 1972.
115. Blackard WG, Hull EW, Lopez SA: Effects of lipids on growth hormone secretion. *Journal of Clinical Investigation* 50:1439-1443, 1976.
116. Quabbe HJ, Bratzke HJ, Siegers U, Elban K: Studies on the relationship between plasma free fatty acids and growth hormone secretion in man. *Journal of Clinical Investigation* 51:2388-2398, 1972.
117. Priem HA, Shanley BC, Malan C: The effect of alcohol administration on plasma growth hormone response to insulin-induced hypoglycaemai in man. *Metabolism* 25:397-403, 1976.
118. Wright J: Endocrine effects of alcohol clinics. *Endocrin and Metab* 7:351-367, 1978.
119. Chalmers RJ, Bennie EH, Johnson RH, Kinnell HG: The growth hormone response to insulin induced hypoglycaemia in alcoholics. *Psychological Medicine* 7:607-611, 1977.
120. Zarrow MX, Rosenberg B: Alcoholic drive in rats treated with propylthiouracil. *American Journal of Physiology* 172:141-146, 1953.
121. Hillborn ME: Thyroid state and voluntary alcohol consumption of albino rats. *Acta Pharmacologica et Toxicologica* 29:95-105, 1971.
122. Richter CP: Loss of appetite for alcohol and alcoholic beverages in rats by treatment with thyroid preparations. *Endocrinology* 59:472-478, 1956.
123. Goldberg: The occurrence and treatment of hypothyroidism among alcoholics. *Journal of Clinical Endocrinology* 20:609-621, 1960.
124. Goldberg M: Thyroid function in chronic alcoholism. *Lancet* ii:746-749, 1962.
125. Cushman, P, Jr, Kreek MJ: Some endocrinologic observations in narcotic addicts, in Zimmerman F, George R (eds): *Narcotics and the Hypothalamus.* New York, Raven Press, 1974, 161-172.
126. Meites J, Bruni JF, VanVugt DA, Smith AF: Relation of endogenous opioid peptrates - Morphine to Neurocuclocrine Functions. *Life Sciences* 24:1325-36, 1979.
127. Labrie F, Dupont A, Borden N, Ferland L, Pelletier G, Giguire V, Lepive J: Physiological role of endorphins in neuroendocrinology. *Endocrinology*, 1980, pp 678-681.
128. Morley JE, Yamada T, Walsh JH, Lamers CB, Wong H, Shulkes A, Damassa DA, Gordon J, Carlson HE, Hershman JM: *Life Sci* 26:2239-2244, 1980.
129. Stimmel G, Cohen M, Hanbury R: Alcoholism and polydrug abuse in persons on methadone maintenance, in Kissin B, Lowinson JH, Millman RB (eds): Recent Developments in Chemotherapy on Narcotic Addiction. *Ann NY Acad Sci* 311:99-110, 1978.
130. Brown B, Kozel NJ, Meyers M, DuPont RL: Use of alcohol by addict and nonaddict populations. *Am J Psychiatry* 130:599-601, 1973.
131. Barr HL, Cohen A, Hannigan P: *Problem drinking by drug addicts and its implications.* Proceedings of National Council on Alcoholism, 1976.
132. Stimmel B, Vernace S, Tobias H: Hepatic dysfunction in heroin addicts: Alcohol vs. viral etiology, abstracted. *Gastroenterology* 60:754, 1971.
133. Stimmel B, Vernace S, Tobias H: Hepatic dysfunction in heroin addicts: The role of alcohol. *JAMA* 222:811-12, 1972.
134. Kreek MJ: Medical complications in methadone patients, in Kissin B, Lowinson JH, Millman RB (eds): Recent Developments in Chemotherapy on Narcotic Addiction. *Ann NY Acad Sci* 311:111-132, 1978.

NEURO-ENDOCRINE EFFECTS OF OPIOIDS

Paul Cushman, Jr., MD

ABSTRACT. A catalogue of human endocrine effects of opioid agonists are reported. These effects are usually attenuated by opioid antagonists. Acute agonists may increase prolactin and decrease LH and testosterone. They may have opposite effects on GH, FSH, TSH. Increased catecholamines, and glucagon may account for opioid-induced hyperglycemia. Opioid antagonists alone may increase LH and less consistenly ACTH/cortisol and decrease prolactin. Opioid-tolerant persons usually show at least partial tolerance to these changes in LH, prolactin, and testosterone. The increase in thyroxine and thyroid binding globulin observed in heroin addicts may relate to relative hypoandrogenicity or liver disease rather than to hyperthyroidism. Disturbed sexual appetite and performance observed in men and women may relate to hormonal changes, or other facets of opiate use or may be symptoms of underlying psychological disorders.

Introduction

Many opiate effects have been known for centuries. However, the recent discovery of the opiate receptor[1-3] and the endogenous opiate-like peptides (EOP), enkephalins and endorphins,[4] has stimulated renewed interest.[5-7] The evidence for possible endocrine roles for both exogenous opioids and EOP will be reviewed. This study reports on human data where available; animal data are included where human data are insufficient.

Opioid actions are believed to commence with binding to a stereospecific receptor, a complex structure which includes both a protein fraction and a lipid component, rich in cerebroside sulfate.[8,9] Numerous data attest to close relationships between receptor binding affinities and opioid effects.[10,11] Further, displacement of agonists from opiate receptors by antagonists correlates with the attenuation, reversal, or blockade of agonists actions. The anatomical localization of these opiate receptors is widespread.[12,13] Besides the many loci in the central nervous system,[14] spinal cord, and gut myenteric plexus that correspond to well-known opioid actions in those loci, receptors have also been detected in tissues of endocrine importance such as adrenal, pancreas, and the hypothalamus.[11-13]

Dr. Cushman is Associate Professor of Pharmacology, Medicine, and Psychiatry, The Medical College of Wisconsin, 8701 Watertown Plank Road, Milwaukee, WI 53226. He is also affiliated with De Paul Rehabilitation Hospital, Milwaukee. This work was supported in part by Grant T01 DA 07181 from the National Institutes of Health.

Advances in Alcohol & Substance Abuse, Vol. 1(1), Fall 1981

The EOP are distributed in centers rich in opiate receptors. The endorphins appear to be a peptide system separate from the pentapeptide enkephalins;[15,16] each has a different distribution. Neural cells seem to contain either endorphins or enkephalins but not both.[15] High concentrations of the endorphins are found in the hypothalamus, pituitary, pre-optic nuclei, thalamus, peripheral blood, and cerebrospinal fluid.[17,18] The arcuate-median eminence region of the hypothalamus has the highest concentration of endorphins in the human brain.[19] The enkephalins are present particularly in the globus pallidus, hypothalamus, amygdala, pre-optic nuclei, spinal cord, adrenal, pancreas, and myenteric plexus of the gut.[20-22] Therefore, both the EOP and opiate receptors are located in many areas which are known to have endocrine activity.

Since the endocrine system involves many component pieces, often interrelated and interlocking, with multiple influences which can affect secretion, degradation, excretion rates, it can be difficult to define rigorously an opioid effect on an isolated hormone. Nevertheless, this review will focus on measurements of hormone concentrations in blood after acute or chronic opioid administration. Opioids can also affect the dynamics of hormone secretion as well as the resting blood hormone levels; therefore, included are examinations of acute or chronic opioids on stimulatory (or inhibitory) influences on blood hormone levels.

It is important to examine hormones after both acute and chronic opioid use. Many important adaptations (tolerance) occur with sustained opioid exposure, requiring larger opioid doses to produce a standard effect. One adaptation, often termed metabolic tolerance, is located primarily at the hepatic metabolic degradation level.[23] This produces faster rates of opioid disposal. Another adaptation of very great clinical importance in analgesia and sedation lies in some ill-understood changes in opioid target tissue, usually termed cellular tolerance.[10,24,25] Cellular tolerance mainly accounts for the large opioid doses that chronic opiate-dependent subjects not infrequently consume—doses which would be lethal in the nontolerant subject.

Studies of the effects of opioid antagonists on hormones have recently aroused extensive interest. First, the antagonist reversal of an opioid action is necessary to establish that the action was caused by an opioid agonist mechanism. Second, possible effects of opioid antagonists, administered without concomitant agonists, have led to inferences about possible roles of opioids in hormonal physiology. If opioid antagonists per se exert consistent effects on a serum hormone level, then these data support the inference that an EOP action regulating that hormone concentration, otherwise concealed, might exist.

One clinically useful antagonist, naltrexone (NTX), has the advantages of long duration of action and oral efficacy.[26] This drug permits the study of chronic opiate antagonism. The most widely studied antagonist is the short-acting, parenteral drug, naloxone (NAL). NAL is generally viewed as a pure antagonist at conventional doses[27,28] but at high doses may have other effects. Some of these effects may be partially opiate-like, notably drowsiness.[27] Other effects include a NAL reversal of the action of N_2O,[29] phenoxybenzamine,[30] barbiturates,[31] gamma-amino butyrate (GABA),[32] and other nonopioid drugs in mice.[33,34] The precise mechanisms of these NAL effects have not been defined; they may result from opiate receptor antagonism or some other effect. Therefore, problems arise in the interpretation of some NAL data, especially when high doses were used. The conventional human dose (0.4 mg/kg) will readily reverse the agonist effects of exogenous opioids, even in the deeply comatose narcotic overdosed patient.[28] Much larger doses (even 10 mg/kg) may be required for demonstration of hormonal effects. It appears likely that the small NAL doses would readily antagonize the actions of exogenous opioids which would have relatively low concentrations both in plasma and at the opiate receptor. Much larger doses of naloxone, perhaps of pharmacological magnitude, may be required to inhibit EOP. Enkephalins are more locally secreted, locally active, and likely to achieve much higher local concentrations in the vicinity of the opiate receptor that exogenous opioids. Until further clarifications of NAL's pharmacological effects, it is perhaps premature to ascribe a change in hormone levels after high dose NAL treatment solely to a change in EOP-receptor relationship. The full physiological significances of both low and high dose NAL effects remain to be established.

An important consideration in extrapolation of rodent data to man lies in dose. Most rat studies have used 2-20 mg/kg of morphine, a dose which would be severely depressing, if not lethal, in man. It should be stressed that these large doses of morphine and other agonists are required for objective opiate agonist effects as analgesia and sedation. The 2-20 mg/kg NAL doses in rats are in the same range as the opiate agonists. Human doses are 10 mg morphine (0.14 mg/kg in a 70 kg person) or 0.4 mg (0.003 mg in a 70 kg person) for NAL. Human doses administered to rats are inactive. Therefore, cross species extrapolation to man of data using high doses in animals should be made cautiously.

There are additional variables arising from the different rates at which exogenous opioids cross the blood brain barrier after intravenous (IV) administration.[35] For example, the more lipid-soluble opioids, such as diacetylmorphine (heroin), cross at much faster rates than deacetylated analogues such as morphine.[36] Given intravenously, endogenous opioids as β-endorphin, seemed to gain selective access to the central nervous system.[37,38] They easily reached the hypothalamus and produced impressive increases in serum prolactin (PRL). But the same dose had unimpressive analgesic actions,[39] suggesting that they did not achieve sufficient concentrations at the opiate receptors involved in analgesia. On the other hand, when delivered to the receptors by appropriate intracranial routes, endorphins and enkephalins are very potent analgesic drugs.[4,5]

Pituitary Polypeptides

The effects of opioids on the unstimulated blood levels of the major pituitary peptides are listed in Table I.

ACTH

It might be expected that the opioids would have some effects in the hypothalamic-pituitary-adrenal (HPA) axis for several reasons. Both ACTH and β-endorphin are part of a larger pituitary peptide[11,40]; they are secreted together as plasma levels of ACTH, β-endorphin, and β-lipotropin rise and

TABLE I

HORMONAL EFFECTS OF ACUTE OPIOIDS IN NORMAL MAN

Category of Hormone	Agonist Alone	Antagonist Alone	Both Agonist Antagonist
Pituitary Peptides			
ACTH	-	++ (43) NC (46)	-
FSH	-	+ (males) NC (females)	-
GH	NC (52-3) +(55)	NC (45, 102-3)	-
LH	++ (75-7)	+ (45)	NC (45)
Prolactin	++ (106-113)	NC (129-30)	NC (131)
TSH	NC (75)	NC (45)	-
Steroids			
Cortisol	+ (56), NC(52-55)	++ (43-5) NC (48)	-
Testosterone	+ (49, 164-6)	NC (166)	-

NC=no change
+=increase
+=decrease

numbers in parentheses denote references

fall in parallel.[11,41] There is also evidence that glucocorticoids may play a role to regulate β-endorphin production.[42]

Yet despite extensive study of ACTH physiology in response to opioid use, simple conclusions cannot be presently reached in man. The preponderance of the human data suggests that no consistent or major effects on ACTH follow either acute or chronic opioid administration, even in opioid-tolerant subjects.

Changes in ACTH secretion are ofen inferred from changes in plasma cortisol in man and corticosterone in rodents. Support for the validity of these inferences has been repeatedly documented since normal responsiveness to exogenous ACTH has been repeatedly observed in both man and rat, regardless of the presence of tolerance.[43-45]

ACTH levels have been infrequently quantitated in human plasma in relation to opioids. The most relevant study[46] described a sharp rise in ACTH levels in 24 subjects after a pharmacologic (10-20 mg) IV NAL bolus compared to their responses after IV saline. Their plasma cortisol levels also rose[46] after IV NAL. Increased cortisol after large doses of IV NAL were independently confirmed by Morley et al.[47,48] Some further data supportive of 10 mg of NAL affecting ACTH/cortisol levels were observed in the 22 subjects undergoing gastroscopy. Cortisol levels rose higher in the IV NAL-treated subjects than those given saline control injections.[48] On the other hand, no changes in plasma cortisol were seen 30 minutes after 0.4 mg IV NAL, nor did NAL alter the cortisol responses to insulin-induced hypoglycemia.[49] Therefore, under some circumstances high doses of IV NAL appear to affect ACTH/cortisol concentrations in plasma.

On the other hand, more physiological doses of IV NAL produced no change in plasma cortisol 30 minutes after a 0.4 mg bolus.[50] Even large doses of IV NAL may not significantly change plasma ACTH, as reported by Lehmann et al,[51] in a small group of normals whose resting plasma "ACTH" was very high compared to most other laboratories. Therefore, under some circumstances high doses of IV NAL appear to increase ACTH/cortisol levels in plasma, but low doses appear not to have such an effect. In the only reported study[25] of ACTH in heroin addicts, Ho et al[47] observed somewhat lower levels than 26 controls in studies that quantitated ACTH at only one moment in time.

Opioids do not seem to exert a consistent acute influence on human plasma cortisol concentrations. No major effect on serum cortisol was observed by Catlin et al[52] after IV infusions of 10-15 mg β-endorphin, a dose which was sufficient to raise serum PRL. Also, no change in normal plasma cortisol[53] or plasma hydroxycorticosteroid levels[54] was observed after parenteral morphine. Mendelson et al[55] also found plasma cortisol to be unaffected by heroin or methadone. These data were obtained after standard analgesic doses. Possibly, higher doses of opioids may have produced different results.

On the contrary, Gold et al[56] found a standard analgesic dose (5 mg) of IV methadone reduced plasma immuno reactive "cortisol" in a small series of subjects from 102 ng/ml to 27 ng/ml. Since the usual range of plasma cortisol levels are normally about 500-2500 ng/ml, the significance of this observation is unclear. Also, lower plasma cortisol plasma levels were observed three to five hours after morphine injections (16 mg) in a few barbiturate-treated normals.[57] Other studies of opioid effects on the stress-stimulated ACTH/cortisol axis also produced conflicting results.[58,59] Tolis et al[53] observed normal cortisol increases during surgery despite 10 mg of IV morphine while Reier et al[60] found blunted cortisol increases after a similar dose of morphine during surgery in his patients. McDonald et al[57] found vasopressin to be less effective in increasing cortisol after 16 mg of IV morphine than after saline. These discrepancies remain to be resolved.

Animal Studies

In the animal, the large number of studies of opioids and corticosterone have been recently reviewed.[49,50,61] Much of the data in rats on the acute effects of opioids on corticosterone (B) are conflicting. Discrepancies may be related to insufficient attention to such extraneous influences on B-concentrations as stress, anesthesia, handling, etc. Yet, most acute studies in the rat report sizeable increases in plasma B concentrations after morphine or other opioids.[50,51,61-63] This effect is blocked by naloxone, apomorphine, barbiturate anesthesia,[49] and dexamethasone.[64] The localization of the opioid effects on plasma B seemed to be at the hypothalamic level. Meites et al[50] reported median eminence lesions in rats blocked the expected opioid increase in plasma B. Tolerance to the apparent stimulations of the pituitary-adrenal axis by opioids may arise with continuing opioid exposure according to several observers.[49,62] It should be recalled that the rat may not be the optimal laboratory animal for studying human pharmacological problems of HPA or hypothalamic-GH secretion. The rat tends to secrete ACTH and growth hormone (GH) in an inverse relationship to each other while man usually secretes both GH and ACTH concomitantly.[65] Thus, there may be important differences in the human and rodent hypothalamic-pituitary mechanisms regulating the HPA axis and GH.

Naloxone also appeared to exert an effect on the HPA axis in rats. Large doses of IV NAL (10-20 mg/kg) given to opiate-naive animal produced a dose-related increase in their plasma B. This effect was viewed either to have been a direct NAL effect on the opioid receptor or possibly as a NAL effect to interfere with an EOP-receptor interaction.[66] While these NAL data in rats imply an EOP influence on HPA axis, nevertheless it is puzzling that both agonists and antagonists produced changes in rat B in the same direction.[67] Thus, there may be separate or multiple systems by which opioids, agonists or antagonists, may affect HPA in rats. High dose NAL may produce its effects in several ways. One is a direct agonist action on a postulated opiate receptor to increase ACTH/cortisol secretion. These purported receptors could be located in a neuroendocrine structure, possibly in the median eminence of the hypothalamus, or they could be elsewhere. But ultimately, the consequences of receptor activity would modulate ACTH/cortisol secretion. Another possibility could be a NAL blockade of an EOP tonic, inhibitory influence on ACTH/cortisol. In this view, NAL could interfere presynaptically with EOP regulaton of CRF release. Changes in CRF would initially produce parallel increases in β-endorphins. Later the β-endorphin would inhibit CRF in a negative feedback loop. As support for this hypothesis, Guillemin et al noted an equimolar increase in β-endorphin and ACTH secretion after a standard stress in the rat.[41] In another possibility, NAL could produce a nonspecific "stress" reaction, probably via its blockade of EOP actions in nonendocrine tissues.

Opioid-Tolerant Subjects

Hormones in the opioid-tolerant person usually were evaluated in methadone-maintained subjects because of greater accessibility and better knowledge about their health and drug use (opioid and other). Studies of HPA axis usually,[68-70] but not always,[47] disclosed normal plasma cortisol levels. In one study of a controlled cycle of morphine addiction,[54] plasma 17 OH cortisosteroids tended to be lower during morphine and to rise sharply with exogenous ACTH or withdrawal. The single study of cortisol production rates reported normal values in methadone-maintained persons.[71] Manipulations of HPA axis with metyrapone or insulin hypoglycemia and studies of circadian periodicity of cortisol in the opioid-tolerant subject usually yielded normal results or no consistent changes.[72,73] IV morphine (30 mg/kg) or β-endorphin increased serum MSH levels in the rat, and this change was blocked by NTX.[74] The physiological importance and relevance for man of this observation are unclear. Table II lists stimulated resting-plasma hormone concentrations in opioid-tolerant persons.

In conclusion, no consistent effects of either acute or chronic opioid use were evident on resting or stimulated ACTH/cortisol in man. Small doses of NAL seem without effect on plasma ACTH/cortisol in man. On the other hand, large doses of NAL raised plasma ACTH and/or cortisol, which may have thereby revealed a tonic inhibitory influence of EOP on ACTH/cortisol or some other NAL effect on ACTH/cortisol. The available animal data were confusing and contradictory.

TABLE II

HORMONES IN OPIOID TOLERANT HUMANS

Hormone	Resting	Stimulated	Stimulus Used
ACTH	↓ (47)	NR (68-70)	metyrapone, hypoglycemia
Aldosterone	N (47)	-	-
Cortisol	N (68-70)	NR (68, 69)	hypoglycemia
Estradiol	N (88)	-	-
FSH	N (98) ↓(84)	↓(84)	LRH
GH	N (53, 70)	NR (105)	arginine, hypoglycemia
Insulin	N (177)	↑(177)	glucose tolerance
LH	N (88-91) ↓(76)	NR (70) ↓(84)	LRH
Prolactin (males)	N (70-72)	↑ (70,72) NR(130)	Opioids, TRH
Testosterone	↓ (164-69) N(91)	-	-
TSH	N (140, 141)	NR (141)	TRH
T4	↑ (139-140) N (141)	- (141)	-

N=normal plasma levels
NR=normal plasma response
↑=increase
↓=decrease

numbers in parentheses donote references

Gonadotropins

Acutely heroin, morphine, and other opioids produced sharp decreases in blood plasma LH levels in human males.[75] This action, well documented by Cicero et al in the male rat,[78-80] started with a rapid drop in serum LH after large doses of opioids (20 mg/kg), followed shortly by a decrease in serum testosterone (T). Serum FSH levels fell only slightly. ED 50 studies of LH reduction by acute opioids in rats paralleled the analgesic potency of the agonist, and the effect was blocked by antagonists.[80] Manifest hypogonadism ensued, including atrophy of male secondary sex characteristics.[79] Blockade by NAL and tolerance to the LH depressing effects of opioid agonists usually occurred with continued opioids.[80] In man LH levels in hyperprolactinemic patients may be particularly susceptible to opioid-depressing effects.[81]

The locus of opioid action affecting LH secretion appeared to be at the hypothalamic level as reflected in studies of surgically formed hypothalamic islands.[39] As further support for this conclusion, Meites et al[50] and Cicero et al[82] showed rat pituitary responses to LRH both in vitro and in vivo preparations to be unaffected by opioids. Rotsztejn et al[83] had some direct in vitro evidence of dopamine-induced LRHR release being blocked by met-enkephalin. On the other hand, Brambilla et al[84] found poor human serum LH/FSH responses to injected LRH in a group of male Italian street opiate addicts. While this suggests that these addicts may have had an opioid-induced LH unresponsiveness, possibly at the pituitary level, their LH hyporesponsiveness may have been primary at the hypothalamus, producing a secondary pituitary disturbance. Thus, the preponderance of data suggests that opioids inhibit LRH release from the hypothalamic median eminence, although direct proof is lacking.[85]

Sex hormones also are known to affect LRH release; the opioids may have an effect on some sex steroid hormone transformation in the hypothalamus and thereby produce changes in LRH release. Rat hypothalami did have decreased aromatization of $\Delta 4$ androstenedione to estrone in the presence of morphine,[86] and changed mitochondrial estradiol—two hydroxylase activities in both acute and chronic opioid treatment.

Acute NAL (10 mg IV bolus) produced a modest rise in serum LH,[45] and oral NTX usually produced impressive acute increases in serum LH levels of both abstinent, former opioid addicts, and normal males.[87] On the other hand, subjects taking NTX chronically had LH levels in the low normal range, suggesting that tolerance to the LH-stimulating effect of antagonists, if any, had occurred.

Therefore, it appears that both opiate agonists and antagonists exogenously administered can exert impressive and opposing acute influences on plasma LH in man. Possibly the antagonist studies may have disclosed a modulation role for EOP in the normal regulation of LH. The biological significances of such roles need further clarification. The major clinical significances of reduced LH levels after opioid use may be to contribute to the lower testosterone (T) blood levels, reduced libido, increased impotency, and other disturbances of sexual function often reported in human opioid users.

Although much less attention has been paid to possible opioid effects on FSH, the data that exist are inconclusive. In male rodents no consistent changes in serum FSH followed acute administration of opioid agonists.[50,79] Low serum levels FSH have been reported in some male heroin addicts.[88] Methadone-tolerant individuals may have slight transient decreases in serum FSH during a short cycle of addiction.[76] In one study, NAL (10 mg IV bolus) produced modest rises in serum FSH.[45]

Systematic study of either FSH or LH in females in relation to exogenous opioids has not yet been performed. NAL did increase the circulating levels of LH but not FSH in hypogonadal women.[81] In normal menstruating women, NAL was without effect on either LH or FSH in the follicular phase but produced pulses of LH one to three hours after the initiation of 1.6 mg NAL/hr infusions at midcycle and in the midluteal phase. The FSH responses to NAL were unchanged. In females during sexual maturation, LH responded to NAL differently from males,[90] suggesting a role for the EOP in sexual development. Therefore, EOP may modulate secretion of gonadotropins during menarche and the normal menstrual cyce. The clinical significance of this observation remain to be determined.

Opiate-Tolerant Subjects

There are abundant clinical findings in opioid-dependent persons consistent with abnormalities in pituitary gonadotropins. These abnormalities likely have multifactorial causes, which could include nutrition, stress, intercurrent illness, and consumption of opioid or nonopioid drugs. Many males had disturbed sexual functions and low plasma T. Many females had menstrual abnormalities and infertility. LH levels in many human opioid-tolerant male subjects were within normal limits,[88,92] although some were low. In one study, methadone-tolerant males had normal LH and T responses to IV LRH.[70] On the other hand, another study in 10 street heroin addicts, studied shortly after their last heroin dose, had low FSH and LH levels at the outset which rose sluggishly after LRH.[84] The discrepancy may relate to differences in tolerance or to details of patients' drug usage.

The menstrual abnormalities commonly seen in female opioid addicts could be opioid related. These changes are likely caused by the addiction process itself, since addicted women usually report normal menses before starting heroin.[92] Of those with normal menses before, amenorrhea or other menstrual abnormalities ensued during addiction in 70% to 90%.[92-94] Most women resumed normal menses within three months after detoxification.[94] Among opiate addicts entering methadone maintenance, the frequency of amenorrhea ranged from 1.5% to 55%.[95,96] Tolerance to these menstrual abnormalities probably arose in some methadone patients since clinical observations disclosed fewer patients reported menstrual abnormalities after months of methadone treatment than at the outset.[97] In a small, well-studied group of methadone-treated women with menstrual abnormalities, there were findings consistent with failure of cyclic ovulation and abnormal cyclic gonadotropin secretion.[98]

Precise data on fertility of narcotic-dependent women are lacking. There are clinical impressions that conception is much more likely to occur during narcotic-free intervals than while receiving narcotics.

Possible mechanisms responsible for the menstrual disturbances have been studied in rats. Morphine will inhibit rat ovulation.[50,99,100] Opiate agonists will also block the rat's FSH and LH surge leading to ovulation failure,[99] which is reversed by NAL or median eminence stimulation.[100,101]

In conclusion, unquestionably large doses of exogenous opioids influence gonadotropins. Opioid agonists decrease serum LH in males, and antagonists increase serum LH levels probably at the hypothalamic level. Neither produces dramatic effects on FSH in men. Opioid-tolerant male subjects tend to have normal LH, suggesting at least partial tolerance had occcurred. In females, opioid antagonists may produce increased LH during puberty and part of the menstrual cycle.

Growth Hormone

Relationships, if any, between opioids and GH are tenuous in man. Resting blood GH levels were unaffected by 10 mg IV morphine[53] or by IV β-endorphin (1-10 mg as an infusion).[52] On the other hand, DAMME, an analogue of enkephalin, given as 0.25 mg IV bolus, did produce an acute increase in serum GH, an effect which was attenuated with concomitant naloxone.[75]

NAL did not effect resting blood GH levels in man.[45,102,103] Although the dynamics of GH secretion have not been well studied in relation to opioids, NAL did not alter the GH responses to the stress of gastroscopy. Large doses of NAL did reduce the GH responses to arginine, but not significantly to L-DOPA[44,45] nor to apomorphine (a dopamine agonist). Nor did NAL alter the physiological influence on GH secretion in man and rats.[104]

In the opiate-tolerant subject, resting GH levels were normal.[53,70] Their responses to IV arginine or insulin hypoglycemia were normal or inconsistently low.[105]

Animal Studies

On the other hand, there are abundant data in the rat showing brisk increases in blood GH in response to administered opioids.[50,51,105-107] Dose of the EOP appears to be an important variable, since Dupont et al found 0.5 μg β-endorphin injected intraventricularly in rats raised PRL while it took 2 μg to raise the serum GH. Attenuated by simultaneous NAL, this GH stimulation seemed to persist for 12 days without evident tolerance in the rat.[108] NAL alone lowered blood GH in rats.[50] Thus, in the rats, there is GH secretion with agonists and decreased regulation with antagonists. These data suggest that opioids are factors in the regulation of GH secretion. It is not yet established whether the GH effects of opioids are at the pituitary or hypothalamus, although in vitro data suggest the latter.[109]

In conclusion, no consistent changes were seen in resting and stimulated Gh levels after acute or chronic opioids in man. The rat shows a GH increase with agonists and decreased Gh with antagonists, effects which may be hypothalamic in location.

Prolactin (PRL)

Both human[52,53,75,110] and animal[50,104,106,107,111-113] data point to a large and reproducible stimulatory effect of opioids on serum PRL. The full biological significance of this finding awaits further clarification of the physiological role for PRL in the nonlactating subject. Recent data in animals suggest a PRL effect on male testes, gonadotropins, and accessory sex organs.[114] Since hyperprolactinemia has been associated with decreased libido, impotence, menstrual abnormalities, and infertility,[110] further study of PRL in relation to these symptoms among opiate users is warranted.

The acute increase in PRL after opioids, which include IV β-endorphin,[115] can be attenuated by NAL,[109] and possibly may be deficient in depressed patients.[116] It is usually attributed to an opioid influence on PRL at the level of hypothalamic nuclei where monoamine and hypothalamic peptidergic pathways lie.[118] Presumably, the opioids affect the neurotransmitter dopamine.[117-123] Since dopamine inhibits pituitary PRL secretion, opiate-induced reduction in dopamine probably released the pituitary from dopamine's tonic inhibition, causing increased PRL secretion. This hypothesis is supported by data showing that the dopamine agonist, apomorphine, can block morphine stimulation of PRL release in rats.[124] Possible other opioid effects resulting in stimulating PRL secretion other than reduction in dopamine need further study.[110,114,125]

Until the mechanism by which PRL is secreted is more clearly defined, the hypothesis that the opioid-induced increases in PRL are solely due to a reduction in dopamine should be tentative. The site of this effect, however, does appear to be the hypothalamus.[126] Pituitary stalk section blocked the β-endorphin-induced release of PRL.[127] Direct instillation of opiate agonists into the basomedial hypothalamic area produced increases in PRL and GH with reductions in LH. Interruption of afferent input to the hypothalamus did not inhibit the opiate effect on PRL.[39] Although some claim an effect of opioids on isolated pituitary tissue releases PRL in vitro,[128] this was not confirmed in other laboratories using similar techniques.[129]

Some studies combining opioids with other stimuli affecting PRL secretion have been done in rats. No further increase in serum PRL followed acute administration of haloperidol (a dopamine receptor blocker) combined with 40 mg of morphine compared to rats given morphine alone.[133] Thus morphine alone may produce maximal stimulation for PRL release. PRL release in response to TRH, however, is submaximal as higher serum PRL levels were seen after 10 mg IV naloxone administered together with TRH.[45] Also, cholinergic[131] but not alphaadrenergic agonists can block opiate-induced PRL release.[124]

Administration of NAL does not affect PRL,[45,132-134] but can readily block the PRL stimulatory effects of exogenous opioids.[122] NAL did not block nonopioid stimulation of PRL secretion.[110]

Opioids appear to have different potencies in studies comparing PRL release to analgesia. A dose level of β-endorphin which produced 50% of maximal PRL release was minimally analgesic in rats.[131] Yet, the dose of an enkephalin analogue DAMME (FK 33-824) which produced a 50% maximal PRL level, showed significant analgesia.[135] Possible explanations for these differences may involve varying tissue and receptor heterogeneity.

In opioid-tolerant subjects, increased PRL usually, but not invariably, followed another opioid dose.[70,72,136] Whether partial tolerance to the PRL effects of opioids occurred is not settled. Methadone may augment PRL response to IV TRH[70] or attenuate it.[132]

In the animal the increase in PRL after acute opioid administration is such that the capability of augmenting PRL may become a biochemical screen for opiate agonist activity.[112] NAL alone decreases resting PRL levels in rats.[50] as well as attenuating the PRL release accompanying opioid agonists. In the primate, PRL fell from 21+3 to 3+0.8 ng/ml 45 minutes after NAL (0.25 mg/kg IV bolus) whereas both methadone and morphine raised PRL to 45-60 ng/ml range and haloperidol over 100 ng/ml.[113] Stress-induced PRL secretion was blocked by NAL.[138]

In conclusion, opioid agonists increase serum PRL in man and animals. NAL attenuates this effect: NAL alone usually decreases PRL in animals but has inconsistent effects in man. The PRL effect is probably located in the hypothalamus primarily involving dopamine. Whether PRL increases among opiate users contribute to their disturbances in reproductive physiology, however, is unclear.

Thyroid Stimulating Hormone (TSH)

In man, acute administration of opioids does not appear to exert a major direct effect either on TSH or thyroid hormones.[53,75] Serum TSH levels were normal in opioid-tolerant subjects,[70,139,140] and TSH rose normally[70,141] in most subjects.[142] Naloxone in man did not change resting or TRH-stimulated serum TSH.[45]

In the rat, high doses of opioids lower serum TSH acutely.[49,50] NAL attenuated the TSH effects of opiates but did not alter TSH levels if given alone.[50] Some chronic studies in rats are consistent with opiate-related inhibition of pituitary-thyroid function. Rat pituitary TSH contents and total thyroid weights went down.[49] The relevance of these animal data for man is unknown.

Hypothalamic Hormones - Vasopressin (AVP)

There is abundant evidence that opioids may exert a diuretic or an antidiuretic effect on man and animals. Thus opioids may affect vasopressin (AVP) directly or other factors involved in water balance. Until further detailed studies of both AVP and these other factors during acute and chronic opioid administration are completed, these apparent contradictions cannot be resolved. In the rat, Aziz et al[143] has found evidence for a biphasic AVP response to opioids. Lower doses stimulate AVP release and higher ones are inhibitory. If comparable data in humans emerge, they may help resolve the problem.

Opioids have been known for years to produce a diuresis.[144,145] In man, Lightman et al[146] found the expected antidiuresis and increased plasma AVP levels of normals subjected to head tilting to be attentuated by NAL. Possibly the EOP may have played a part in modulating AVP response to this volume stimulus. Studies on AVP release in humans given DAMME are conflicting. Following DAMME administration, there is an increase in free water clearance. In dehydrated and in saline-infused normals, either no change in AVP or a decrease in plasma AVP was noted.[147,148] The discrepancy may be related to dose, as infusions of 1 mg DAMME were effective while those of 0.4 mg were not.

Nutt and Jasinski reported that oxilorphan and butorphanol, both partial agonists and antagonists, had diuretic actions in man.[149] NAL alone was without effect. Miller reported that acute oxilorphan in well-hydrated and water-deprived man produced increased water clearance, plasma osmolality, but unchanged urinary AVP.[150] Previously Miller[151] had reported apparent suppression of antidiuretic activity in rats after oxilorphan and butorphanol, despite increases in plasma osmolality.

Greidanus et al[74] reported decreased vasopressin in the resting and stimulated rat after morphine (10 mg/kg subcutaneously) or 25 ng of an enkephalin analogue intracerebrally. While opioids may impact on several aspects of vasopressin physiology, there is some evidence for a direct action on vasopressin-secreting cells. Iversen et al[152] observed opioids to inhibit electrically stimulated vasopressin release from rat pituitary stalks. Rossier et al[155] placed lesions in the rat hypothalamic paraventricular and supraoptic nuclei, and the leucine enkephalin content fell sharply.[153] They believed that the enkephalins are involved in the control of antidiuretic hormone release from the magnocellular neurosecretory neurons in some way.

On the other hand, antidiuresis after opioids has been recognized for years.[154-157] This effect is usually attributed to a release of antidiuretic hormone, although an effect on renal water metabolism, or other effect, is possible. Bisset et al[158] found 10 mg doses of enkephalin increased rat urine vasopressin. Weitzman et al[154] reported β-endorphon increased rabbit vasopressin, yet, they did not find increased release of AVP from rat neural tissue in vitro upon endorphin exposure.

Oxytocin

Oxytocin release after suckling, its physiological stimulus, was inhibited by morphine and other opiate agonists in mice.[160] No comparable human data have been reported. There are no clinical reports of lactation difficulties in opiate-tolerant individuals.

Releasing Hormones

The study of hypothalamic-releasing hormones after acute and chronic opioids is still in its infancy. There is abundant circumstantial evidence suggesting that opioids are important influences on releasing hormones. As previously cited, LH levels fell after acute opioid administration and rose after acute administration of antagonists. These effects are attributed to alterations in LRH levels.[161] Similarly, the sharp rise in prolactin after acute opioids is likely to be primarily a change in hypothalamic PRL releasing or inhibiting hormones although a pituitary effect is possible.[162] Somatostatin concentrations in the rat brain also may be affected by morphine.[163,164]

Target Organ

Adrenal

The cortisol responses to acute and chronic opioids have already been discussed under ACTH. There is no evidence of any impairment of adrenal steroid responsivity to ACTH after acute or chronic opioids. However, both the adrenal medulla and cortex are rich in opiate receptors.[165,166] The physiological importance and significance of these observations are unknown. As with cortisol, aldosterone is not influenced by enkephalins or endorphins although β-lipotropin (LPT) has recently been shown to augment aldosterone secretion.[167] Thus LPT should be included with hyperkalemia, hyponatremia, and ACTH as influences on aldosterone secretion.

Adrenal Medullary Secretion

Adrenal medullary secretion in relation to opioids has not been adequately studied. Opioid stimulation of catecholamines in animals has been postulated[168-69] and recently documented.[170] Yet paradoxically, the surgically induced increases in both epinephrine and nonepinephrine[171] were attenuated by acute morphine administration in dogs. Possibly these catecholamines were secreted in response to pain, which the opiate may have alleviated.

Testes

Testosterone

Male plasma testosterone (T) levels fell after acute opioid administration under controlled conditions.[49,172] Initial exposure to heroin, methadone, and alpha methylmethadol (LAAM) were all reported to produce reduced plasma (T).[172-174] These data are consistent with the often,[91,140] but not universal findings of low plasma T levels observed among opioid-dependent persons. After chronic methadone administration, plasma T levels tended to scatter, with many in the normal ranges suggesting that partial tolerance had occurred in some.[175] Furthermore, the quantity of opioid administered was a variable, with daily methadone amounts of $\geq$ 40 mg being associated with much higher frequencies with low plasma T than daily doses of less than 40 mg.[55,172] Recovery of plasma T and LH after opiate detoxification was rapid.[173]

Most of these discrepancies in reported data may relate to the uncertain biological significance of a single plasma T level and/or to the degree of tolerance that the specific patient may have developed. Since plasma T and LH reflect prior secretory episodes, the interpretation of single plasma values is difficult. Mendelson and co-workers solved this problem by continuous plasma sampling and measuring integrated levels at short intervals. Under these conditions, plasma T fell during acute opioid exposure, but after ten days, the decreases were much smaller.[77]

Acute administration of NTX did not alter integrated plasma T but did increase LH in both normal and detoxified opiate-dependent males. With more chronic NTX use, integrated plasma T levels tended to rise while LH levels tended to fall off.[77] Responsivity of plasma LH and T to naltrexone and opioids in the immediate postdetoxification stage was especially striking, suggesting that supersensitivity of these hormones to opioids may have been present.

Androgenicity

Hypoandrogenicity may occur in opioid-addicted persons, although the clinical manifestations may be subtle. One manifestation may be the increased binding affinities of thyroid binding globulin (TBG). Augmented binding affinities of TBG, usually associated with exogenous estrogens or relative hypoadrogenicity, have been frequently observed in opioid addicts.[139,140] Another possible manifestation of hypoandrogenicity may be in sexual behavior. Male addicts commonly report reduced libido, impaired potency, and delayed time for completion of ejaculation during opioid use, which improved swiftly upon detoxification.[175] To what extent these sexual problems relate to plasma androgens is far from clear.

Animal data, elegantly worked out in rats by Cicero et al[78-80] and confirmed by Thomas and Dombrowsky[176] in mice, showed initial reductions in LH, followed by reduced T, and later reduced secondary sex characteristics. The locus of opioid effects appeared to be at the hypothalamic level, with the pituitary, gonad, and secondary sex organs seconardily involved. Both morphological and functional abnormalities were found in male prostrate and seminal vesicles. Binding of androgens to these sites seemed to be excluded.[78] Tolerance to these effects seemed to arise with time.

TABLE III

ACUTE OPIOIDS IN THE RAT

Effects of Naloxone, Morphine, and Methionine Enkephalin on Serum Prolactin, LH, FSH, TSH, and GH (ng/ml)

n=10/Group	PRL	GH	LH	FSH	TSH
Controls 0.87% NaCL	$9.0 \pm .4^a$	131 ± 23	19 ± 1	341 ± 12	232 ± 33
Naloxone 0.2 mg/kg	$4.6 \pm .4^b$	77 ± 10^b	44 ± 5^b	361 ± 15	272 ± 40
Naloxone 2.0 mg/kg	$4.2 \pm .3^b$	103 ± 40	52 ± 8^b	490 ± 36^b	157 ± 22
Naloxone 5.0 mg/kg	$4.0 \pm .3^b$	48 ± 6^b	45 ± 8^b	446 ± 29^b	191 ± 25
Morphine 2.0 mg/kg	$10.1 \pm .8$	839 ± 172^b	8 ± 1^b	340 ± 12	122 ± 13
Morphine 10.0 mg/kg	20.2 ± 2.3^b	1211 ± 185^b	9 ± 2^b	387 ± 23	77 ± 7^b
Morphine 15.0 mg/kg	18.5 ± 1.2^b	1775 ± 172^b	13 ± 2	333 ± 13	71 ± 0^b
MET-ENK 5.0 mg/kg	$11.5 \pm .6$	215 ± 27	11 ± 2^b	314 ± 20	96 ± 17^b
NAL & MOR 0.2+2.0 mg/kg	$3.6 \pm .4^b$	383 ± 71^b	17 ± 3	384 ± 9	210 ± 13
NAL & MOR 0.2+10.0 mg/kg	9.0 ± 1.1	902 ± 168^b	14 ± 4	369 ± 16	134 ± 17^b
NAL & MET-ENK 0.2+5.0 mg/kg	$5.4 \pm .8^b$	138 ± 37	17 ± 3	350 ± 18	191 ± 18

a $\bar{x} \pm$ S.E.M.
b $p < 0.05$ compared with controls.
MET-ENK = met-enkephalin.
NAL = naloxone.
MOR = morphine. (from Bruni, Van Vugt, Marshall and Meites, reprinted from ref. 109 with permission).

Semen Analyses

In the only study in this area to date, Cicero et al[177] described low semen volumes, normal sperm counts, and some quantitative differences in some semen constituents in opioid addicts compared to controls. Methadone recipients were more abnormal than the heroin addicts studied.

Ovary

There are formidable problems in the study of the ovarian component of the complex hypothalamic-pituitary-ovarian axis in females. The clinical impressions of infertility and observations of oligo-amenorrhea in many opiate dependent persons imply that important disturbances in this axis exist.[92-94] This is enhanced by the previously summarized data that opioids may inhibit cyclic gonadotropins and ovulation. Yet, methadone-treated women had normal estrogen feedback effects on LH and normal withdrawal uterine bleeding after stopping exogenous progesterone.

In the laboratory animal, opiates exogenously administered have repeatedly induced inhibition of ovulation.[98,178]; this inhibition can be blocked with NAL. Also sexual behavioral changes have been well charted in female animals with opioid administration; these can also be blocked by NAL.[179]

Plasma estradiol (E-2) as well as progesterone and FSH in normal women are not affected by NAL infusions of 1.4 mg/hr for four hours.[89] On the other hand, systematic study of E-2, or progesterone, in relation to acute opioids has not been reported in normal women. Since most of the plasma estrogens in males are derived from peripheral aromatization of androgens precursors, low plasma E-2 levels might be expected in opioid-dependent persons. Azizi et al found normal mean plasma E-2 in a small group of males. Only a few had low E-2. Paradoxically, those with low E-2 were not necessarily those with low plasma T levels.[88] Unfortunately, data on sex hormone binding globulin, an important factor in the interpretation of plasma E-2 levels, are lacking in humans. Estradiol production rates, usually low normal in a small group of chronic methadone male recipients, rose with detoxification before returning to normal.[71]

Thyroid

There are probably no major or consistent changes in thyroid function in man as a result of opioid use. Acute opioids in normal man produced only slight and insignificant increases in serum TSH levels.[75,139] NAL also did not change serum TSH.[45] On the other hand, euthyroid opioid addicts frequently had increased serum T-3 or T-4 levels, without increased TSH or free T-4.[139,140] Since low levels of tri-iodithronine (T-3) resin uptakes were also present, augmented binding affinities of TBG were postulated. This was confirmed by direct analyses. A decrease in TBG binding was observed during methadone treatment.[139] Perhaps the changes of TBG may relate to the use of street opiates, some diluent, or to a nonopioid consequence of narcotic addiction. One such possibility could be a consequence of viral hepatitis, common among opiate addicts.[139] Another possibility could be the well-known effects of androgens and estrogens on TBG binding affinities. Among opiate-dependent persons, both TSH[141] and total plasma T-3 responded normally to injected TRH.[142]

In the rat, TSH levels acutely fell with 10-15 mg/kg of morphine or 5 mg/kg of met-enkephalin but not with lower doses.[72] NAL alone was without effect but could attenuate opiate-induced decreases in TSH. Some rats treated with acute and chronic morphine had reduced thyroid uptake and release, reduced thyroid weights, and lowered pituitary TSH contents.[49] No comparable data have been reported in humans.

Miscellaneous

While modest increases in immunoreactive insulin (IRI) in blood followed acute opioids,[75] the effect is of little clinical significance. NAL alone produced modest increases in IRI but no change in plasma in glucagon.[45] The pancreas, rich in opiate receptors and opioids,[180] has been shown to respond to opioids acutely.[181] Although both glucagon and insulin rose in isolated pancreatic tissue,[182,183] the glucagon effect appeared to be of greater significance. Normal dogs had increased glucagon without change in insulin levels[183] but amylase and bicarbonate decreased.[184] Thus, both endocrine and exocrine pancreatic secretion in animals can be affected.[185]

The well-known hyperglycemic response to acute opiates[186] has been usually attributed to a release of catecholamines with attendant glycogenolysis.[187] However, the evidence for such a catecholamine effect is inconclusive. Possibly augmented glucagon may account for the hypoglycemia through its glycogenolytic effect since hyperglycemia occurred in the alloxan-diabetic dog after acute opioids.[187] Yet paradoxically, among opiate-dependent persons, plasma glucose was normal and rose slowly while immunoreactive insulin remained higher than the controls in oral glucose tolerance testing.[188] Since these observations are not as yet replicated, their significance in unclear.

REFERENCES

1. Snyder, SH, Pert CB, Pasternak GW: The opiate receptor. *Ann Intern Med* 81:534-540, 1974.
2. Kosterlitz HW, Hughes H: Some thoughts on the significance of enkephalin, the endogenous ligand. *Life Sci* 17:91-96, 1975.
3. Simon EJ, Hiller JM, Edelman I: Stereospecific binding of the potent narcotic analgesic (3H) etorphine to rat brain homogenate. *Proc Natl Acad Sci USA* 70:1947-1949, 1973.
4. Goldstein A: Opioid peptides (endorphins) in pituitary and brain. *Science* 193:1081-1086, 1976.
5. Verebey K, Volavka J, Clouet D: Endorphins in psychiatry. *Arch Gen Psychiatry* 35:877-888, 1978.

6. Bunney WE, Pert CB, Klee W: Basic and clinical studies of endorphins. *Ann Intern Med* 91:239-350, 1979.

7. Guillemin R: Beta-lipotropin and endorphins: Implications of current knowledge. *Hosp Pract* 13(11):53-60, 1978.

8. Loh HH, Law PY, Ostwald T, Cho TM, Way EL: Possible involvement of cerebroside sulfate in opiate receptor binding. *Fed Proc* 37:147-152, 1978.

9. Lee NM, Smith AP: A protein-lipid model of the opiate receptor. *Life Sci* 26:1459-1464, 1980.

10. Snyder SH: Receptors, neurotransmitters and drug responses. *N Engl J Med* 300:465-472, 1979.

11. Snyder SH: Brain peptides as neurotransmitters. *Science* 209:976-983, 1980.

12. Pert CB, Kuhar MJ, Snyder SH: Autoradiographic localization of opiate receptor in rat brain. *Life Sci* 16:1849-1854, 1975.

13. Watanabe M, Diab IM, Schuster CR, Roth LJ: ¹H morphine localization in brain, in Ford DH, Clouet DH (eds): *Tissue Responses to Addictive Drugs*. New York, Spectrum Publications, 1975, pp 61-68.

14. Snyder SH: Opiate receptors in the brain. *N Engl J Med* 296:266-271, 1977.

15. Bloom F, Battenberg E, Rossier J, Ling N, Guilleman R: Neurons containing β-endorphin in the rat brain exist separately from those containing enkephalin: Immunocyrochemical studies. *Proc Natl Acad Sci USA* 75:1591-1595, 1978.

16. Watson SJ, Akil H, Richard CW, Barchas JD: Evidence for two separate opiate peptide neuronal systems. *Nature* (London) 275:226-228, 1978.

17. Rossier J, Vargo TM, Minick S, Ling N, Bloom FE, Guillemin R: Regional dissociation of β-endorphin and enkephalin contents in rat brain and pituitary. *Proc Nat Sci* 74:5162, 1977.

18. DuPont A, Barden N, Cusan L, Mérand Y, Labrie F, Vaudry H: Beta-endorphin and met-enkephalins: Their distribution, modulation by estrogens and haloperidol and role in neuroendocrine control. *Fed Proc* 39:2544-2550, 1980.

19. Wilkes MM, Watkins WB, Stewart RD, Yen SSC: Localization of quantitation of β-endorphin in human brain and pituitary *Neuroendocrinology* 30:113-121, 1980.

20. Hughes J, Kosterlitz HW, Smith TW: The distribution of methionine-enkephalin and leucine-enkephalin in the brain and peripheral tissues. *Br J Pharmacol* 61:639-647, 1977.

21. Polak JM, Bloom SR, Sullivan SN, Facer P, Pearse AGE: Enkephalin-like immunoreactivity in the human gastrointestinal tract. *Lancet* 1:972-974, 1977.

22. Verebey K, Volavka J, Mule S, Resnick R: Methadone in man: Pharmacokinetic and excretion studies in acute and chronic treatment. *Clin Pharmacol Ther* 18:180-190, 1976.

23. Fraser HF, Kay DC, Gorodetzky CW: Evidence for the importance of N-dealkylation in opioid pharmacology. *Drug Alcohol Depend* 3:1-22, 1978.

24. Mellet LB, Woods LA: Distribution and fate of morphine in the non-tolerant and tolerant monkey. *J Pharmacol Exp Ther* 116:77-83, 1956.

25. Mushlin BE, Grell R, Cochin J: Studies on tolerance. Role of interval between doses on the development of tolerance to morphine. *J Pharmacol Exp Ther* 196:280-287, 1976.

26. Resnick RB, Schuyten-Resnick E, Washton AM: Treatment of opioid dependence with narcotic antagonist: A review and commentary, in DuPont RI, Goldstein A, O'Donnells (eds): *Handbook on Drug Abuse*. Washington, DC, US Govt Printing Office, 1979, pp 97-104.

27. Jasinski DR, Martin WR, Haertzen CA: The human pharmacology and abuse potential of n-allyinoroxy morphine (naloxone). *J Pharmacol Exp Ther* 157:420-426, 1967.

28. Johnstone RE, Jobes DR, Kennell EM, Behar MG, Smith TC: Reversal of morphine anesthesia with naloxone. *Anesthesiology* 41:361-367, 1974.

29. Berkowitz BA, Finck AD, Ngai SH: Nitrous Oxide Analgesia: Reversal by naloxone and development of tolerance. *J Pharmacol Exp Ther* 203:539-547, 1977.

30. Spiehler VR, Paalzow L: Naloxone antagonism of phenoxybenzamine antinociception in the mouse tail stimulation test. *Life Sci* 24:2125-2132, 1979.

31. Furst Z, Foldes FF, Knoll J: Influence of Naloxone on barbiturate anesthesia and toxicity in the rat. *Life Sci* 20:921-926, 1977.

32. Gilbert PE, Martin WR: Antagonism of pentobarbital by naloxone in the chronic spinal dog, abstracted. *Fed Proc* 36:964, 1977.

33. Holtzman SG: Behavioral effects of separate and combined administration of naloxone and d-amphetamine. *J Pharmacol Exp Ther* 189:51-60, 1974.

34. Fertziger AP, Fischer R: Interaction between narcotic antagonist (naloxone) and lysergic acid diethylamide LSD in the rat. *Psychopharmacology* 54:313-314, 1977.

35. Jacquet YF: β-endorphin, blood-brain barrier and schizophrenia. *Lancet* 1:831-837, 1980.

36. Oldendorf WH: Drug penetration of the blood brain barrier, in Zimmerman E, George R, (eds): *Narcotics and the Hypothalamus*. New York, Raven Press, 1974, pp 213-222.

37. Foley KM, Inturrisi CE, Kourides IA, Kaiko RF, Posner JB, Houde RW, Li CH: Intravenous and intraventricular administration of beta-endorphin in man: Safety and disposition, in Van Ree JM, Terenius L (eds): *Characteristics and Functions of Opioids* (Development in Neuroscience, vol 4). Amsterdam, Elsevier/North Holland, 1978, pp 421-422.

38. Foley KM, Kourides IA, Inturrisi CE, Kaiko RF, Zaroulis CG, Posner JB, Houde RW, Li CH: β-endorphin: Analgesic and hormonal effects in humans. *Proc Natl Acad Sci USA* 76:5377-81, 1979.

39. Grandison L, Fratta W, Giudotti A: Location and characterization of opiate receptor regulating pituitary secretion. *Life Sci* 26:1633-1642, 1980.

40. Mains RE, Eipper BA, Ling N: Common precursor to corticotropins and endorphins. *Proc Natl Acad Sci USA* 74:3014-3018, 1977.

41. Guillemin R, Vargo T, Rossier J: β-endorphin and adrenocorticotropin are secreted concomitantly by the pituitary gland. *Sciences* 197:1367-1369, 1977.

42. Sabol SL: Regulation of endorphin production by glucocorticoids in cultured pituitary tumor cells. *Biochem Biophys Res Commun* 82:560-567, 1978.

43. Volavka J, Cho D, Mallya A: Naloxone increases ACTH and cortisol levels in man. *N Engl J Med* 300:1056-1057, 1979.

44. Morley JE, Baranetsky NG, Carlson HE: Endocrine effects of naloxone. The Endocrine Society Program of 60th Annual Meeting 25, 1978.

45. Morley JE, Baranetsky NG, Wingert TD: Endocrine effects of naloxone-induced opiate receptor blockade. *J Clin Endocrinol Metab* 50:251-257, 1980.

46. Lehmann H, Nair NPV, Kline NS: β-endorphin and naloxone in psychiatric patients: Clinical and biological effects. *Am J Psychiatry* 136:762-766, 1979.

47. Ho WWK, Wen HL, Fung KP, Ng YH, Au KK, MA L: Comparison of plasma hormonal levels between heroin addicted and normal subjects. *Clin Chim Acta* 75:415-419, 1977.

48. Spiler IJ, Moltich ME: Lack of modulation of pituitary hormone stress response by neural pathways involving opiate receptors. *J Clin Endocrinol Metab* 50:516-520, 1980.

49. Fishman J: The opiates and the endocrine system, in Fishman J (ed): *Bases of Addiction* Berlin, Dahlem Konferenzen, 1977, pp 257-280.

50. Meites J, Bruni JF, Vanvugt DA, Smith AF: Relation and endogenous opioid peptides and morphine to neuroendocrine functions. *Life Sci* 24:1325-1336, 1979.

51. Kokka N, George R: Effects of narcotic analgesics, anesthetics, and hypothalamic lesions on growth hormone and

adrenocorticotropic hormone secretion in rats, in Zimmerman E, George R (eds): *Narcotics and the Hypothalamus* New York, Raven Press, 1974, pp 137-159.

52. Catlin DH, Poland RE, Gorelick DA, Gerner RH, Hui KK, Rubin RT, Li CH: Intravenous infusion of β-endorphin decreases serum prolactin, but not growth hormone or cortisol in depressed subjects and withdrawing methadone addicts. *J Clin Endocrinol Metab* 50:1021-1023, 1980.

53. Tolis G, Hickey J, Guyda H: Effects of morphine on serum growth hormone, cortisol, prolactin and thyroid stimulating hormone in man. *J Clin Endocrinol Metab* 41:797-800, 1975.

54. Eisenman AJ, Fraser HF, Brooks JW: Urinary excretion and plasma levels of 17-hydroxycorticosteroids during a cycle of addiction to morphine. *J Pharmacol Exp Ther* 132:226-231, 1961.

55. Mendelson JH, Meyer RE, Ellingboe J, Mirin SM, McDougle M: Effects of heroin and methadone on plasma cortisol and testosterone. *J Pharmac Exp Ther* 195:296-302, 1975.

56. Gold PW, Extein I, Pickar D, Rebar R, Ross R, Goodwin FK: Suppression of plasma cortisol in depressed patients by acute intravenous methadone infusion. *Am J Psychiatry* 137:862-863, 1980.

57. McDonald RK, Evans FT, Weise YK, Patrick, RW: Effect of morphine and nalorphine on plasma hydrocortisone levels in man. *J Pharmacol Exp Ther* 125:241-247, 1959.

58. Briggs EN, Munson PL: Studies on the mechanism of stimulation of ACTH secretion with the aid of morphine as a blocking agent. *Endocrinology* 57:205-219, 1955.

59. George JM, Rier CE, Lanese RA, Rower JM: Morphine anesthesia blocks cortisol and growth hormone response to surgical stress in humans. *J Clin Endocrinol Metab* 38:736-741, 1976.

60. Reir CE, George JM, Kilman JW: Cortisol and growth hormone response to surgical stress during morphine analgesia. *Anesth Analg* 52:1003-1009, 1973.

61. Van Vugt DA, Meites J: Influence of endogenous opiates on anterior pituitary function. *Fed Proc* 39:2533-2538, 1980.

62. Munson PL: Effects of morphine and related drugs on the corticotropin (ACTH) stress reaction. *Prog Brain Res* 39:371-372, 1973.

63. Simon M, George R, Garcia J: Acute morphine effects on regional brain amines, growth hormone and corticosterone. *Eur J Pharmacol* 34:21-26, 1975.

64. Zimmerman E, Critchlow V: Inhibition of morphine-induced pituitary-adrenal activation by dexamethasone in the female rat. *Proc Soc Exp Biol Med* 143:1224-1226, 1973.

65. Kokka N, Garcia JF, George R, Elliott, HW: Growth hormone and ACTH secretion: Evidence for an inverse relationship in rats. *Endocrinology* 90:735-743, 1972.

66. Eisenberg RM: Effects of naloxone on plasma corticosterone in the opiate naive rat. *Life Sci* 26:935-943, 1980.

67. Eisenberg RM, Sparber SB: Changes in plasma corticosterone as a measure of acute dependence upon levorphanol in rats. *J Pharmacol Exp Ther* 211:364-369, 1979.

68. Cushman P, Bordier B, Hilton JG: Hypothalamic-pituitary-adrenal axis in methadone treated heroin addicts. *J Clin Endocrinol Metab* 30:24-29, 1970.

69. Kreek MJ: Medical complications in methadone patients. *Ann NY Acad Sci* 311:110-134, 1978.

70. Dent R, Tolis G: Hypothalamic-pituitary target organ axis in patients on methadone maintenance, abstracted. Presented at the 58th Annual Endocrine Society Meeting, 217, 1976.

71. Hellman L, Fukushima DK, Roffwarg H, Fishman J: Changes in estradiol and cortisol production rates in men under the influence of narcotics. *J Clin Endocrinol Metab* 41:1014-1019, 1975.

72. Cushman P, Kreek MJ: Some endocrinologic observations in narcotic addicts, in Zimmerman E, George R, (eds): *Narcotics and the Hypothalamus.* New York, Raven Press, 1974, pp 161-173.

73. Renault PF, Schuster CR, Heinrich RL, Van der Kolk B: Altered plasma cortisol response in patients on methadone maintenance. *Clin Pharmacol Ther* 13:269-273, 1972.

74. Van Wimersma, Greidanus TB, Thody TJ, Verspaget H, DeRotte GA, Goedemans HJH, Croiset G, VanRee JM: Effects of morphine and β-endorphin on basal and elevated plasma levels of a MSH and vasopressin. *Life Sci* 24:570-586, 1979.

75. Stubbs WA, Jones A, Edwards CRW, Delitala G, Jeffcoat WJ, Besser GM, Bloom SR, Alberti KGMM: Hormonal and metabolic responses to an enkephalin analogue in normal man. *Lancet* 2:1225-1227, 1978.

76. Martin WR, Jasinski DR, Haertzen CA, Kay DC, Jones BE, Mansky PA, Carpenter RW: Methadone - A reevaluation. *Arch Gen Psychiatry* 28:286-295, 1973.

77. Mendelson JH, Ellingboe J, Kuehnle JC, Mello NK: Heroin and naltrexone effects on pituitary-gonadal hormones in man: Tolerance and supersensitivity. *Natl Inst Drug Abuse Res Monogr Ser* 27:302-208, 1979.

78. Cicero TJ, Bell RD, Meyer ER, Schweitzer J: Narcotics and the hypothalamic-pituitary-gonadal axis: Acute effects on luteinizing hormone, testosterone, and androgen-dependent systems. *J Pharmacol Exp Ther* 201:76-83, 1977.

79. Cicero TJ, Meyer ER, Bell RD, Koch GA: Effects of morphine and methadone on serum testosterone and luteinizing hormone levels and on secondary sex organs of the male rat. *Endocrinology* 98:367-372, 1976.

80. Cicero TJ, Wilcox CE, Bell RD, Meyer ER: Acute reductions in serum testosterone levels by narcotics in the male rat: Stereospecificity blockade by naloxone and tolerance. *J Pharmacol Exp Ther* 198:340-346, 1976.

81. Quigley ME, Sheehan KL, Casper RF, Yen SSC: Evidence for an increased opioid inhibition of luteinizing hormone secretion in hyperprolactinemic patients with pituitary microadenoma. *J Clin Endocrinol Metab* 50:427-431, 1980.

82. Cicero TJ, Badger TM, Wilcox CE, Bell RD, Meyer ER: Morphine decreases luteinizing hormone by an action on the hypothalamic pituitary axis. *J Pharmacol Exp Ther* 203:548-555, 1977.

83. Rotszejn WH, Drouva SV, Pattou E, Kordon C: Met-enkephalin inhibits in vitro dopamine induced LHRH release from mediobasal hypothalamus of male rats. *Nature* 274:281-2, 1978.

84. Brambilla F, Resele L, DeMaio D, Nobil P: Gonadotropin response to synthetic gonadotropin hormone releasing (GNRH) in heroin addicts. *Am J Psychiatry* 136:314-316, 1979.

85. Cicero TJ: Effects of exogenous and endogenous opiates on the hypothalamic-pituitary-gonadal axis in the male. *Fed Proc* 39:2551-255, 1980.

86. Norton B, Hahn E, Fishman J: Effects of narcotics on steroid hormone metabolism in the rat. The Endocrine Society, 61st Annual Meeting, abstracted, 1979, p 929A.

87. Mendelson JH, Ellingboe J, Kuehnle J, Mello NK: Effects of naltrexone on mood and neuroendocrine function in normal adult males. *Psychoneuroendocrinology* 3:231-236, 1979.

88. Azizi F, Vagenakis AG, Longcope C, Ingbar SH, Braverman LE: Decreased serum testosterone concentration in male heroin and methadone addicts. *Steroids* 22:467-472, 1973.

89. Quigley ME, Yen SSC: The role of endogenous opiates on LH secretion during the menstrual cycle. *J Clin Endocrinol Metab* 51:179-181, 1980.

90. Blank MS, Panerai AE, Friesen HG: Opioid peptides modulate luteinizing hormone secretion during sexual maturation. *Science* 203:1129, 1979.

91. Cushman P: Plasma testosterone in narcotic addiction. *Am J Med* 55:452-458, 1973.

92. Santeen RJ, Sofsky J, Bilic N, Lippert R: Mechanism of action of narcotics in the production of menstrual dysfunction in women. *Fertil Steril* 26:538-548, 1975.

93. Gaulden EC, Littlefield DC, Putoff OE, Seivert AL: Menstrual abnormalities associated with heroin addiction. *Am J Obstet Gynecol* 90:155-160, 1964.

94. Stoffer SS: A gynecological study of drug addicts., *Am J Obstet Gynecol* 101:770-783, 1968.

95. Wallach RC, Jerez E, Blinick G: Pregnancy and menstrual function in narcotic addicts treated with methadone. *Am J Obstet Gynecol* 105:1226-1229, 1969.

96. Weiland WE, Yunger M: Sexual effects and side effects of heroin and methadone. Proceedings of Third National Conference on Methadone Treatment, Washington DC (USPHS publication 2172). 1970, pp 50-53.

97. Kreek MJ: Medical safety and side effects of methadone in tolerant individuals. *JAMA* 223:665-668, 1973.

98. Santen RJ: How narcotics addiction affects reproductive function in women. *Contemporary OB/Gyn* 3(4):93-96, 1974.

99. Barraclough CA, Sawyer CH: Inhibition of the release of pituitary ovulatory hormone in the rat by morphine. *Endocrinology* 57:329-337, 1955.

100. Packman PN, Rothchild JA: Morphine inhibition of ovulation: Reversal by naloxone. *Endocrinology* 99:7-10, 1976.

101. Pang, CN, Zimmerman E, Sawyer CH: Morphine inhibition of the pre-ovulatory surges of plasma luteinizing hormone and follicle stimulating hormone in the rat. *Endocrinology* 101:1726-1732, 1977.

102. Lal S, Nair NPV, Cervantes P, Pulman J, Guyda H: Effect of naloxone or levallorphan on serum prolactin concentrations and apomorphine-induced growth hormone secretion. *Acta Psychiatr Scand* 59:173-179, 1979.

103. Janowsky D, Judd L, Huey L, Roitman NM, Parker D, Segal D: Negative naloxone effects on serum prolactin. *Lancet* 2:637, 1978.

104. Martin JB, Tolis G, Woods I, Guyda H: Failure of naloxone to influence physiological growth hormone and prolactin secretion. *Brain Res* 168:210-215, 1979.

105. Cushman P: Growth hormone in narcotic addiction. *J Clin Endocrinol Metab* 35:352-358, 1972.

106. Rivier C, Vale W, Ling N, Brown M, Guillemin R: Stimulation in vivo of the secretion of prolactin and growth hormone by β-endorphin. *Endocrinology* 100:238-241, 1977.

107. Takahara J, Kageyama J, Yonoki S, Yakushiji W, Yamuchi J, Kageyama N, Ofugi T: Effects of 2-bromo-a-ergocryptine on β-endorphin induced growth hormone, prolactin, and luteinizing hormones release in urethane anesthetized rats. *Life Sci* 22:2205-2208, 1978.

108. DuPont A, Cusan L, Garon M, Labrie F, Li CH: β-endorphin: Stimulation of growth hormone release in vivo. *Proc Nat Acad Sci USA* 74:358-359, 1977.

109. Bruni JF, Van Vugt D, Marshall S, Meites J: Effects of naloxone, morphine and methionine enkephalin on serum prolactin luteinizing hormone, follicle stimulating hormone, thyroid stimulating hormone and growth hormone. *Life Sci* 21:461-466, 1977.

110. Tolis G: Prolactin: Physiology and pathology. *Hosp Practice* 15:85-100, 1980.

111. Sheppard NC, Kronheim S, Primstone B: Effect of substance P, neurotensin and enkephalins on somatostatin release from the rat hypothalamus in vitro. *J Neurochem* 32:647-649, 1979.

112. Gold MS, Redmond DE, Donabedian RK: Prolactin secretion, a measurable central effect of opiate-receptor antagonists. *Lancet* 1:323-324, 1978.

113. Gold MS, Redmond DE, Donabedian RK: The effect of opiate agonist and antagonist on serum prolactin in primates. Possible role for endorphins in prolactin regulation. *Endocrinology* 105:284-289, 1979.

114. Bartke A: Role of prolactin in reproduction in male animals. *Fed Proc* 39:2577-2581, 1980.

115. Berger PA, Watson SJ, Akil H, Elliott GR, Rubin RT, Pfefferbaum A, Davis KL, Barchas JD, Li CH: β-endorphin and schizophrenia. *Arch Gen Psychiatry* 37:635-640, 1980.

116. Extein I, Pottash ALC, Gold MS, Sweeney DR, Martin DM, Goodwin FK: Deficient prolactin response to morphine in depressed patients. *Amer J Psychiatry* 137:845-846, 1980.

117. Tolis G, Dent R, Guyda H: Opiates, prolactin and dopamine receptor. *J Clin Endocrinol Metab* 47:200-203, 1978.

118. Clemens JA, Sawyer BD: Evidence that methdone stimulates prolactin release by dopamine receptor blockade. *Endocr Res Commun* 1:373, 1974.

119. Enjalbert AM, Rubergs, Arancibia S, Prian N, Kordon C: Endogenous opiates block dopamine inhibition of prolactin secretion in vitro. *Nature* 280:595-596, 1979.

120. Van Loon GR, Kim C: Beta-endorphin induced increase in striatal dopamine turnover. *Life Sci* 23:961-970, 1978.

121. Ferland L, Fuxe K, Eneroth P, Gustafsson JA, Skett P: Effects of methionine enkephalin on prolactin release and catecholamine levels and turnover in the median eminence. *Eur J Pharmacol* 43:89-90, 1977.

122. Van Vugt DA, Bruni JF, Sylvester PW, Chen HT, Ieiri T, Meite J: Interactions between opiates and hypothalamic dopamine on prolactin release. *Life Sci* 24:2361-2368, 1979.

123. Deyo SN, Swift RM, Miller RJ: Morphine and endorphin modulate dopamine turnover in rat median eminence. *Proc Natl Acad Sci USA* 76:3006-3009, 1979.

124. Shaar CJ, Clemons JA: The effects of opiate agonists on growth hormone and prolactin release in rats. *Fed Proc* 39:2539-2543, 1980.

125. Boyd AE, Reichlin S: Neural control of prolactin secretion in man. *Psychoneuroendocrinology* 3:113-130, 1978.

126. Rossier, J, Battenberg E, Pittman Q, Bayon A, Koda L, Miller R, Guillemin R, Blam F: Hypothalamic enkephalin neurones may regulate the neurohyphyses. *Nature* (London) 277:653-655, 1979.

127. Wardlaw SL, Wehrenberg, Ferin N, Frantz AG: Failure of β-endorphin to stimulate prolactin in the pituitary stalk sectioned monkey. *Endocrinology* 107:1663-1666, 1980.

128. Lien EL, Fenichel RL, Garsky V, Sarantakis D, Grant NH: Enkephalin stimulated prolactin release. *Life Sci* 19:837-840, 1976.

129. Shaar CJ, Frederickson RCA, Dininger NB, Jackson L: Enkephalin analogues and naloxone modulate the release of growth hormone and prolactin-evidence for regulation by an endogenous opioid peptide in the brain. *Life Sci* 21:853-860, 1977.

130. Ferland L, Kelly P, Denizeau F, Labrie, F: Role of dopamine and serotonin in the stimulatory effects of opiates in prolactin secretion, in Van Ree JM, Terenius L (eds): *Characteristics and Functions of Opioids* (Developments in Neuroscience vol 4) Amsterdam, Elsevier/North Holland, 1978, pp 353-354.

131. Sylvester PW, Chen HT, Meites J: Interactions of morphine with dopaminergic and cholinergic drugs on release of prolactin in the rat. *IRCS J Med Sci* 6:510-515, 1978.

132. Gold MS, Pottash ALC, Extein I, Redmond DE, Kleber HD: Decrease in serum prolactin by naloxone: Evidence against antidopamine and antipsychotic effects. *Am J Psychiatry* 136:1339-1340, 1979.

133. Janowsky D, Judd L, Huey L, Roitman K, Parker D: Naloxone effects on serum growth hormone and prolactin in man. *Psychopharmacology* 65:95-97, 1979.

134. Deyo SN, Swift RM, Miller RJ, Fang VS: Development of tolerance to the prolactin releasing action of morphine and its modulation by hypothalamic dopamine. *Endocrinology* 106:1469-1474, 1980.

135. Roemer D, Buescher HH, Hill RC, Pless J, Bauer W, Cardinaux F, Closse A, Hauser D, Huguenin R: A synthetic enkephalin analogue with prolonged parenteral and oral analgesia activity. *Nature* 268:547-549, 1977.

136. Kreek MJ, Khuri E: Effects of methadone maintenance on prolactin release, abstracted. The Endocrine Society, 61st Annual Meeting. 965A, 1979.

137. Kley HK, Oellevich M, Wiegelman W, Hermmann J, Rudorff KH, Nieschlag E, Kruskemper HL: The effect of methadone on hypophyseal and peripheral glandular hormones during withdrawal. *Horm Metab Res* 9:484-488, 1977.

138. Chihara K, Arimura A, Coy DH, Schally AV: Studies on the interaction of endorphins, substance P, and endogenous somatostatin on growth hormone and prolactin release in rats. *Endocrinology* 102:281-290, 1978.

139. Webster JB, Coupal JJ, Cushman P: Increased serumthyroxine levels in euthyroid narcotic addicts. *J Clin Endocrinol Metab* 37:928-934, 1973.

140. Azizi F, Vagenakis AG, Portnay GI, Braverman LE, Ingbar SH: Thyroxine transport and metabolism in methadone and heroin addicts. *Ann Intern Med* 80:194-199, 1974.

141. Shenkman L, Massie B, Mitsuma T, Hollander CS: Effects of chronic methadone administration on the hypothalamic-pituitary-thyroid axis. *J Clin Endocrinol Metab* 35:169-170, 1972.

142. Chan V, Wang C, Young R: Effects of heroin addiction on thyrotropin (TSH), thyroid hormones and prolactin secretion. The 58th Endocrine Society Annual Meeting, 178A, 1976.

143. Aziz LA, Forsling ML, Woolf CJ: The action of morphine on vasopressin release in the rat. *J Physiol* 300:24, 1980.

144. Gudelsky GW, DeVane GW, Porter JC: Morphine induced inhibition of the release of arginine vasopressin (AVP), abstracted. The Endocrine Society 62nd Annual Meeting, 14, 1980.

145. Marchand C, Denis G: Diuretic effect of chronic morphine treatment in rats. *J Pharmacol Exp Therap* 162:331-337, 1968.

146. Lightman SL, Forsling ML: Evidence for endogenous opioid control of vasopressin release in man. *J Clin Endocrinol Metab* 50:569-578, 1980.

147. Grossman A, Besser GM, Milles JJ, Baylis PH: Inhibition of vasopressin release in man by an opiate peptide. *Lancet* 2:1108-1110, 1980.

148. Lightman SL, Langdon N, Forsling ML: Effects of the opiate antagonist naloxone and the enkephalin analogue DAMME on the vasopressin response to hypertonic stimulus in man. *J Clin Endocrinol Metab* 51:1447-1449, 1980.

149. Nutt JG, Jasinski DR: Diuretic action of the narcotic antagonist oxilorphan. *Clin Pharmacol Ther* 15:361-367, 1974.

150. Miller M: Role of endogenous opioids in neurohypophysial function in man. *J Clin Endocrinol Metab* 50:1016-1020, 1980.

151. Miller M: Inhibition of ADH release in the rat by narcotic antagonists. *Neuroendocrinology* 19:241-251, 1975.

152. Iversen LL, Iversen SD, Bloom FE: Opiate receptors influence vasopressin release from nerve terminals in rat neurohypophysis. *Nature* 284:350-351, 1980.

153. Rossier J, Pittman Q, Bloom F, Guillemin R: Distribution of opioid peptides in the pituitary: A new hypothalamic-pars nervoas enkephalinergic pathway. *Fed Proc* 39:2555-2560, 1980.

154. Weitzman RE, Fishman DA, Minick S, Ling N, Guillemin R: β-endorphin stimulates secretion of arginine vasopressin in vitro. *Endocrinology* 101:1643-1646, 1977.

155. Debodo RC: The antidiuretic action of morphine and its mechanism. *J Pharmacol Exp Ther* 82:74-85, 1944.

156. Inturrisi CE, Fujimoto JM: Studies on the antidiuretic action of morphine in the rat. *Eur J Pharmacol* 2:310-307, 1968.

157. Tseng LF, Loh HH, Li CH: Beta endorphin: Antidiuretic effects in rats. *Int J Pep Protein Res* 12:173-176, 1978.

158. Bisset GW, Chowdery HS, Feldberg W: Release of vasopressin by enkephalin. *Br J Pharmacol* 62:370-371, 1978.

159. Weitzman RE: Effects of β-endorphin, morphine, and naloxone on arginine vasopressin and the EEG. *Neurosci* 4:1895-7, 1979.

160. Haldar HM, Sawyer WH: Inhibition of oxytocin release by morphine and its analogs. *Proc Soc Exp Biol Med* 157:476-480, 1978.

161. Rotsztejn WH, Drouva SV, Pattou E, Kordon C: Effect of morphine on the basal and dopamine-induced release of LHRH from mediobasal hypothalamic fragments in vitro. *Eur J Pharmacol* 50:285-286, 1978.

162. Judd AM, Hedge GA: The role of opioid peptides in thyrotropin and prolactin secretion. *Physiologist* 23(4):19, abstract 98, 1980.

163. Morley JE, Yamada Y, Walsh JH, Lamers CB, Wong H, Shulkes A, Damassa DA, Gordon J, Carlson HE, Hershman JM: Morphine addiction and withdrawal alters brain peptide concentrations. *Life Sci* 26:2239-2244, 1980.

164. Martin JB, Audet J, Saunders A: Effects of somatostatin and hypothalamic ventromedial lesions on GH release induced by morphine. *Endocrinology* 96:839-847, 1975.

165. George R: Hypothalamus: Anterior pituitary gland, in Clouet DH (ed): *Narcotic Drugs Biochemical Pharmacology*. New York, Plenum Press, 1971, pp 283-299.

166. Yang H-YT, Hexum T, Costa E: Opioid peptides in adrenal gland. *Life Sci* 27:1119-1125, 1980.

167. Matsuaka H, Mulrow PJ, Li CH: β-liptropin a new aldosterone stimulating factor. *Science* 209:307-308, 1980.

168. Schusdziarra V, Harris V, Unger RH: Morphine-induced hyperglycemia: Role of insulin and glucagon. *Endocrinology* 107:461-463, 1980.

169. Guaza C, Torrellas A, Gorrell J, Borrells: Effects of morphine upon the pituitary-adrenal system and adrenal catecholamines: A comparative study in cats and rats. *Pharmacol Biochem Behav* 11:57-63, 1979.

170. Appel NM, Ho D, DeSouza EP, Van Loon GR: Adrenal denervation blocks the epinephrine response to intracerebral β-endorphin. *Physiologist* 23(4):19, abstract 762, 1980.

171. Taborsky GJ, Halter JB, Porte D: Morphine suppresses the increase of catecholamines during surgery, abstracted. The Endocrine Society, 61st Annual Meeting, A205, 1979.

172. Mendelson JH, Mendelson JE, Patch VD: Plasma testosterone levels in heroin addiction and methadone maintenance. *J Pharmacol Exp Ther* 192:211-217, 1975.

173. Mendelson JH, Mello NK: Plasma testosterone levels during chronic heroin use and protracted abstinence. *Clin Pharmacol Therap* 17:529-533, 1975.

174. Mendelson JH, Inturrisi CE, Renault P, et al: Effects of acetymethadol on plasma testosterone. *Clin Pharmacol Ther* 19:371-374, 1976.

175. Cushman P: Sexual behavior in heroin addiction and methadone maintenance. Correlation with plasma luteining horomone. *New York State J Med* 72:1261-5, 1972.

176. Thomas JA, Dombrowsky JT: Effect of methadone on the male reproductive system. *Arch Int Pharmacodyn* 215:215-221, 1975.

177. Cicero TJ, Bell RD, Wiest, WH, Allison JH, Polakoski K, Robins E: Function of male sex organs in heroin and methadone users. *N Engl J Med* 292:882-887, 1975.

178. Johnson JH, Rosecrans JA: Blockade of ovulation by methadone in the rat: A central nervous system-mediated acute effect. *J Pharmacol Exp Ther* 213:110-113, 1980.

179. Ostrowski NL, Stapleton JM, Noble RG, Reid LD: Morphine and naloxone's effects on sexual behavior of the female golden hamster. *Pharmacol Biochem Behavior* 11:673-681, 1979.

180. Ambinder RF, Schuster MM: Endorphins: New gut peptides with a familar face. *Gastroenterology* 77:1132-1140, 1979.

181. Ipp E, Dobbs R, Unger RH: Morphine and β-endorphin influence the secretion of the endocrine pancreas. *Nature* 276:190-191, 1978.

182. Kanter R, Fujimoto W, Ensinck J: Opiates modulate insulin and glucagon secretion. *Diabetes* 28:395, abstract 202, 1979.

183. Ipp E, Rubinstein AH: Opioid peptides and stress hyperglycemia. *Lancet* 2:1083, 1980.

184. Konturek SJ, Tasler J, Cieszkowski M, Jaworek J, Coy DH, Schally AV: Inhibition of pancreatic secretion by enkephalin and morphine in dogs. *Gastroenterology* 1978: 74:851-855, 1978.

185. Boda RC, Cotui FW, Benaglia AE: Studies on the mechanism of morphine hyperglycemia. *J Phar Sxp Ther* 61:48-57, 1937.

186. Feldberg W, Shaligram SV: The hyperglycaemic effect of morphine. *Brit J Pharmacol* 46:606-618, 1972.

187. Moore KE, McCarthy LE, Borison HL: Blood-glucose and brain catecholamine level in the cat following the injection of morphine into the cerebrospinal fluid. *J Pharmacol Exp Ther* 148:169-175, 1965.

188. Reed JL, Ghodse AH: Oral glucose tolerance and hormonal response in heroin-dependent males. *Br Med J* 2:582-585, 1973.

OPIOIDS AND PSYCHOLOGICAL DISORDERS

Karl Verebey, PhD

ABSTRACT. Recent evidence suggests that small peptides are intimately involved in both normal and abnormal behavior. The endogenous opioids have been shown to have similar pharmacological properties as narcotic drugs. The ability of these exogenous agents to alter mood and relieve anxiety is well known. This paper reviews the clinical psychopharmacology of exogenous opioid agonists and antagonists, developing the hypothesis that the level of functional endorphins may be related to maintenance of psychological homeostasis. The role that may be played by endogenous opioids in psychological disorders, as well as the potential benefit of narcotic drugs in treatment of refractory psychotic states, is considered.

Introduction

Separate investigations, one directed toward the elucidation of the mechanism of opioid drug action and the other toward identifying the biochemical basis of mental illness, seemed to arrive at similar conclusions: that small peptides are intimately involved in both normal and abnormal behavior. The endogenous opioid peptides produce the same pharmacological responses in animals as the exogenous opiates which are analgesia, catatonia, locomotor hyperactivity, and others.[1-6] Some of the behavioral effects of narcotic analgesics in normal human subjects are fear and anxiety relief, relaxation, "coasting," and euphoria.[7] In the literature there are also numerous studies in which opioids were administered to human subjects having psychotic or neurotic symptoms. In many of these reports behavioral improvement was noted and the therapeutic value of opioids in maintaining an improved psychological state recognized.[8-25]

Consequently, special attention will be paid to the psychotropic effects of opioids. If endorphin deficiency or excess is indeed responsible for certain psychiatric or addictive disorders, the therapeutic value of exogenous opioids or opiate antagonists may need to be explored.

Finally, the combination of the experimental observations on endorphins

---

Dr. Verebey is Director of Clinical Pharmacology, Division of Substance Abuse Services, Testing and Research Laboratory, State of New York and Associate Professor of Clinical Psychiatry, State University of New York - Downstate Medical Center, 80 Hanson Place, Brooklyn, NY 11217. The author expresses his thanks to Dr. Rhea Dornbush for her comments and suggestions and to Mrs. Elizabeth McLeod for the typing of the manuscript.

Advances in Alcohol & Substance Abuse, Vol. 1(1), Fall 1981

and clinical reports on exogenous opiates suggests a relationship between opiate and alcohol addictions and certain psychological disorders, implying a common underlying biological deficit related to the endorphin system. These observations, hypothesis, and related issues will be reviewed and evaluated.

Opiates, Pain, and Analgesia

The most important use of morphine and its congeners in clinical medicine is for analgesia. Narcotic analgesics (opiates) are the only class of drugs which can effectively attenuate severe intractable physical pain. Although hundreds of opioid compounds were synthesized in the past 50 years, morphine remains the standard to which all other narcotic analgesics are compared. The precise mechanisms of morphine's analgesic activity is not known, but it is thought that it is mainly effective by exerting a calming, soothing, and fear-relieving effect. Thus patients treated with morphine or other opiates state that their pain is still felt, but they do not care about it; it does not bother them. The opiates' direct interference with the pain source is insignificant, if any, and reduction of neurotransmission through the sensory afferent pain pathway accounts for only a fraction of their analgesic effects. Consequently, the most potent pain relievers known to mankind are efficacious in relieving intractable physical pain by their control of the emotional components of pain.[7]

The fact that some psychotic episodes are emotionally painful events is recognized by most medical professionals. Strangely, however, the simple association was seldom recognized that if the mechamism of opiate action in alleviating physical pain is achieved mainly through the control of pain components such as fear, anxiety, and rage, then there is a good chance that opiates would also be effective in psychotic episodes in which paranoia, anxiety, and rage are common components. In books of psychopharmacology, lists of drugs which are known neuroleptics, however, do not include opiates. The omission of opiates is an oversight, or opiates are not effective in the treatment of psychosis, or there is no solid information on this topic. Some answers to these possibilities may be uncovered in the literature.

Opiate Receptors and Endorphins in the Brain

The dense distribution of opiate receptors, as well as endorphins in the limbic system, provided anatomical evidence for the possibility that opiates may effect emotional responses.[26,27] Although opiate receptors are found all over the peripheral nervous system and other organs as well, they are exceptionally highly concentrated in the limbic structures of the brain which control emotional responses. Specifically, the amygdala and the hypothalamus are related to fear and punishment responses; the interception of the septal nuclei triggers aggression and rage; and the pre-optic region of the thalamus is associated with pleasureful experiences, reward, and feelings of well-being.[26] These last reponses are known opiate effects and possibly stimulation of the pre-optic region of the thalamus results in the euphorigenic feelings reported after opiate administration.[28]

The endorphins have been shown experimentally to possess most of the pharmacological effects of exogenous opiate agonists such as morphine, meperidine, heroin, methadone, etc.[1-6] The similarity of endorphins and opiates is helpful in elucidating the physiological and psychological roles of endorphins because a rich background research literature is available on the psychopharmacology of opiate agonists.

History of Opiate Use

Historical accounts of opiate use for therapeutic purposes as well as behavior modification are rich.[29] In Homer's *Odyssey* a passage presents evidence of the psychotropic effects of the substance used, presumably an opiate, "Now Helen, the daughter of Zeus, turned her thoughts elsewhere. Straightway, she cast into the wine of which they drank, a drug which quenches pain and strife and brings forgetfulness to every ill."[30] In 1680 Sydenham wrote about opium: "Among the remedies which it has pleased almighty God to give to man to relieve his sufferings, none is so universal and so efficacious as opium."[7] The historical records indicate that the uses of opioids were very diverse, including the suppression of cough, sedative euphorient for social and ceremonial events, and for the relief of physical pain and anxiety of various etiology.[29,30] As described by Kraepelin,[31] Weygandt,[32] and Abse,[33] opiate extracts were widely used especially in Germany and England during the 19th and the beginning of the 20th century for the treatment of depression. The literature is not very clear about the therapeutic effects of opium tincture in such patients but the dosage regimen is well described.[32] Today, with advances in pharmacology, it becomes clear that because morphine absorption is very poor from the gut,[7] the amount absorbed after oral administration was very little. Individual variation in bioavailability of opiates may be the reason why the treatment was more successful in some individuals than in others.

Opioid Interaction with Addiction and Mental Illness

Opiates may have prophylactic and therapeutic effects on mental illness based on clinical observations in addicts, ex-addicts, and subjects who are dependent on opioids only intermittently. Most case studies describing the psychotropic effects of opiates are uncontrolled observations. But the large number of similar observations collectively should provide more convincing evidence suggesting a serious evaluation of exogenous opioids in the treatment of various psychiatric conditions.

After the introduction of methadone for the maintenance treatment of heroin addicts,[34] large numbers of subjects were treated with methadone and substantial numbers of addicts appeared to have had prior psychological problems.[35] McKenna described the significant psychotropic effects of methadone in emotionally disturbed patients.[9] Three representative case studies were described with different psychological problems including mania, depressive psychosis, agitated depression, and paranoid schizophrenia. He states that for these subjects methadone was a "primary psychotropic agent to interrupt their psychotic symptoms." The three subjects all experienced periods of intense anxiety, depression, self-doubt and subsequently found symptomatic relief with an opiate. Methadone provided for them a sense of self-esteem previously lacking and also gave them a new energy or zest for life which allowed them to pursue relationships without their previous handicaps of fear, doubt, and imminent failure. Each subject made repeated attempts to become drug free but they became psychotic during or shortly after these attempts and returned to opiate use to abolish or attenuate their psychotic disturbances. "None of these patients took opiates for the attainment of a high. They were not victims of peer pressure for their addiction, but were actively seeking any substance to relieve their painful psychological problems. They were specific in their drug of choice and were not deterred by threats of criminal prosecution."[9]

Several investigators working with methadone maintenance programs recognized methadone as a "bonafide antipsychotic drug." Wurmser described a subject who resumed his studies and lived an orderly life while taking methadone regularly.[8] Since drug-free living was the long-term goal of most methadone maintenance programs, detoxification was usually encouraged. In addicts with underlying psychoses, these attempts were disastrous. One such subject, after detoxifying, described unbearable inner tension and suicidal feelings. He promptly recompensated after he took methadone again, and the violent rage disappeared within a day. He stated: "Methadone has kept me from a show down with myself. When I stop methadone, I cannot put up with any frustration and I cannot get enjoyment out of anything. Methadone shields me, methadone is a house of warmth; when I step out of it I see how miserable everything is." This patient without an opiate was overwhelmed by his intense feelings of loneliness, disillusionment, emptiness, and rage.[8] As Khantzian points out, methadone helps to restore a psychological homeostasis and controls aggression and antisocial behavior.[11]

In the opinion of Resnick et al,[36,37] Khantzian,[12] Wurmser,[8] and McKenna,[9] significant numbers of addicts use opiates to relieve their psychological problems rather than for purely hedonistic purposes. Khantzian recognized the effectiveness of opiates in relieving dysphoric states of mind and controlling anxiety, rage, and aggression. The psychopharmacological action of methadone is conceptualized by its stabilizing, antiaggression effects. While providing stabilization, it counteracts the disorganizing influences of rage and aggression and thereby reverses regressed states and makes a healthier adaptation possible.[22] Methadone maintenance patients showed less liability to angry projections and possessed a greater capacity for sustained constructive behavior. In general, a shift is observed from liability to stability and from egocentricity to concerned interest in others.[11] Wurmser, after observing a large number of opiate addicts, concluded that the symptoms of rage, vengefulness, shame, paranoia, hurt, and rejection were reduced as soon as they were on methadone. In a few of them, the symptoms disappeared altogether; in others they occasionally surfaced but much less severely.[8] He also observed as Khantzian[11] and Gold et al[38] that withdrawal of certain patients from methadone leads to psychosis and reinduction to methadone resulted in rapid recompensation. Khantzian and Wurmser both viewed "craving" in some addicts as not only a sign of physical dependence but more importantly a desire for relief from threatening and dysphoric feelings associated with unmitigated aggression.[8,11]

Why these observations were not recognized for their therapeutic significance can only be speculative at this time. The patients were treated for heroin addiction rather than for underlying psychological problems. The few investigators who properly identified the orally effective, long-acting opiates as potential antipsychotic agents also realized the current socio-political and medico-legal problems. Without the needed scientific rationale for the use of opiates in psychiatric patients, there was little hope for gaining the Institutional Review Board's approval for further research in this area.

Resnick et al as early as 1970 recognized that addicts are a heterogeneous group.[36] Through a questionnaire, they rated individuals based on the importance opiates played in their lives. Many of their patients viewed heroin use as an effective measure in reducing anger, tension, and disappointments and increasing their ability to work, study, to relate to others, and to express themselves. Resnick suggests that this group of subjects may fit the Dole and Nyswander[34] paradigm in which opiate dependence was related to a state of metabolic deficiency (endorphin deficiency?). For this group of patients, methadone substitution for heroin or other perenteral opiate preparations may provide the pharmacotherapy necessary for a more stabilized, normal functioning. Methadone maintenance subjects belonging to this group may be identified by the result of their efforts of detoxification from methadone. When the doses reach 10 to 15 mg, some subjects have no significant problems, while the above-mentioned group will experience acute psychotic episodes. This can be promptly reversed by the administration of 30 to 40 mg of methadone.[8] Goldstein has shown that complete detoxification of many addicts is possible when a long-term, gradual dose reduction schedule is followed.[39] Subjects who are unable to detoxify even on the slow reduction schedule probably belong to the group labeled as having a biological deficit or "metabolic deficiency." Methadone patients who are successful in a slow detoxification schedule belong to another group. These subjects use heroin for their social interactions, while the drug has no major role in improving their daily functioning. These subjects may fit Wikler's description, which stipulates opiate addiction as a result of conditioning by environmental stimuli.[40] These subjects can live opiate free without major psychological problems after slow, gradual detoxification from methadone. But if they are told at one point that they are not receiving active drug anymore, they immediately show signs of acute withdrawal. The major difference between the groups is that the "metabolic deficiency" group becomes psychotic when the doses of methadone are reduced below 10 to 15 mg while the other group does not. An excellent example of the group which can be easily detoxified are the heroin-using Vietnam veterans described by Robins.[41] Soldiers, while under stress in the combat zone, used heroin to help cope with the horrible conditions in Vietnam. However, after the stress was removed by their return to the U.S., most stopped using heroin. Less than 1% of the addicted veterans continued the use of heroin. These data would support the notion that while a healthy endorphin system is functional in such individuals, they would not become permanently dependent on opioids. But is also points out that when the environmental stress is high and opiates are available, opiate use is likely to become popular.

Still another group of subjects is described by Powell, called the "chipers."[42] They are a very elusive group to study because they use opiates only intermittently and do not take on the stereotypic addict life-style. Because of the pattern of their opiate use, they do not develop tolerance or physical dependence, and their habits goes undetected. This group uses opiates as self-medication of various psychological problems, but somehow they are able to control the dose and the frequency of their opiate use so that only a few of their intimate friends are aware of it. Although this group of subjects does depend psychologically on opiates, they are able to conform to the social mores by holding responsible jobs and by having socially acceptable personal lives. The "chipers" existence negates the myth that everyone is liable to become addicted to opiates after trying heroin or morphine. This idea was further denounced by Pittel: "dependence is most likely to occur among individuals who lack the psychological resources needed to deal with inner conflicts and/or environmental frustrations. The opiates are desired by such individuals to compensate for the absence of inner structure."[43] Although it is provocative, a suggestion may be reasonable that a functional endorphin system is necessary for what Pittel calls "an inner structure."

The personalities of addicts and speculation over the reasons for their dependence on opiates were also hypothesized. Wikler writes that former heroin addicts in general are noncompetitive individuals who prefer to handle their anxieties of pain, sexuality, and aggression by avoiding situations which provoke them. Opiate addiction often begins in adolescence and is related to the intensity of conflicts in the area of sexuality and assumption of aggressive masculine roles. The almost instantaneous relief for such emotional suffering serves to heighten the addicts' esteem for opiates.[44] Not only opiate abuse but also alcohol abuse, schizophrenia, and affective disorders often being during the mid or late adolescent years. There is a possibility that during these neuroendocrinologically explosive years, some juveniles develop a temporary deficiency of endorphins which results in the particular psychopathology. If this can be substantiated, temporary exogenous opiate treatment may abridge the deficiency period and perhaps prevent the concomitant development of life-long psychosis or substance abuse.[45]

The fact that opiates provoke aggressive, assaultive behavior is more of a myth than reality. Nyswander describes that the choice of drug reveals what makes the user feel at his best. The narcotic addict is more comfortable when his hostility and aggresive feelings are blunted as with opiates. The significance of the opiate is to make the addict feel completely at peace with himself and the world. He has succeeded in killing two birds with one stone; in his passivity he experiences the feelings of satisfaction that usually come to an aggressor.[46]

Paradoxically, opiates seem to offer alternative treatment in various psychiatric disorders yet due to their socio-political status, use or even testing of opiate efficacy in mental illness is severely restricted. Jaffe writes that in the United States the use of medically prescribed opiate analgesics for pain relief or treatment of gastrointestinal disorders is quite proper; however, the self-administration or prescription of the same drugs in the same dosages for the relief of depression or tension is considered flagrant abuse. For example, when the alternative to the use of opiates is the compulsive use of alcohol, an overt psychosis, or severe depression, the use of opiates can be more helpful than destructive. The opiates seem to suppress anxiety, anger, and aggression, thus permitting the users of opiates to make passive adaptation to their inner tensions.[47]

Even though the antipsychotic effects of opiates were observed by many investigators, in most methadone maintenance programs an effort has been made to exclude patients with mental illness. Despite this general policy, Salzman et al admitted patients exclusively with psychiatric history.[48] In general, the disturbed patients seemed to benefit from the methadone maintenance program indicated by the fact that 50% of the patients were able to hold jobs compared to only 10% before methadone. Weissman believes that in certain individuals, treatment with methadone should be lifelong. The use of methadone dampens physiologically some of the unchanneled tension, and individuals can gradually learn new and more efficient ways of binding tension in a socially acceptable fashion. Methadone serves the tension-reducing role previously played by the subject's acting out behavior.[49] On a similar note, Winkelstein proposed that in some cases of opiate dependence it is useless to attempt further psychiatric treatment to achieve abstinence. One such patient almost killed his father in a rage. He then took opiates to avoid acting out his overt aggressive behavior. Another case is of a paranoid schizophrenic who, by using opiates, has made a reasonably good work adjustment. He is isolated in a file room and does excellent work. He received several promotions with increase in salary, but he needs his daily dose of opiates.[50] These subjects indefinitely require maintenance doses of methadone to keep them in some state of stability.

Evaluation of six years of records of a drug-abusing population provided evidence for the prophylactic effects of opiates against the development of psychiatric illness.[51] McLellan et al reported that at the beginning of the study, the psychiatric examinations showed low symptom levels in various drug-abusing groups. By the end of six years a large percentage of stimulant and depressant users had serious psychoses and depression while the opiate users showed no deterioration from their control values. These investigators also recognized the specific psychopharmacological effects of opiates. Their clinical impression was that opiates may function to medicate underlying psychological problems by reducing the symptoms of anxiety, depression, and paranoia.[51]

Levinson in 1971 proposed outright the use of methadone for the treatment of schizophrenic patients. He stressed that the organizing and antianxiety effects of methadone should help psychotic patients in mental institutions become functional. He believes that methadone maintenance should provide a much more humane and effective control of psychotic symptoms than some of the currently used neuroleptics in controlling rage, paranoia, and anxiety. Thus, methadone would likely improve the physical and mental conditions of many institutionalized patients.[52]

The Effects of Methadone on Suicidal Tendency

At present there is no reliable drug for the treatment of suicidal ideation. For this reason the observation of Litman is important. While working in a California-based suicide control agency, he observed that methadone was very effective in the control of suicidal tendency. When detoxification from methadone was attempted, suicidal ideation returned. The author concluded that "depressive suicidal components are often present in drug addicts and that, indeed, narcotics are used as self-medication to prevent depressive pain and as an alternative to suicide."[23] Fredrick's report on both the depression scale and the assessment of morbid attitudes reveals fewer expressions of anxiety, resentment, and depression for methadone users compared to other addicts (abstinent or on heroin). However, the greatest difference was in the expectation of violent death, where the percentage of subjects on methadone was less than half of those abstaining from methadone treatment. The author finds that methadone may be helpful in bringing about a happier and better adjusted attitude by decreasing the level of depression and attitudes towards violence, aggression, and morbidity.[53] A more recent case study by Berken et al described a 19-year-old woman with psychotic rage and a compulsion toward self-mutilation and suicidal attempts among other serious psychopathology.[54] Conventional, medically accepted psychopharmacological agents were ineffective in controlling her symptoms. As a last resort the investigators obtained permission from the FDA to use methadone in this patient. The authors describe that "the 'normalizing' effect of methadone proved more satisfactory for this patient than any other treatment she had received." These investigators, similarly as others in this section, made their observations at a methadone maintenance clinic. They noticed that addicts with histories of crimes of rage, current aggressive rage, or repressed rage who received methadone could recognize the onset of rage and could verbalize their needs rather than acting out in violence.[54]

Similarities and Differences Between Opioid Agonists and Antipsychotic Agents

Is there any biological correlation between opioids and neuroleptic agents which would justify the observed antipsychotic actions of opioids? Some of the biochemical and neurophysiological data on opiates and currently used neuroleptics indicate considerable similarity of actions between the two classes of drugs. There are several theories depicting dopamine accumulation as a possible cause of schizophrenia.[55-57] Hartman described schizophrenia as a single deficit condition and a multiplicity of causes or aggravating factors. The single basic deficit is vulnerability to stress, described as a constant pressure which can be conceptualized as unneutralized psychic energy. For some relatively healthy individuals it takes a major stressful event to precipitate a psychotic episode while others are on the brink of psychosis chronically.[55] The author suggests that increased levels of dopamine produces the build-up of what he calls "unneutralized psychic energy." Hartman described a self-experiment in which he administered to himself a precourser of dopamine (dopa) and fusaric acid, an inhibitor of the enzyme dopamine β-hydroxylase, which is necessary for the conversion of dopamine to norepinephrine. This combination theoretically would increase the levels of dopamine in the brain. The temporary psychosis created by these chemicals was described by the author.[55]

Fitting this theory, the mechanism of antipsychotic action of various neuroleptics, such as chlorpromazine and haloperidol, is dopamine receptor blockade.[58,59] This action was also demonstrated for morphine and methadone.[60-62]

Haloperidol and morphine are equally effective in blocking morphine withdrawal body shakes in rats while increasing the spontaneous electrical activity in the nigro striatal nerve endings.[63-68] Neuroleptic drugs directly compete with dopamine for the post synaptic dopamine receptor, by inhibiting the actions of dopamine on dopamine-sensitive adenylate cyclase[58,59] while opiates do not inhibit this enzyme.[60,61] However, the similarity of the behavioral and neurochemical responses of opiates and neuroleptics suggests a common final pathway in their mechanisms of action in various brain regions. Another biochemical correlation is that both neuroleptics and methadone are able to increase the levels of serum prolactin,[69] possibly by acting through the hypothalamic-adrenergic system. In fact, prolactin release is an accepted test for screening by the pharmaceutical industry for potential antipsychotic agents.

Electroencephalographic (EEG) studies of Fink[70] and Martin et al[71] in human subjects evaluated the changes in electrical activity of the brain after the administration of neuroleptics and methadone. Although the methods of EEG evaluations were somewhat different in the two studies, the electrical changes were quite similar after phenothiazines and methadone. Further comparison of the two classes of drugs will be continued when their pharmacology, side effects, and toxicity are compared in the next section.

The Therapeutic Possibilities for Opioids and Their Antagonists in Mental Disease

The potential involvement of the endorphin system in mental disease was promptly hypothesized by several investigators. Their differences in approach were mainly on whether an excess or a deficiency of endorphins is responsbile for the observed pathophysiology of psychosis.

In order to evaluate the possible use of narcotic antagonists in mental disease it is helpful to review the psychopharmacology of these agents.

Mixed narcotic agonist-antagonists such as cyclazocine and nalorphine have been shown to have agonists activity[72,73] as well as dysphoria and psychotomimetic effects.[74] Naloxone and naltrexone have been generally considered to be relatively pure antagonists, but some agonist-like physiological effects were described by Martin et al and Verebey et al after naltrexone administration in ex-addicts: a decrease in respiratory rate, body temperature, and pupillary constriction.[74,75] Jones et al administered 20 mg naloxone intravenously in volunteers who have never been addicted. This also caused some effects: tremors, EEG changes, increase in body temperature, and changes in mood. Those changes showed considerable interindividual variability, but naloxone had clearly different effects than placebo in this double-blind experiment. Many of the effects were those observed during mild withdrawal syndromes in addicts.[76] Buchsbaum et al have observed an increased sensitivity to pain (in pain-sensitive normal subjects) after 2 mg of naloxone administered intravenously. Pain-insensitive subjects reported the opposite effect after the same dose. Similar group differences were observed in somatosensory-evoked potentials using the same subjects.[77] Naltrexone produced minor changes in ex-addicts: an increase in attention and perception and some dysphoria. Naltrexone was shown to be extremely safe in acute and chronic treatments, an important consideration for use in chronic psychiatric conditions.[75]

The usual tests for pharmacological activity of narcotic antagonists involved the reversal of opiate agonist-induced effects or the evocation of abstinence signs in opiate-dependent subjects.[78] The ability of the antagonists to act on the naturally occurring endorphins has been suggested but not proved by the results of experiments involving analgesia in several species. Analgesia can be produced by focal electrical brain stimulation in rats.[79,80] and in man.[81,82] It can also be elicited by stress (footshock) in rats.[83] Brief transcutaneous stimulation[84] and acupuncture[85,86] elicit analgesia in man. In most of these experiments, analgesia was to some extent antagonized by naloxone. However, in other experiments, naloxone was less effective[87] or ineffective[88] in antagonizing the analgesia induced by electrical stimulation in the mesencephalic gray matter in rats.

The Use of Narcotic Antagonists to Counteract Endorphin Excess

Terenius et al discovered increased CSF levels of endorphins in chronic psychotic patients; these levels decreased after successful treatment with neuroleptics.[89] Therefore, the logical therapeutic measure implicated by these observations was the administration of a narcotic antagonists. Naloxone (0.4 mg i.m.) was administered to six chronic schizophrenic patients. Four patients reported a dramatic reduction of hallucinations for several hours after naloxone.[90] Attempts of replication and extension of similar studies using naloxone to treat schizophrenic patients yielded negative results.[91-93] Various alterations in experimental design were implemented because of questions about the size of the doses, patient selection, and even the drugs used. A recent review by Volavka describes in detail all of the past and recent clinical findings on the narcotic antagonists naloxone and naltrexone in schizophrenia, mania, and depression.[94] In essence his findings were that low doses of naloxone (up to 6.0 mg) had no effect on mania, schizophrenia, and depression whereas doses of 10 to 20 mg yielded some promising results in occasional patients. Small doses of 0.4 to 1.2 mg naloxone are effective in reversing serious opiate overdose-related respiratory depression, indicating high

potency and specificity of naloxone in displacing opioids from the opiate
receptors. The fact that in mental illness 20 to 50 times more naloxone is
necessary for a limited success than its normal narcotic antagonistic dose
indicates another mechanism than effecting the opiate receptor.

The Use of Opioid Agonists for the Supplementation of Endorphin Deficiency

In contradistinction to the endorphin excess theory, Jacquet and Marks
suggested that endorphin deficiency may result in some mental disease.[3]
Their suggestion was based on the apparent similarity between the extrapyramidal rigidity seen in patients taking neuroleptic drugs and the rigidity
elicited in rats by β-endorphin. Along with the extrapyramidal side effects
the neuroleptics are effective antipsychotic agents. Thus they suggested that
β-endorphin may have similar pharmacological effects as the neuroleptics.
Testing this hypothesis Kline et al injected 6 to 10 mg of β-endorphin to a
total of 15 patients with various psychiatric diagnoses, including schizophrenia, depression, personality disorders, and mental deficiency.[95,96] Some of the
patients became more talkative and less anxious followed by a period of
sedation. Improvement of depressive and schizophrenic symptoms was apparent after these injections of β-endorphin. Several subsequent studies were
undertaken by other investigators using β-endorphin and their synthetic
analogues in mental diseases instituting several changes in the experimental
conditions. Berger et al studied the effects of β-endorphin in nine chronic
schizophrenic patients using a double blind cross-over design. A 20 mg
injection of β-endorphin produced beneficial EEG changes by increasing
alpha waves and also by releasing prolactin similarly as other opiate agonists. Consequently the treatment showed a statistically significant improvement of the patients' symptoms but these benefits were not apparent clinically.[97] Gerner et al investigated the effects of β-endorphins in both schizophrenic and depressed patients. Temporary but significant improvement was
seen in the depressed patients, but there was no significant change in the
schizophrenic patients. In fact, six of the eight schizophrenic subjects had
worse symptoms than before β-endorphin.[98]

The results of other studies are discussed in a recent review by Olson et al.[99]
The most interesting data emerged from the studies utilizing some of the
synthetic endorphin analogues, destyrosine-γ-endorphin (DTγE) and FK-
33-824, a potent analogue of Met-enkephalin. Verhoven et al administered
DTγE to schizophrenic patients and found improvement in all six patients.[100]
This study, however, was not double blind, but their second study was.
Using 8 patients, 1 mg of DTγE was injected daily for eight days. After four
days, in most patients the psychotic symptoms were greatly reduced.[101] Two
studies were conducted with the potent met-enkephalin analogue FK-33-824.
Krebs and Roubicek reported short-term improvement in the patients' psy-

chotic symptoms[102] as did Nedapil and Ruther.[103] The comparative evaluation of these studies is difficult because of the differences in patient selection
and the variations in psychiatric evaluation by the different groups. Also, the
clinical trials involving endorphins and their synthetic analogues are hin-
dered by lack of availability and the very high cost of these substances.
Nevertheless, there is considerable promise in these preliminary results to
warrant further studies.

β-endorphin, although the naturally occurring substance in brain, may not
be the optimal substance for therapeutic use. The effectiveness of β-endorphin
in treating mental disease would suffer from the same difficulty as would the
short-acting narcotic agonists such as heroin and morphine: they would have
to be administered systematically at short intervals. And since β-endorphin is
a peptide, it would be rapidly degraded by various peptidases, limiting the
bioavailability of the active molecules in the circulatory system and at their
sites of action. If opioid agonists and/or antagonists prove to be useful
therapeutically in mental disease, the longeracting, orally effective methadone
and 1-α-acetylmethadol and the long-acting narcotic antagonist, naltrexone,
provide more suitable characteristics for chronic treatment.

There are indications in the literature that there may be a multiplicity of
opiate receptors,[104-106] this further complicates the therapeutic approach using opiates in mental disease. The main questions are: which receptor is
involved in a particular psychopathology and is there any drug or synthetic
peptide which has more selectivity for that particular receptor?

However, the principal pharmacology of endorphins is quite similar to
that produced by exogenous opiates. If the endorphins are therapeutically
effective in any disease, it seems reasonable to anticipate that the exogenous
opiates may be effective as well. Animal literature[1,6,107] clearly indicates that
endorphins produce tolerance and physical dependence. Thus, these substances will have addiction liability and reduced effects of the same doses
(tolerance) in clinical use as well. At present, very little information is available on the safety and toxicity of endorphins. However, there is an abundant
literature on exogenous opiates, eg, morphine and methadone, which may be
utilized until more specific information on the endorphin becomes available.

Effects of Chronic Opiate Use: Safety and Toxicity

Addiction liability is the major safety problem of long-term opiate treatment. It is interesting to note that apparently no addiction resulted from the
old opiate treatments of depression.[31,32] An authoritative textbook describing the therapeutic use of opium in affective disorders flatly states that:
"there is no danger of addiction." But the textbook does not specify whether
the possibility of drug-seeking behavior in these patients has ever been specifically explored.[108] However, we may perhaps assume that it presented no

major problem to the clinician in those days. Wikler's schizophrenic patients treated with morphine have developed physical dependence reflected by the withdrawal syndrome when the treatment was stopped. However, none of their three patients exhibited any interest in morphine at any time during or after the study.[109] Thus, it may be suggested that psychotic patients can develop physical dependence on opiates without taking on the life-style of street addicts. Similar observations were made in "normal" individuals treated for pain. When opiates are used for medical reasons, the chances of developing drug-seeking behavior are very slight.[43,110,111]

The gross fluctuations in performance normally associated with the single dose of short-acting narcotics such as heroin were eliminated by maintenance on methadone.[112,113] Measurements using the Eysenck Personality Inventory showed that subjects undergoing methadone maintenance therapy were not more anxious or unable to cope with stress than a group of apparent normals.[114] Some opiate users stated that methadone did not impair function, but in fact improved their ability to do useful work. Observations made under experimental conditions showed that as long as adequate amounts of opiates were available to the subjects, their aggressive and antisocial behavior was practically eliminated, personal hygiene was maintained, and assigned responsibilities were discharged satisfactorily.[25] Psychological tests of performance revealed little or no impairment, and the sensorium remained clear, while anxiety was reduced.[25,115]

Good health and productive work are compatible with dependence on opiates. Addicts receiving high daily oral doses of methadone carried out their daily tasks and held responsible positions. Nyswander stated that opiate addicts were not unusual in appearance when maintained at the proper dose of opiates. Their retention and recall of simple mathematics and conceptual thinking were intact, with no evidence of mental deterioration.[46] A study of Gearing and Schweitzer of 17,500 methadone maintenance patients found increased social productivity and decreased antisocial behavior among patients in methadone maintenance treatment vs before treatment.[116] Cutting described a physician who was functioning well both physically and mentally after 62 years of addiction.[117] Thus, moderate morphine use does not necessarily interfere with regular activities during a normal life span.

Although clinical experience suggests that chronic intake of controlled amounts of opiates is not necessarily detrimental to the general health, there are some undesirable side effects of chronic opiate consumption. The most common symptoms and signs in patients receiving high maintenance doses of methadone are sweating, constipation, minor sleep disorders, decreased testosterone levels, decreased libido and fertility, and abnormal menses.[118-122] Tolerance develops to many of these effects during the repeated intake of methadone.[121]

In comparison with the existing antipsychotic drugs, opiates have a number of clinical advantages and disadvantages. Opiate overdose is very dangerous; however, it is easier to treat than an overdose of tricyclic antidepressants or phenothiazines, since specific narcotic antagonists are available for the treatment. Withdrawal syndrome following the discontinuation of opiates is certainly much more unpleasant than that occurring after stopping neuroleptics. However, the recent introduction of clonidine seems to eliminate the unpleasant symptoms of withdrawal,[123] and the effects of chronic opiate treatment subside at some point after the treatment is stopped. This is not true of neuroleptics; tardive dyskinesia is irreversible in many cases. Recent research indicates that tardive dyskinesia may be associated with significantly mortality.[124] Thus, the dangers of opiates should be weighed against the serious toxic effects of currently used psychoactive drugs.[125,126] Treating nonaddicts with opiates will raise ethical problems. The medical profession as well as the public have shown increasing acceptance of opiates as analgesics for patients with cancer as well as for the treatment of other diseases.[127] It is perhaps possible to view some psychoses as mentally painful psychological states, in a sense similar to painful physical states, that require an analgesic.

In addition to the heuristic value of therapuetic studies using opiates, there is an obvious and practical need for more effective treatment of mental disease. Special subjects for initial trials of opiates would include therapy-resistant schizoprenics, particularly those showing aggressive behavior, taking advantage of the potent antiaggression effects of opiates.[54] Another group would be patients showing first signs of tardive dyskinesia, who cannot discontinue neuroleptic therapy without serious deterioration of psychiatric symptoms. Such patients could be effectively managed with methadone, especially because chronic methadone use in humans does not result in extrapyramidal side effects. Another group of prospective patients are psychotic depressives who are considered for electroconvulsive treatment, but who cannot receive it for medical or other reasons. For these latter patients, it would seem useful, safe, and interesting to replicate the old "opium cure" using low doses of methadone instead of the opium tincture.

Theoretical Models of the Endorphin System

The relationship between opioids and psychosis has been suggested explicitly or implicitly by a large number of investigators.[2,3,12,22,36,89,128,129] Other researchers have formulated hypotheses about the endorphins in addictions[45,130–132] and in the mechanisms of pleasure and reward systems.[45,129,133] These three issues will be discussed separately.

Psychological Homeostasis

Verebey et al suggested that one of the physiological roles of endorphins is the preservation of "psychological homeostasis."[75] This is based on the quasi-equivalency of endorphins with opiate agonists[1-6] and on the opioids' psychopharmacological effects, which are the promotion of stress tolerance, tranquilization, and fear relief among others. A crude but descriptive term for the role of endorphins would be "brain shock absorbers." Following stressful stimuli, the autonomic response is usually a sympathetic discharge which is likely to result in dopamine and norepinephrine hyperactivity in the limbic system of the brain. This would possibly trigger signs and symptoms of psychoses. However, in "normal" individuals simultaneously with the sympathetic discharge, a stress-induced release of endorphins[134] would promptly antagonize dopamine and would also produce inhibitory modulation to most stimulant neuronal activities.

Recent evidence by Pickar et al indicates that a rise and fall of endorphin levels is a possible mechanism of manic-depressive psychosis.[135] Plasma levels of endorphins were high when the patient exhibited mania. This was followed by some decrease in endorphin plasma levels, paralleled by a mixed psychological state and further decrease in endorphin levels leading to a motorically retarded depression. The same patient at a later date while in the manic state had increased opioid activity in her plasma again. This mechanism stipulates that certain levels of endorphins are needed for a psychological equilibrium and that appropriate adjustment of these levels may be therapeutically effective at least in manic-depressive illness.

Apparent endorphin deficiency can result by various mechanisms. Deficiency may be realized by slow biosynthesis or too rapid enzymatic deactivation of endorphins. Or if the endorphins are present in sufficient amounts in brain storage, then the release mechanisms may be defective or the receptors may be nonfunctional. The concomitant endorphin deficiency symptoms would include the low pain threshold, anxiety, supersensitivity to stress, rage, aggression, depression, paranoia, suicidal ideation, and low self-esteem. In fact, these are some of the symptoms seen in various psychiatric disorders. By simple logic the treatment approach would be three-pronged. The healthiest would be the reactivation of the endorphin system by stimulation of production, facilitation of release, or inhibiting enzymatic decay of endorphins. The second approach would be the supplementation of long-acting synthetic endorphins, and the third route which is available immediately and with which we have a great deal of experience is the use of long-acting, orally effective opiate agonists. Supplementation of endorphins or opiates would not be effective, however, if the problem lies with the receptors.

Finally another more complex possibility is that the endorphin system is only one of the behaviorally active peptide systems in the CNS and that all of the peptide systems plus the well-known neurotransmitter systems interact to produce the integrated responses manifested as normal or abnormal behavior.

The Possible Link Between Opiate and Alcohol Dependence

The effects of alcohol have been often compared to those of opiates, especially because both substances cause analgesia, euphoria, tranquilization[136,137] as well as similar neurochemical and physiological effects.[138] Wikler et al reported that a 60 ml dose of 95% ethanol in human subjects raises the pain threshold approximately 35% to 40% while not altering other sensory perceptions.[139] Euphorigenic activity might be the principal property of ethanol causing dependence liability. The euphoria is a "high" manifested by a diminution of anxiety resulting in a positively reinforcing, relaxed, and physically active state. The paradoxical question has long been debated: Is alcohol a stimulant or depressant? Alcohol is not a stimulant according to a respected textbook of pharmacology, but like other general anesthetics, it is a primary and continuous depressant of the CNS.[137] The mechanisms of action for the stimulating effect of alcohol are explained through a depressant mechanism. The theory is that the activity of certain inhibitory centers in the CNS are depressed by low doses of alcohol and that this inhibition results in a "false sense" of stimulation. This simple explanation, although logical and possibly partially true, has certain shortcomings. First it presumes that there is greater sensitivity of inhibitory neurons to alcohol than that of other neurons. Second, it is not clear how the inhibition of the inhibitory centers cause—in addition to stimulation—euphoria, analgesia, and antianxiety effects. It would be easier to understand the euphorigenic effects of alcohol if alcohol could be shown to release endogenous, opiate-like substances thus providing the known opiate pharmacological effects, ie, analgesia, euphoria, and anxiety relief.[136] Perhaps the stimulatory effects of alcohol could be viewed as a counteraction of the anxiety-related immobilization seen in stressed or depressed individuals.

Some interesting and provocative reports are supportive of both the direct and indirect interactions between alcohol and endorphins at the opiate receptors. Lorens and Sainati present evidence for the ability of naloxone to block the excitatory effects of ethanol in the rat.[140] Naloxone injected one hour after ethanol administration immediately reversed the excitatory effects of ethanol. The authors suggest the possibility that ethanol releases endogenous opioids which act at the opiate receptors and enhance locomotor activity similarly as seen after the administration of an opiate agonist or after direct electrical stimulation of lateral hypothalamic centers. The implication of the study is that endorphin release might underlie the positive reinforcing properties of ethanol.[140] If the hypothesis is tenable, opiate antagonists (naloxone or naltrexone) should be able to block alcohol-induced analgesic, euphoria, and catatonia and possibly improve alcoholic stupor by displacing endorphins from opiate receptor sites. A preliminary report provided encouraging results. Schenk et al[141] selected four subjects who were severely intoxicated with alcohol; their blood alcohol levels ranged from 1.5 to 3.2 mg %. Following the administration of naloxone at various doses from 4 to 28 mg intravenously, the authors observed that nearly unconscious alcoholic subjects spontaneously awoke and were able to talk and perform fairly well on motor tests and coordination tasks. In addition, the previously unresponsive corneal reflex could be stimulated. Changes in an objective measure, blood gas analysis, were also striking after naloxone injection. It showed a marked incease in pO_2 levels 15 minutes after naloxone from 58 to 104 mm Hg while the pCO_2 levels dropped from 61 to 48 mm Hg. It is interesting to note that in another study β-endorphin was shown to produce respiratory depression in dogs, and this effect was also promptly reversible by naloxone administration as manifested by pO_2 increase and pCO_2 decrease.[142] Jeffcoate et al was able to prevent the impairment of psychomotor performance in human volunteers induced by alcohol when they injected 0.4 mg naloxone i.v. before alcohol administration.[143] The performance scores measured by the "four choice serial reaction-time test" were the same after baseline measurements and after naloxone plus alcohol administration. The authors explain the role of naloxone as possibly being blockers of endogenous opioids which are released by alcohol.

Using psychometric testing, another interesting hypothesis has been presented by Senter et al.[144] These authors found that euphoria experienced by alcoholics, induced by the consumption of large amounts of alcohol, is far greater than that experienced by social drinkers. The authors suggest that the sustaining of drinking behavior in alcoholics might arise from the intense alcohol-induced euphoria, providing the positive reinforcing effects. This hypothesis is an alternative to the theory that alcohol dependence is due to the tension reduction of alcohol as a negative reinforcement. Based on opiate pharmacology, both theories may be partly correct. However, it would be interesting to know whether or not the higher euphoria observed in Senter's work would be paralleled by higher levels of endorphins in the plasma of alcoholics.

The general implication of these research data is that if narcotic antagonists can block certain alcohol-related effects, there is a likelihood for a common mechanism of action by alcohol and opiates. Although alcohol dependence and opiate dependence appear different superficially, the primary reinforcing effects in both may be related to their ability to stimulate directly or indirectly the opiate receptors in the brain.

Satisfaction, Reward, and Euphoria May Be Mediated
Through the Opiate Receptors

Byck as early as 1976 recognized the possibility that endogenous opioids might be responsible for the autonomic regulation of analgesia, sleep, euphoria, and respiration.[129] Furthermore, he points out that anhedonia, or the inability to feel happy, is a common characteristic of psychosis, depression, and anxiety. The first is the lack of endorphin at opiate receptors. Secondly, ample endorphins are present in the brain, but the opiate receptors are not functioning properly. Administration of opioids or endorphins in the second case would not improve the sense of well-being or any other condition resulting from receptor dysfunction. Byck further postulated that substances which increase binding of agonists at the opiate receptor will cause euphoria while decreased binding of agonists or increased binding of antagonists may result in dysphoria. Sodium is known to increase antagonist binding and decrease agonist binding. Lithium acts similarly to sodium, and it is known to be effective in manic depressive illness, possibly by decreasing agonist binding.[129] For these reasons, sufficient quantities of endorphins at the receptor are only one requirement. The sodium ion content of the interstitial fluid is another factor influencing preferential binding of the opiate receptors which finally determine the particular mood.

Stein and Belluzzi tested in an animal model whether release of enkephalins or possibly release of catecholamines is responsible for the activation of the "reward" receptors in the brain.[133] Their animal data clearly implicate enkephalin as the "natural euphorigen or reward transmitter." N_2O or nitrous oxide is an analgesic-anesthetic gas. It is well-known that this substance causes euphoria, thus the common name for the drug "laughing gas." Berkowitz et al reported that naloxone was able to eliminate the N_2O-related analgesia in mice.[145] This indicates that nitrous oxide may also act through the endogenous opioid system.

What are the social implications of the discovery of natural substances and receptors which may regulate the sense of well-being? If pleasure states are induced naturally via the endorphins, then how can society condemn the self-medicators of exogenous euphorigens when they turn to external sources? This question is especially poignant when an opiate is used to compensate a genetically deficient or functionally dormant endorphin system. The uncritical, hedonistic, and self-destructive abuse of drugs should still be seriously discouraged; however, drug use should not be restricted if it means psychological stabilization and functional rehabilitation. In this respect, current drug laws are inadequate because no recognition is given to possible biological need and/or drug-related benefits. Further elucidation of the role of opioid peptides in human behavior will perhaps unravel some of the mysteries of euphoria, reward, and satisfaction. Such scientific advances may lead to rational medical, legal, and social approaches by eliminating substance abuse and providing free access for the beneficial use of opiates in therapeutic medicine and psychiatry.

Conclusion

This review brings into focus the fact that opiates are not entirely foreign molecules to the human organism based on the similar pharmacology of the naturally occurring brain peptides and the exogenous opioids. This indicates that normal human subjects are constantly under the influence of morphine-like substances. An acceptance of these facts may liberate opiates from the prevailing social stigma and legal attitudes which identify them entirely with addiction. Further research on endorphins may elucidate their precise role in behavior, thus their excess or deficiency states may be properly treated.

The clinically observed antipsychotic effects of opiates seem very reasonable based on the anatomical distribution of opiate receptors and endorphins and on the biochemical and neurophysiological similarity between the effects of opiates and neuroleptic drugs. The clinical observations, although stimulating, also exposed many important questions for future research to answer. The anecdotal clinical evidence seems to imply the effectiveness of opiates in many diverse psychopathological states. It would be necessary to identify the diagnostic category of responding conditions. Since tolerance is an important characteristic of opioids, it would be important to determine how it will effect their use in chronic treatment? Furthermore, the above data will help to determine the therapeutic regimen and dosage forms.

The timeliness of this research is exemplified by the numerous recent reports on the problems of tardive dyskinesia in patients chronically treated with antipsychotic drugs. These patients would be left without any medication after the discontinuation of antipsychotic agents. Effective psychoactive drugs without extrapyramidal side effects are needed. The orally effective long lasting opiate agonists might be excellent candidates for this purpose.

REFERENCES

1. Loh HH, Tseng LF, Wei E, et al: Beta-endorphin is a potent analgesic agent. *Proc Natl Acad Aci USA* 73:2895-2898, 1976.
2. Bloom F, Segal D, Ling N, et al: Endorphins: Profound behavioral effects in rats suggest new etiological fractions in mental illness. *Science* 194:630-632, 1976.
3. Jacquet YF, Marks N: The C-fragment of β-lipotropin: An endogenous neuroleptic or antipsychotogen. *Science* 194:632-635, 1976.
4. Graf L, Szekely JI, Ronai, AZ, et al: Comparative study on analgesic effect of met⁵-enkephalin and related liptropin fragments. *Nature* 263:240-242, 1976.
5. Plotnikoff NP, Kastin AJ, Coy DH, et al: Neuropharmacological actions of enkephalins after systemic administration. *Life Sci* 19:1283-1288, 1976.
6. Wei E, Loh H: Physical dependence on opiate-like peptides. *Science* 193:1262-1263, 1976.
7. Jaffee JH, Martin WR: Narcotic analgesics and antagonists, in Gilman AG, Goodman LS, Gilman A (eds): *The Pharmacological Basis of Therapeutics*, ed 6. New York, Macmillan Co, 1980, pp 494-502.
8. Wurmser L: Methadone and the craving for narcotics: Observations of patients on methadone maintenance in psychotherapy. *Natl Conf Methadone Treat Proc* 4:525-528, 1972.
9. McKenna GJ: The use of methadone as a psychotropic agent. *Natl Conf Methadone Treat Proc* 5:1317-1324, 1973.
10. Blake DA, Distasio C: A comparison of level of anxiety, depression and hostility with methadone plasma concentration in opioid-dependent patients receiving methadone on a maintenance dosage schedule. *Natl Conf Methadone Treat Proc* 5:1308-1316, 1973.

11. Khantzian EJ: A preliminary dynamic formation of the psychopharmacologic action of methadone. *Natl Conf Methadone Treat Proc* 4:371-374, 1972.

12. Khantzian EJ, Mack JE, Schatzberg EF: Heroin use as an attempt to cope: Clinical observations. *Am J Psychiatry* 131:160-164, 1974.

13. Wellisch DK, Gay GR, Wesson DR, et al: The psychotic heroin addict. *J Psychedelic Drugs* 4:46-49, 1971.

14. Wellisch DK, Gay GR: The walking wounded: Emergency psychiatric intervention in a heroin addict population. *Drug Forum* 1:137-144, 1972.

15. Maxman JS, Sliberfarb PM, Plakun E: Pentazocine abuse and problems of withdrawal. *Brit J Psychiat* 126:370-1371, 1975.

16. Waddell KJ, Smith RK, Stewart GT: Changes in MMPI scores of black heroin addicts maintained on methadone. *Natl Conf Methadone Treat Proc* 4:435-438, 1972.

17. Gay GR, Winkler JJ, Newmeyer JA: Emerging trends to heroin abuse in the San Francisco Bay area. *J Psychedelic Drugs* 4:53-55, 1971.

18. Wikler A: A psychodynamic study of a patient during experimental self-regulated re-addiction to morphine. *Psychiatr Q* 26:270-292, 1952.

19. Gay GR, Way EL: Some pharmacological perspectives on the opiate narcotics with special consideration of heroin. *J Psychedelic Drugs* 4:31-39, 1971.

20. Dimijian GC: Contemporary drug abuse, in Goth A (ed): *Medical Pharmacology*. St. Louis, CV Mosby Co, 1976, pp 299-303.

21. Chappel JN: Methadone and chemotherapy in drug addiction. *JAMA* 228:725-728, 1974.

22. Khantzian EJ: Opiate addiction: A critique of theory and some implications for treatment. *Am J Psychother* 28:59-70, 1974.

23. Litman RE, Shaffer M, Peck ML: Suicidal behavior and methadone treatment. *Natl Conf Methadone Treat Proc* 4:482-485, 1972.

24. Comfort A: Morphine as antipsychotic drug. *Lancet* 1:95, 1977.

25. Wikler A, Rasor RW: Psychiatric aspect of drug addiction. *Am J Med* 14:566-570, 1953.

26. Simon EJ, Hiller JM, Edelman I: Stereospecific binding of the potent narcotic analgesic (3H) etorphine to rat-brain homogenate. *Proc Natl Acad Sci USA* 70:1947-1949, 1973.

27. Smith TW, Hughes J, Kosterlitz HW, et al: Enkephalin: Isolation, distribution and function, in Kosterlitz, HW (ed): *Opiates and Endogenous Opioid Peptides*. Amsterdam, North-Holland Publishing Co, 1976, pp 57-62.

28. Pert CB, Snyder SH: Opiate receptors: Demonstration in nervous tissue. *Science* 179:1011-1044, 1973.

29. Kurland AA: Historical notes, in Mule SJ (ed): *Psychiatric Aspects of Opiate Dependence*. West Palm Beach, Fla, CRC Press, 1978, pp 1-38.

30. Gay GR, Way EL: Some pharmacological perspectives on the opiate narcotics with special consideration of heroin. *J Psychedelic Drugs* 4:31-39, 1971.

31. Kraepelin E: *Die Psychiatrische Klinik*. Leipzig, East Germany, Barth, 1905, p 11.

32. Weygandt W: *Lehrbuch der Nerven- und Geistes-Krankheiten*. Halle, West Germany, Marhold Verlagsbuchhandlung, 1935, p 507.

33. Abse DW, Dahlstrom WG: The value of chemotherapy in senile mental disturbances. *JAMA* 174:2036-2042, 1969.

34. Dole VP, Nyswander M: A medical treatment for diacetylmorphine (heroin) addiction. *JAMA* 193:646-650, 1965.

35. Kleber HD, Gold MS: Use of psychotropic drugs in treatment of methadone maintained narcotic addicts. *NY Acad Sci* 311:81-98, 1978.

36. Resnick RB, Fink M, Freedman AM: A cyclazocine typology in opiate dependence. *Amer J Psychiat* 126:1256-1260, 1970.

37. Resnick RB, Schuyten-Resnick E, Washton A: Narcotic antagonists in the treatment of opioid dependence: Review and commentary. *Comprehensive Psychiat* 20:116-125, 1979.

38. Gold MA, Pottach ALC, Sweeney DR, Kleber HD, Redmond DE: Rapid opiate detoxification: Clinical evidence of antidepressant and antipanic effects of opiates. *Am J Psychiatry* 136:982-983, 1979.

39. Goldstein A: *Pharmacological basis of methadone treatment*. Proceedings of the Fourth National Conference on Methadone treatment, San Francisco, 1972. National Association for Prevention of Addiction of Narcotics, New York, 1972, p 27.

40. Wikler A: Conditioning factors in opiate addiction and relapse, in Wilner DM, Kessenbaum GG (eds): *Narcotics*, New York, McGraw-Hill Book Co, 1965.

41. Robins L: *The Vietnam drug user returns: Final report, Sept. 1973*. Special Action Office Monograph, ser A, no 2, Washington, DC, US Government Printing Office, 1974.

42. Powell DH: A pilot study of occasional heroin users. *Arch of Gen Psychiat* 28:586-594, 1973.

43. Pittel SM: Psychological aspects of heroin and other drug dependence. *J Psychedelic Drugs* 4:40-45, 1971.

44. Wikler A, Rasor RW: Psychiatric aspects of drug addiction. *A J Med* 14:566-570, 1953.

45. Verebey K, Blum K: Alcohol euphoria: Possible mediation via endorphinergic mechanisms. *J Psychedelic Drugs* 11:305-311, 1979.

46. Nyswander M: *The Drug Addict as a Patient*. New York, Grune & Stratton Inc, 1956, pp 57-82.

47. Jaffe JH: Drug addiction and drug abuse, in Goodman LA, Gilman A (eds): *The Pharmacological Basis of Therapeutics*. New York, Macmillan Co, 1970.

48. Salzman B, Frosch WA: Methadone maintenance for the psychiatrically disturbed. *Natl Conf Methadone Treat Proc* 4:117-118, 1972.

49. Weissman A: The significance of diagnosis in the treatment of narcotic addicts. *International J Addict* 5:717-730, 1970.

50. Dole VP, Nyswander M: Methadone maintenance and its implication for theories of narcotic addiction. *Trans Assoc Amer Physicians* 79:122-136, 1966.

50. Winkelstein C: Psychotherapy of a borderline schizophrenic with heroin addiction. *J Hillside Hosp* 5:78-90, 1956.

51. McLellan TA, Woody GE, O'Brien CP: Development of psychiatric illness in drug abusers. *New Engl J Med* 310:1310-1314, 1979.

52. Levinson P: Addiction induction - Will it be tested? *Perspect Biol Med* 14:671-674, 1971.

53. Fredrick CJ, Resnick HLP, Wittlin BJ: Self-destructive aspects of hard core addiction. *Arch Gen Psychiat* 28:579-585, 1973.

54. Berken GH, Stone MM, Stone SK: Methadone in schizophrenic rage: A case study. *Am J Psychiatry* 135:248-249, 1978.

55. Hartman H: Schizophrenia: A theory. *Psychopharmacology* 49:1-15, 1976.

56. Snyder SH, Taylor JJ, Coyle JL, Myerhoff JL: The role of brain dopamine in behavioral regulation and the action of psychotropic drugs. *Amer J Psychiat* 127:199-207, 1970.

57. Snyder SH, Banerjee SP, Yamamura HJ, Greenberg D: Drugs, neurotransmitters and schizophrenia *Science* 184:1243-1253, 1974.

58. Kebabian JW, Petzold GJ, Greengard P: Dopamine-sensitive adenylate cyclase in caudate nucleus of rat brain, and its similarity to the "dopamine receptor." *Proc Natl Acad Sci USA* 69:2145-2149, 1972.

59. Clement-Cormier YD, Kebabian JW, Petzold GL, et al: Dopamine-sensitivity adenylate cyclase in mammalian brain: A possible site of action of antipsychotic drugs. *Proc Natl Acad Sci USA* 71:1113-1117, 1974.

60. Iwatsubo K, Clouet DH: Dopamine-sensitive adenylate cyclase of the caudate nucleus of rats treated with morphine or haloperidol. *Biochem Pharmacol* 24:1499-1503, 1975.

61. Carenzi A, Guidotti A, Revuelta A, et al: Molecular mechanisms in the actions of morphine and viminol. (R2) on rat striatum. *Pharmacol Exp Ther* 194:311-318, 1975.

62. Sasame HA, Perez-Cruet J: Evidence that methadone blocks dopamine receptors in the brain. *J Neurochem* 19:1953-1957, 1972.

63. Lal H, Numan R: Blockade of morphine withdrawal body shakes by haloperidol. *Life Sci* 18:163-168. 1976.
64. Bunney BS, Walters JR, Roth RH, et al: Dopaminergic neurons: Effect of antipsychotic drugs and amphetamine on single cell activity. *J Pharmacol Exp* 185:560-571, 1973.
65. Iwatsubo K, Clouet DH: Effect of morphine and haloperidol on the electrical activity of rat nigrostriatal neurons. *J Pharmacol Exp Ther* 202:429-436, 1977.
66. Ahtee L: Catalepsy and stereotypes behavior in rats treated chronically with methadone: Relation to brain homovanillic acid content. *J Pharm Pharmacol* 25:649-651, 1973.
67. Clouet DH, Ratner M: Catecholamine biosynthesis in brains of rats treated with morphine. *Science* 168:854-856, 1970.
68. Gauchy C, Agid Y, Glowinski J: Acute effects of morphine on dopamine synthesis and release and tyrosine metabolism in the rat striatum. *Eur J Pharmacol* 22:311-319, 1973.
69. Gold MS. Donabedian RK. Dillard M, et al: Antipsychotic effect of opiate agonists. *Lancet* 2:398-399, 1977.
70. Fink M: *EEG in Clinical Psychiatry*. New York, John Wiley & Sons, 1953, pp 331-353.
71. Martin WR, Jasinski DR, Haeztzen CA, Kay DS, Jones BE, Mansky PA, Carpenter RW: Methadone - A re-evaluation. *Arch Gen Psychiat* 288:286-290, 1973.
72. Haertzen CA: Subjective effects of narcotic antagonists, in Braude MC, Harris LS, May EL (eds): *Narcotic Antagonists*. New York, Raven Press, 1973, pp 383-398.
73. Martin WR, Gorodetsky CS: Demonstration of tolerance to and physical dependence on N-allylnor morphine (nalorphine). *J Pharmacol Exp Ther* 150:437-442, 1965.
74. Martin WR, Jasinski DR. Mansky PA: Naltrexone, an antagonist for the treatment of heroin dependence. *Arch Gen Psychiatry* 28:784-791, 1973.
75. Verebey K, Volavka J, Clouet D: Endorphins in psychiatry: An overview and a hypothesis. *Arch Gen Psychiatry* 35:877-888, 1978.
76. Jones R: Naloxone-induced mood and physiologic changes in normal volunteers, in Usdin E, Bunney WE Jr (eds): *Endorphins in Mental Illness*. London, Macmillan Press, 1978.
77. Buchsbaum MS. Davis GC. Bunney WE: Naloxone alters pain perception and somatosensory evoked potentials in normal subjects. *Nature* 270:620-622, 1977.
78. Gorodetsky CW: Assays of antagonist activity of narcotic antagonist in man, in Braude MC, Harris LS, May EL, et al (eds): *Narcotic Antagonists*. New York, Raven Press, 1974, pp 291-297.
79. Mayer DJ, Hayes RL: Stimulation-reduced analgesia: Development of tolerance and cross-tolerance to morphine. *Science* 188:941-943, 1975.
80. Akil H, Mayer DJ, Liebeskind JC: Antagonism of stimulation-produced analgesia by naloxone, a narcotic antagonist. *Science* 191:961-962, 1976.
81. Hosobuchi Y, Adams JE. Linchitz, R: Pain relief by electrical stimulation of the central gray matter in humans and its reversal by naloxone. *Science* 183-186, 1977.
82. Richardson DE, Akil A: Pain reduction by electrical brain stimulation in man. I. Acute administration in periaqueductal and periventricular sites. II. Chronic self-administration in the periventricular gray matter. *J Neurosurg* 47:178-194, 1977.
83. Akil H, Madden J, Patrick RL, et al: Stress-induced increase in endogenous opiate peptides: Concurrent analgesia and its partial reversal by naloxone, in Kosterlitz HW (ed): *Opioids and Endogenous Opioid Peptides*. Amsterdam, North-Holland Publishing Co, 1976, pp 63-70.
84. Melzack R: Prolonged relief of pain by brief, intense transcutaneous somatic stimulation. *Pain* 1:357-373, 1975.
85. Pomeranz B, Chiu D: Naloxone blockade fo acupuncture analgesia: Endorphine implicated. *Life Sci* 19:1757-1762, 1976.
86. Mayer DJ, Price DD, Rafi A: Antagonism of acupuncture analgesia in man by the narcotic antagonist naloxone. *Brain Res* 121:368-372, 1977.
87. Pert A, Walter M: Comparison between naloxone reversal of morphine and electrical stimulation induced analgesia in the art mesencephalon. *Life Sci* 19:1023-1032, 1976.
88. Yaksh TL, Yeung JC, Rudy TA: An inability to antagonize with naloxone the elevated nociceptive thresholds resulting from electrical stimulation of the mesencephalic central gray. *Life Sci* 18:1193-1198, 1976.
89. Terenius L, Wahlstrom A, Agren H: Naloxone (Narcan) treatment in depression: Clinical observations and effects of CSF endorphins and monoamine metabolites. *Psychopharmacology* 54:31-33, 1977.
90. Gunne LM, Lindstrom L, Terenius L: Naloxone-induced reversal of schizophrenic hallucinations. *J Neural Transm* 40:13-19, 1977.
91. Volavka J, Mallva A, Baing S, et al: Naloxone in chronic schizophrenia. *Science* 196:1227-1228, 1977.
92. Davis GC, Bunney WE, DeFraites EG, et al: Intravenous naloxone administration in schizophrenia and affective illness. *Science* 197:74-77, 1977.
93. Janowsky DS, Segal DS, Bloom F, et al: Lack of effect of naloxone on schizophrenic symptoms. *Am J Psychiatry* 134:926-927, 1977.
94. Volavka J: Naloxone and naltrexone in psychoses, in Emrich HM (ed): *Modern Problems of Pharmacopsychiatry, The role of endorphins in neuropsychiatry*. Basel, Karger Publishing Company, 1981.
95. Kline NS, Li CH, Lemann HE, et al: β-Endorphin-induced changes in schizophrenic and depressed patients. *Arch Gen Psychiatry* 34:111-113, 1977.
96. Kline NS, Lehmann HE: Studies of β-endorphin in psychiatric patients, in Usdin E, Bunney WE Jr (eds): *Endorphins in Mental Illness*. London, Macmillan Press, 1978.
97. Berger PA, Watson SJ, Akil H, Elliott GR, Rubin RT, Pfefferbaum A, Davis KL, Barchas JD, Li CH: β-Endorphin and schizophrenia. *Arch Gen Psychiat* 37:635-640, 1980.
98. Gerner RH, Catlin DH, Gorelick DA, Lui KK, Li CH: β-Endorphin: Intravenous infusion causes behavior change in psychiatric in patients. *Arch Gen Psychiat* 37:642-647, 1980.
99. Olson RD, Kastin AJ, Olson GA, Coy DH: Behavioral effects after systemic injection of opiate peptides. *Psychoneuroendocrinology* 5:47-52, 1980.
100. Verhoven WM, van Praag HM, Botter PA, Sunier A, van Ree JM, DeWied D: [des-tyr r] a endorphin in schizophrenia. *Lancet* 8072:1046-1047, 1978.
101. Verhoven WM, van Praag HM, van Ree JM, DeWied D: Improvement of schizophrenic patients treated with (des-tyr)-gamma-endorphin (DT gamma E). *Arch Gen Psychiat* 36:294-298, 1979.
102. Krebs E, Roubicek J: EEG and clinical profile of synthetic analogue of methionine-enkephalin-FK-33-824. *Pharmacopsychiatry* 12:86-93, 1979.
103. Nedapil N, Ruther E: Effects of the synthetic analogue of methionine enkephalin FK-33-824 on psychotic symptoms. *Pharmacopsychiatry* 12:277-280, 1979.
104. Martin WR: Opioid antagonists. *Pharmacol Rev* 19:463-521, 1967.
105. Martin WR, Eades CG, Thompson JA, et al: The effect of morphine and nalorphine like drugs in the non-dependent and morphine dependent chronic spinal dog. *J Pharmacol Exp Ther* 197:517-523, 1976.
106. Lord JAH, Waterfield AA, Hughes J, et al: Endogenous opioid peptides: Multiple agonists and receptors. *Nature* 267:495-499, 1977.
107. Pert A: Behavioral pharmacology of D-alanine-methionine-enkephalin amide and other long-acting opiate peptides, in Kosterlitz HW (ed): *Opiate and Endogenous Opioid Peptides*. Amsterdam, North-Holland Publishing Co, 1976, pp 87-94.
108. Mayer-Gross W, Slater E, Roth M: *Clinical Psychiatry*. London, Cassell & Co Ltd, 1960, p 223.
109. Wikler A, Pescor MJ, Kalbaugh EP, et al: Effects of frontal lobotomy on the morphine-abstinence syndrome in man. *Arch Neurol Psychiatry* 67:510-521, 1952.

110. Jaffe JH: Opiate dependence and the use of narcotics for the relief of pain. *Mod Treat* 5:1121-1135, 1968.
111. Beecher HK: *The Measurement of Subjective Responses: Quantitative Effects of Drugs.* New York, Oxford University Press, 1959.
112. Rothenberg S, Schottenfeld S, Meyer RE, et al: Performance differences between addicts and non-addicts. *Psychopharmacology* 52:299-306, 1977.
113. Gordon NB, Appel PW: Performance effectiveness in relation to methadone maintenance. *Natl Conf Methadone Treat Proc* 4:425-427, 1972.
114. Gasser ES, Langrod J, Valdes K, et al: The Eysenck Personality Inventory with methadone maintenance patients. *Br J Addict* 69:85-55, 1974.
115. Grevert P, Masover B, Goldstein A: Failure of methadone and levomethadyl acetate (levo-alpha-acetylmethadol, LAAM) maintenance to affect memory. *Arch Gen Psychiatry* 34:849-853, 1977.
116. Gearing FR, Schweitzer MD: An epidemiologic evaluation of long-term methadone maintenance treatment of heroin addiction. *Am J Edidemiol* 100:101-112, 1974.
117. Cutting WC: Morphine addiction for 62 years. *Stanford Med Bull* 1:39-41, 1942.
118. Cicero TJ, Bell RD, Wiest WG, et al: Function of the male sex organs in heroin and methadone users. *N Engl J Med* 292:882-887, 1975.
119. Kay DC: Human sleep and EEG through a cycle of methadone dependence. *Electroencephalogr Clin Neurophysiol* 38:35-39, 1975.
120. Yaffe J, Strelinger RW, Parwatikar S: Physical symptom complaints of patients on methadone maintenance. *Natl Conf Methadone Treat Proc* 5:507-522, 1973.
121. Kreek MJ: Medical safety and side effects of methadone in tolerant individuals. *JAMA* 223:665-668, 1973.
122. Leen NJ, Senay EC, Renault PF, et al: Neurological assessment of patients on prolonged methadone maintenance. *Drug Alcohol Dependence* 1:305-311, 1976.
123. Gold MS, Pottash AC, Sweeney DR, Kleber HD: Opiate withdrawal using Clonidine. *JAMA* 243:343-346, 1980.
124. Mehta D, Mallya A, Volavka J: Mortality of patients with tardive dyskinesia. *Am J Psychiatry* 135:371-372, 1978.
125. Leestma JE, Koenig KL: Sudden death and phenothiazines a current controversy. *Arch Gen Psychiatry* 18:137-148, 1968.
126. Davis JM, Casper R: Antipsychotic drugs: Clinical pharmacology and therapeutic use. *Drugs* 14:260-282, 1977.
127. Holden C: New look at heroin could spur better medical use of narcotics. *Science* 198:807-809, 1977.
128. Herz A: Recent developments in opiate research and their implications for psychiatry. *Arch Psychiatr Nervenkr* 221:183-197, 1976.
129. Byck R: Peptide transmitters: A unifying hypothesis for euphoria, respiration, sleep and the action of lithium. *Lancet* 2:72-73, 1976.
130. Snyder SH: Opiate receptor in normal and drug altered brain function. *Nature* 257:185-189, 1975.
131. Hughes J: Enkephalin and drug dependence. *Br J Addict* 71:199-209, 1976.
132. Goldstein A: Opioid peptides endorphins in pituitary and brain. *Science* 193:1081-1086, 1976.
133. Stein L, Belluzzi JD: Brain endorphins and the sense of well-being: A psychobiological hypothesis, in Costa E, Trabucchi M (eds): *Advances in Biochemical Psychopharmacology*, vol 18. New York, Raven Presss, 1978, pp 299-311.
134. Teschemacher H, Breidenbach T, Konig A, Luckhardt M: Plasma levels of β-endorphin and β-lipotropin in humans under stress. In *Abstracts Third Congress of the Hungarian Pharmacological Society*, Budapest, Aug. 1979.
135. Pickar D, Cutler NR, Naber D, Post RM, Pert CB, Bunney WE: Plasma opioid activity in manic-depressive illness. *Lancet* ii:937, 1980.
136. Jaffe JH, Martin WR: Narcotic analgesics and antagonists, in Goodman LS, Gilman A (eds): *The Pharmacological Basis of Therapeutics.* New York, Macmillan Co, 1975.
137. Richie MJ: The aliphatic alcohols, in Goodman, LA, Gilman A (eds): *The Pharmacological Basis of Therapeutics.* New York, Macmillan Co, 1975.
138. Blum K, Hamilton ML, Wallace JE: Alcohol and opiates: A review of common neurochemical and behavioral mechanisms, in Blum K (ed): *Alcohol and Opiates*, 1977.
139. Wikler A, Goodell H, Wolff HG: Studies on pain: The effects of analgesic agents on sensations other than pain. *Journal of Pharmacology and Experimental Therapeutics* 83:294-299, 1945.
140. Lorens SA, Sainati SM: Naloxone blocks the excitatory effects of ethanol and chlordiazepoxide on lateral hypothalamic self-stimulation behavior. *Life Sci* 23:1359-1364, 1978.
141. Schenk GK, Enders P, Engelmier MP, Ewert T, Herdemerten S, Kohler KH, Lodenmann E, Matz D, Pach J: Application of the morphine antagonist naloxone in psychiatric disorders. *Arzneimittel-Forschung Drug Research* 28:1274-1277, 1978.
142. Moss IR, Friedman E: β-endorphin. Effects on respiratory regulation. *Life Sci* 23:1271-1276, 1978.
143. Jeffcoate WJ, Herbert M, Cullen MH, Hastings AG, Walder CP: Prevention of effects of alcohol intoxication by naloxone. *Lancet* Dec. 1, 1979, pp 1157-1159.
144. Senter RJ, Heintzelman M, Dorfmeuller M, Hinkle H. A comparative look at ratings of the subjective effects of beverage alcohol. *The Psychological Record* 29:49-56, 1979.
145. Berkowitz BA. Finck AD, Ngai H: Nitrous oxide analgesia: Reversal by naloxone and development of tolerance. *J Pharmacol Exp Ther* 203:539-547, 1977.

SELECTIVE GUIDE TO CURRENT REFERENCE SOURCES ON TOPICS DISCUSSED IN THIS ISSUE

Jane S. Port
Dorothy R. Hill
Doris Jaeger
Harriet Meiss
Merril Schindler

Each issue of *Advances in Alcohol and Substance Abuse* will feature a section offering suggestions on where to look for further information on that issue's theme. Our intent is to guide readers to sources which will provide substantial information on the specific theme presented, rather than on the entire field of alcohol and substance abuse. We aim to be selective, not comprehensive, and in most cases we shall emphasize current rather than retrospective material.

Some reference sources utilize designated terminology (controlled vocabularies) which must be used to find material on topics of interest. For these we shall indicate a sample of available search terms so that the reader can assess the suitability of sources for his/her purposes. Other reference tools use key words or free text terms (generally from the title of the document, agency, or meeting listed). In searching the latter, the user should look under all synonyms for the concept in question.

Readers are encouraged to consult with their librarians for further assistance before undertaking research on a topic.

Suggestions regarding the content and organization of this section will be welcomed.

1a. INDEXING AND ABSTRACTING SOURCES—Publisher, start date, and frequency of publication are noted.

The authors are affiliated with the Gustave L. & Janet W. Levy Library, The Mount Sinai Medical Center of New York, One Gustave L. Levy Place, New York, NY 10029.

Biological Abstracts. Philadelphia, PA, BioSciences Information Service, 1926– , semimonthly.

 See: Keyword subject index.

Chemical Abstracts. Columbus, OH, American Chemical Society, 1907– , weekly.

 See: Pharmacodynamics, Hormone pharmacology, Biochemical interactions, and Toxicology sections in biochemistry issues, published on alternate weeks.

 See: Keyword subject indexes.

Excerpta Medica. Section 40—Drug Dependence. Amsterdam, Netherlands, Excerpta Medica, 1972– , monthly.

 See: Brain metabolism—endogenous opiate-like peptides section.

 See: Beta endorphin, drug abuse, drug dependence, opiate, opiate receptor in index.

Index Medicus, (including Bibliography of Medical Reviews). Bethesda, MD, National Library of Medicine, 1960– , monthly.

 See: *MeSH* terms, such as: drug abuse, drug dependence, endorphins, narcotics, narcotic dependence, receptors, endorphin, substance abuse, substance withdrawal syndrome, and subheadings such as antagonists and inhibitors, pharmacodynamics, toxicity.

Index to Scientific Reviews. Philadelphia, Institute for Scientific Information, 1974– , semiannual.

 See: Permuterm keyword subject index.

 See: Citation index. (references from the items indexed)

Psychological Abstracts. Arlington, VA, American Psychological Assn, 1927– , monthly.

 See: Physiological intervention—drug stimulation, Psychopharmacology sections.

Science Citation Index. Philadelphia, Institute for Scientific Information, 1961– , bimonthly.

 See: Permuterm keyword subject index.

 See: Citation index. (references from the items indexed)

1b. ON-LINE BIBLIOGRAPHIC DATA BASES—Examples of search entry points are noted for selected data bases. Consult a librarian for search formulation.

BIOSIS—BioSciences Information Service (includes *Biological Abstracts* citations).

 Use: classification numbers for neuropharmacology, pharmacological toxicology, physiology, and biochemistry of the nervous system, drug metabolism, clinical pharmacology—studies in humans, addiction, neuroendocrinology.

 Use: keywords.

CHEM SEARCH (includes Chemical Abstracts citations).
>   Use: keywords.
CONFERENCE PAPERS INDEX.
>   Use: keywords.
EXCERPTA MEDICA.
>   Use: Excerpta Medica (MALIMET) descriptors and keywords.
MEDLARS—Medical Literature Analysis and Retrieval System (includes *Index Medicus* citations).
>   Use: *MeSH* terms noted in section "1a" of this review under *Index Medicus.*
National Institute for Mental Health Data Base.
>   Use: alcohol biochemistry and metabolism, drug neuroendocrinology, psychopharmacology headings.
>   Use: keywords.
SCI SEARCH (includes *Science Citation* Index citations).
>   Use: keywords from titles.
>   Use: citations to existing literature. (references from the items indexed)
SSIE Current Research—Smithsonian Science Information Exchange.
>   Use: SSIE subject descriptors.

2. BOOKS.

Current Catalog. Bethesda, MD, National Library of Medicine, annual.
>   See: *MeSH* terms noted in section "1a" of this review under *Index Medicus.*
Medical Books and Serials in Print 1980: An index to literature in the health sciences. New York, R.R. Bowker Co, 1980, annual.
>   See: Drug abuse, drug metabolism, neuropsychopharmacology, opium habit, others in subject index.

3. US GOVERNMENT PUBLICATIONS.

Monthly Catalog of United States Government Publications, Washington, DC, US Government Printing Office, monthly.
>   See: Following agencies—Alcohol, Drug Abuse and Mental Health Administration, National Institute on Drug Abuse, National Institute on Alcohol Abuse and Alcoholism.
>   See: keyword title index.

4. HANDBOOKS, DIRECTORIES, GRANT SOURCES, ETC.

Akey, DS, ed. *Encyclopedia of Associations,* 15th ed, Detroit, Gale Research Co, 1980, 3 vols.
>   See: keyword subject index under drug and pharmacology terms.
Annual Register of Grant Support, 14th ed, Chicago, Marquis Academic Media/Marquis Who's Who, Inc, © 1980.

See: Medicine, Pharmacology sections. Example of agencies listed: National Institute on Drug Abuse, Division of Research, 5600 Fishers Lane, Rockville, MD 20857; National Institute on Alcohol Abuse and Alcoholism, 5600 Fishers Lane, Rockville, MD 20857.

Research Awards Index. U.S. National Institutes of Health. Division of Research Grants, annual.

See: Drug abuse, drugs, neuropharmacology, neurotransmitters, pharmacology, and many other headings in index volume.

5. JOURNAL LISTINGS AND SELECTED JOURNAL TITLES.

Ulrichs International Periodicals Directory, 19th ed, 1980, New York, R.R. Bowker Co, annual.

See: Drug abuse and alcoholism, biology—biological chemistry, pharmacy, and pharmacology in subject index. Selected journal titles: *American Journal of Psychiatry, Brain Research, Drug and Alcohol Dependence, European Journal of Pharmacology, Psychopharmacology Bulletin* (Note: each issue contains a recurring bibliography to papers on psychopharmacology), *Substance and Alcohol Actions/Misuse.*

6. AUDIOVISUAL PROGRAMS.

National Library of Medicine Audiovisuals Catalog. Bethesda, MD, National Library of Medicine 1979–   , annual.

See: Drug abuse and drug dependence headings.

The Videolog: Programs for the Health Sciences 1979. New York, Esselte Video, Inc, 1979.

See: Drug abuse and drug dependence in subject index.

7. GUIDES TO UPCOMING MEETINGS.

Scientific Meetings. San Diego, Scientific Meetings Publications. Quarterly.

See: Subject indexes, association listing.

World Meetings. Medicine. New York, Macmillan Publishing Co, Inc, quarterly.

See: keyword subject index, sponsor directory, and index.

World Meetings: Outside United States and Canada.

See: keyword subject index, sponsor directory, and index.

World Meetings: United States and Canada.

See: keyword subject index, sponsor directory, and index.

8. PROCEEDINGS OF MEETINGS

Index to Scientific and Technical Proceedings, Philadelphia, Institute for Scientific Information, monthly.

See: Permuterm subject index, sponsor and other indexes.

9. SPECIALIZED RESEARCH CENTERS.

Palmer, AM, ed. *Research Centers Directory*, 6th ed, Detroit, Gale Research Co, © 1979. Supplements (*New Research Centers*).
  See: Alcohol and alcoholism, drug abuse, drugs, pharmacy, and pharmacology in index.

10. SPECIAL LIBRARY COLLECTIONS.

Ash, L, comp. *Subject Collections*, 5th ed, New York, R.R. Bowker Co, 1978.
  See: Drug habit, drugs, drugs—physiological effects, pharmaceutical research, pharmacology, pharmacopoeias, and formularies.
Young, ML & Young HC *Directory of Special Libraries and Information Centers. Vol. 3: Health Sciences Libraries.* Detroit, Gale Research Co, © 1979.